Leaving Neverland

Why Little Boys Shouldn't Run Big Corporations

Daniel Prokop

Published for Daniel Prokop
by
Continuum Australia Pty Ltd
62 New Brighton Road
NEW BRIGHTON, NSW 2483
AUSTRALIA, MATE

www.leavingneverland.net
info@leavingneverland.net
www.facebook.com/LeavingNeverland

Copyright © Daniel Prokop 2010
Cover design by Martin Chatterton

National Library of Australia
Cataloguing- in- Publication data

Prokop, Daniel
Leaving Neverland.
Why Little Boys Shouldn't be Allowed to Run Big Corporations.
ISBN: 978-0-9808288-3-2
Second Edition

Work Ethic, Responsibility, Moral Development
158.7

All rights reserved. Apart from any fair dealing for the purposes of private study, research, criticism or review, as permitted under the Copyright Act, no part may be reproduced or stored by any process or means without written permission. Inquiries should be made to the publisher.

Every effort has been made to appropriately acknowledge sources and seek permission or make use within the provisions of the copyright act. If any mistakes or omissions have been made, the author and publishers will be pleased to rectify matters at the first opportunity.

It is the intention of the publishers that 5% of any profits from this book will be donated to support Rites of Passage programs around the world.

NEVERLAND:

The imaginary island home of Peter Pan and the lost boys. A place where you never grow up. Michael Jackson's former retreat. An accurate description of the 21st century and the 20th century, the 19th century, the 18th century the 17th century, the 16th century, the 15th century, the 14th century, the 13th century, the 12th century...

Author's Note:

This book is not intended to be a Rites of Passage, planetary management or parenting manual. The material contained herein is general information and some content is highly satirical and written using the *sarcastica* true type font. Even if you have a good understanding of satire, in no way is any information contained herein to be construed as advice of any kind (except that little boys in men's bodies do need to grow up and that contemporary Rites of Passage programs should be run in every high school). Nor is any of the material contained in this book intended to be the definitive source of information on how to run planet Earth, run a Rite of Passage, parent or grow up.

Covering my ass (cont'd): the author and publisher of this publication exclude any liability suffered by any person, corporation or other entity for any loss, damage or injury caused by or arising from reliance upon any statement or opinion made or information provided in this publication. Using any information contained or referred to herein is your confirmation that you will not rely on the same as professional advice or as a substitute for professional advice.

If you like Leaving Neverland please tell other people about it. I welcome feedback and you can connect with me via the Leaving Neverland Facebook page or the newsletter that you can sign up for on the website. Please enjoy.

With Gratitude

Thank you to my family. I am very blessed to have you in my life. This book would not have been possible without your love and support. Thank you to Samuel, my first born, to Aelysha, my daughter and to my wise and beautiful wife Beth for being my partner, for your friendship, your listening, your passion and advice. I honour your amazing restraint, "I told you so," is not part of who you are☺. Beth, I honour your creativity and your amazing ability to open a door, walk away with grace and leave me to go through, or not. This work is the richer for the insights gained from the rooms beyond those doors. Thank you to Martin Chatterton for your timely and sage suggestions and the amazing cover design. In no particular order, thank you to: the Northern Rivers Writers Centre, all the men from Sun Lodge, Chris McAllister for website support, Owen Rigby with proofing, Ray Ellis, Milan Votrubec, Alistair Ping, Rex Finch, Pat McIntosh, Laurel Cohn editing, to the Pathways Foundation, Paul McMahon for the laughs, Tracks Trust, NZ (and in particular Adge Tucker and Jim Horton for holding this work so beautifully). To Paul Henley: thank you for your commitment to this work, your courage, humour and unflinching support. Thank you to Leonie, Simone and all the women who have given so much to bring balance and make this work available for our girls. Thank you for all those who have walked the paths that we may follow. To my mother, you are gone but not forgotten.

<u>Quotes by Daniel Prokop from "Leaving Neverland":</u>

"Mankind has become Pankind."

"In a desperate attempt to stay young forever we have achieved eternal childishness, rather than eternal youth."

"None of the King of Pop's horses and none of the King of Pop's enablers could put the King of Pop's childhood back together again."

"We live in an adolescent society, Neverland… where never growing up seems more the norm than the exception."

"Unfortunately the 'warrior' archetype accidentally dropped the soap in the shower and he has been getting boned senseless by the 'soldier/lobbyist archetype' ever since."

"As the supposed adults in our society we have a lot of work to do to re-brand adulthood into something aspirational rather than something to be avoided at all costs (including your life)."

"Behind every threat to the future of the human race lurks a boy in a man's body with both his hands in the jar of cookies that our ancestors set aside for future generations. It is time to Leave Neverland."

Contents

"Life is too important to be taken seriously."
— Oscar Wilde

"The BP president said yesterday that the company would survive. That's like someone running over your dog and saying, 'Don't worry, my car is fine." —Jimmy Fallon

"Even amidst tragedy there is laughter, sometimes farce. The degree of farce depends on who is running the tragedy."
—Daniel Prokop

"The oil company said it was the rig company's fault. The rig company said it was Halliburton. And somehow, each time they passed the blame, Goldman Sachs made a hundred million dollars."—Bill Maher

"Congress says they are looking into this Bernard Madoff scandal. Oh Great!! The guy who made $50 Billion disappear is being investigated by the people who made $1.5 Trillion disappear!" — unknown

1

A Little About Little Boys – An Introduction

(by Daniel Prokop)

The Global Financial Crisis was proudly brought to all of us by the little boys in designer suits that convinced suggestible authorities that they should be left in charge of the banking cookie jar. Of course they helped themselves to our cookies because "self regulation" to a child means "quick grab every cookie you can while no one is looking." The only real surprise is that people are surprised at all the missing cookies.

Different little boys were left to play in a warm, deep bathtub called the Gulf of Mexico. Even though the water was way, way over their heads the boys said that they didn't need any supervision. They boasted that their expensive toys were so safe that they were happy to bet the lives of their workers on them. Unfortunately their biggest toy caught fire and sank to the bottom of the tub. It cost 11 men their lives spewed over 4.9 million barrels of crude oil into the Gulf of Mexico. The oily ring on the tub may never come off and the combination of oil and dispersant is affecting the flow of the North Atlantic Current BUT cutting corners on safety could also have resulted in increased profit.

This was not an isolated or unprecedented incident. There are many examples where similar childish arrogance has created messes that rarely get a column inch of international press coverage, especially when they happen in remote or poor places like the Niger Delta, Ecuador or Papua New Guinea.

A Little About Little Boys

It is rare that the overgrown children that often run big corporations are flushed out of their ivory boys clubs and separated from a sycophantic crowd. They are not used to being held accountable for their salaries or the preventable human and environmental suffering caused by the operations they are vastly overpaid to run on a take no responsibility first and take no responsibility last basis.

Apparently, when you run a corporation that has an economic output greater than most countries you expect to be treated like royalty, only better. (In 2008, ranked by revenue, 65 of the top 100 world economies were corporations[1].) Under critical public scrutiny they cannot hide their callous lack of compassion for the great unwashed, the workers, the common folk or as the Chairman of BP refers to them - "the small people." They also do not seem to have much regard for the environment: "Louisiana isn't the only place that has shrimp."

If you are alarmed, pissed off or just concerned with what is happening in many parts of the world then this book is for you. If you think that it is time to say "Just drop the cookies and back away from the jar," then this book is for you. If you are interested in a solution for Leaving Neverland that can be rolled out rapidly using the existing education infrastructure then keep reading.

We live in an adolescent society where Peter Pan is hailed as a hero and growing up and taking responsibility is seen as bad, boring, even stupid. Why would any culture worship perpetual childhood? If there are no adults then who will take responsibility for the environment, for ensuring a fair and equitable financial system, for keeping people safe, for helping those not able to help themselves, for keeping communities strong? Oh...

Never growing up seems more the norm than the exception. Little boys wearing expensive suits and adult bodies should not be allowed to run big corporations. They shouldn't be allowed to run governments, armies, religions, small businesses and charities either and just quietly, they make pretty shabby husbands and fathers too. Mankind has become Pankind and whilst "lost boys" abound there is an alarming increase in the number of "lost girls."

Finally, finally, the appalling arrogance of spoilt *über* boys and the avoidable suffering that they have caused is generating a global wave of anger and frustration and about time too. We can ride this wave of frustration right into growing up and right out of Neverland.

It is time for us to grow up. It is actually that simple. As healthy responsible adults working together we can create solutions to the social and environmental challenges that we face. Some of the little boys that have not been playing nice will have their big toys taken off them and some of them will be told they need some 'time out' in special sandpits called prisons. We can expect tears before bedtime, some impressive tantrums and that some of these perpetual boys will try to take their bats and balls and play in places where no one can stop them. A few are going to become very, very angry and quite vicious, well, even more vicious.

The difficulty with the solution, of course, is that growing up is much easier said than done. Just shouting "Grow up!" or "Act your age, not your shoe size!" does not work, though you are welcome to give it a try.

Fortunately there is a timely solution to the growing up conundrum that lies at the heart of this book. There is a vehicle for achieving the transformation from being a child to being a young adult which has been road tested for tens of thousands of years. It can be done many different ways and it can be made accessible to everyone. The vehicle, the catalyst for growing up that traditional societies all relied upon is called a community based Rite of Passage.

A Rite of Passage is non-denominational and is simply a supported event or ceremony that marks the transition from one life stage to another. There are many stages that we pass through on our life's journey. Most life stage transitions do not happen on their own without help from people who have already crossed the threshold. Without Rites of Passage many people, me included, can get stuck. The stage of life known as adolescence is particularly sticky, so to speak. Some people never escape adolescence. Some corporations will never even try.

The onset of puberty in adolescence means that there is a lot happening physiologically for young people and emotionally the flood of hormones can at times short circuit reason. A lot happens for the parents of teenagers too, especially now with parents having children older and older. A mother going through menopause whilst her child goes through adolescence can be a volatile mix. The parental pedestal also conveniently crumbles at this time and we are suddenly parenting adolescents that have the same or more body mass than we do without the benefit of the parental awe we have enjoyed for so long.

Parents play a huge role in either assisting or hindering a young person's ability to leave Neverland. Do we abandon them to self initiate or do we provide an assisted Rite of Passage? It is our choice. HINT: Leaving young people to self initiate has not worked and the consequences affect us all.

A Little About Little Boys

In the western world, it seems that most adults don't want to grow up but have lost the joy and freedom of being childlike and in a desperate attempt to stay young forever have achieved eternal childishness, rather than eternal youth.

Most people would agree that children shouldn't be allowed to run corporations the size of countries or in fact anything larger than a sandpit built for one. And yet it happens, frequently. Too often errant corporations have been given the benefit of the doubt or of public disinterest or of public disinformation or all three.

This book weighs up the consequences of living in an adolescent society, skewers and explains how to spot overgrown children, explores how we got where we are and offers a timely solution.

The behavioural differences between a Peter Pan and a healthy adult are vast. Understanding the differences are the keys to restoring balance. As well as my own personal journey out of the Neverland of corporate life and my experience with contemporary, community based Rites of Passage this book includes commentary by the pin up boy for people who refuse to grow up, Peter Pan (yes, that Peter Pan).

In the interests of fairness and transparency Peter argues on behalf of a never ending Neverland. Peter urges children to rise up and drive the last adults into the sea. Actually, it's not as dramatic as that, but Peter has been busy upgrading Neverland Classic into the expanded and socially networked Neverland 2.0.

Peter shares his strategies for never growing up. These strategies have helped him fly from one highly successful corporate career to another. "The Seven Habits of Highly Effective Bullying" is one of Peter's favourite chapters. He also offers advice for parents on how to parent for perpetual childhood. I find Peter's strategies amusing and they would be hilarious if they weren't actually so close to the truth of daily experience.

How many more GFCs or BP Gulf oil spills do we need before we finally decide that it is time for us to leave Neverland? For our sake, for our children's sake, *ffs, we need to leave and as the Neverland departure lounge fades into the distance, the little boys (and little girls) that are behaving appallingly will be replaced by adults and we can start to live happily and co-operatively ever after. * ffs = for our future's sake.

---

[1] From revenue data compiled by Josh Morgan at Gnock.com
http://gnock.com/wp-content/uploads/2010/03/topecon_rev.html

2

Getting Forked into Growing Up

(by Daniel Prokop)

This is a good place for me to introduce myself. I am a script writer, a comedy show radio host, an inventor, a migrant, a parent educator and a stand up comedian. I have been a labourer at the Port Kembla Steelworks, made pizzas, cleaned toilets, washed dishes, even worked at McDonalds (it's ok, my kids know). I've picked kiwi fruit in NZ, put myself through University and worked on a turkey farm where they were doing artificial insemination. Personal development: been there, still doing that. I am also a father of two children and a husband and we all live together which is a bit nuclear.

I've been around the block a few times, nearly fifty times if you call one year a block. I studied little boys in their "natural" corporate environment, from within the belly of an oily beast. The beast was the biggest corporation in the world at the time. Hint: the logo looks like a scallop shell. It was a huge, big budget sandpit where I played at a senior level for 13 years, which still surprises me. I owned a franchised business in a major shopping centre and employed twelve staff for 9 years (okay, that one still surprises me too) and I have worked for a harm prevention charity. Three vastly different sandpits all linked by similar childish behaviour, some of it my own.

I have seen the infantile and puerile celebrated, watched bullying and irresponsible behaviour rewarded and worked in

5

environments where growing up was *verboten* (forbidden). We live in a world where the "hood" from "childhood" is frequently never replaced by the "hood" from "adulthood." I think the child's hood gets a bit whiffy if it never gets changed.

In this book, I'm going to talk a lot about growing up and I don't want readers thinking that I am suffering from 'Less like Peter Pan than thou syndrome.' I successfully dodged growing up for a long time. Peter Pan and me, we used to be tight, we were Bro's, well, we lived in the same big house, the house of Neverland. I was happy to stay in Neverland forever but at the age of 32 I got forked. I had been told to "get forked" a number of times before this but being young; I mistook it for abuse rather than good advice.

My fork came out of nowhere. I had just picked up Beth, my girlfriend, from the international airport and at some point on the kiss, kiss, "I've missed you for the past six weeks", happy reunion drive home, things went weird. I heard, as if through a fog, the words... "I think I'm pregnant." I swear I never saw that train coming. There was a horrible crash and screaming, lots of screaming and some pathetic whining. Fortunately, my inner train wreck did not affect my outer ability to maintain control of a motor vehicle. The only outer manifestation of my inner carnage was a temporary loss of the power of speech, which was a good thing. Somehow we made it home safely, all three of us.

My fork was this, a baby, my baby, was going to be born whether I liked it or not and I had two choices: 1) Stay and become a good Dad or 2) run away. The third possibility of staying and being a crap dad is really a variation of Option 2. I must admit that Option 2 was very attractive because there was a big problem with Option 1. I knew that to become a good dad, I would have to grow up and I didn't want to grow up. I really did not want to grow up, I wanted to stay in Neverland forever and I didn't want to leave because of a baby.

There was a part of me that knew I hadn't been taking responsibility for myself, my life and if I couldn't take responsibility for me, how could I be expected to take responsibility for another human being, a helpless baby? I was terrified of responsibility, of being tied down, of getting it wrong, of being a Dad. Fortunately my wife to be, Beth, was very patient (very patient). Beth didn't push me and I was allowed time to just struggle. I was grumpy and bad tempered for a while; not very communicative either. There was little support and no "Expectant Dad" programs around to help me. Eventually, finally and to an extent miraculously, I got my head around the fact that I was

6

going to become a Dad. Some internal switch got flicked and I have loved, really loved my journey of fatherhood. Getting forked was the best thing that has ever happened to me and I have strongly recommended it to a few very "special" people.

When Samuel was born, because of a birth complication, I was the first person to hold him. I was quickly replaced by something much more useful, a nipple, but I had had my moment, a magic new Dad moment with my baby. It was just amazing for me to hold this beautiful, tiny human being in my arms. I'm sure time stopped or maybe it just stopped for me. As well as a healthy baby boy, a new love was also birthed that day. A tender, protective, totally unconditional, connected and indescribable (I tried) kind of love that I had never experienced before. I had become a parent and I could have missed that moment. If my son, Samuel, had waited until I was ready to grow up and become a Dad, he could still be waiting.

Our baby became a child and the child just kept getting bigger and bigger, as they do when they are healthy. I didn't want Samuel to wait until he was 32 before he started to grow up. To this end, I had been watching for some time the development of a program called "Pathways to Manhood" that was being run locally. I knew it was a bush camp for boys and their dads or a mentor and that they needed leaders to help run more camps. I also knew that it had something to do with boys growing up and setting their feet on the long road to healthy manhood. The program's name: "Pathways to Manhood", is kind of a clue as to its intention☺. I knew very little about Rites of Passage back then, but the words "Rites of Passage" sounded kind of important to me.

As Samuel got older my internal imperative to do something got annoyingly stronger. Eventually, (thanks Elyjah) I got involved as a trainee leader with the Pathways Foundation. I had done a lot of mixed rituals where both men and women were involved and to be honest, I wasn't thrilled about doing smelly "men's business." I was busy, it cost money, <excuse #3>,<excuse #4> and <optional excuse #5> but I followed through with the Leadership Training because I am committed to being the best Dad I can be for Sam, even if that means stretching my personal comfort zones. In the small print of my being the best Dad I can be, I reserve the right to moan and complain about sprained comfort zones, just so you know.

My first camp as a trainee leader was amazing. Seven days in nature, no electricity, no phones, open fires, no women, great food, lots of flatulence, no running water. A rough bush camp, 30 men drawn together with the sole intention of supporting 14 boys to make the transition from boy to young man in a safe, non competitive environment. For some men, the camp was the first time that they had ever been in a space where they were not judged by the type of job they had, how much they made, where they lived, the car they drove, or the clothes they wore. In this safe space I watched men relax; really relax as they set aside the unconsciously adopted defensive male warrior pose.

I watched the transformation of boys' relationships with their fathers, with other men and with themselves unfold. We all witnessed courageous men sharing stories of their lives from their hearts without hubris. We sat around fires, shared food, laughter, games and challenges and over the week the boys left the camp and they rejoined us as young men. The young men were acknowledged and honoured by older men for completing their Rite of Passage, for stepping over the metaphorical line in the sand dividing boyhood from manhood.

As a group of men, we returned to our families and the wider community, to the anxious mums and uncles and grandparents and siblings. The community acknowledged the young men and celebrated their safe return to the hearth. Over the week away, a number of the men had said that they wished that they had had something like a Pathways to Manhood, a Rite of Passage when they were growing up. I agree whole heartedly.

It was a gift to see the difference in the fathers, the young men and how they were with their families, with the women who had kept the home fires burning so that we could be away. At different times over the week, the beauty and power of the work had brought me to tears, especially when I imagined myself with my son Samuel, guiding him through his Rite of Passage.

Little did I know that Rites of Passage would so get under my skin that it would become an itch that I can never seem to scratch. In an ever changing world, I don't know many things for certain but I do know that contemporary, community based Rites of Passage make a world of difference to young people and to their families, they are every child's rite. More than at any other time in this planet's history, we need healthy men and women rather than overgrown boys and girls as parents, as politicians, as generals and as business and community leaders. Whilst it is self evident that little boys should not be allowed to run big corporations it is alarmingly common.

Peter Pan has never quite forgiven me for forking off and leaving Neverland, for starting to grow up. I still see Peter on the odd occasion, like when I jump back over the line in the sand and behave like a little boy instead of a man. So whilst I do visit Neverland (strictly for research purposes) I don't live there anymore and I have some awareness of when I am behaving that way. After my tantrum I can clean up the mess and get on with what needs getting on with.

It is almost impossible to not be concerned about alarming increases in rates of depression across all age groups, environmental degradation, the inequities of the global financial system, <pet worry #4>,<pet worry #5> etc. We face many challenges. Peter Pan with the support of a coalition of the willing has had great success in creating a Cult of Perpetual Youth (CoPY). Neverland is promoted as if it is Nirvana which it is not.

Neverland: "Stay young forever by never growing up."

Neverland: "Be happy and childlike forever."

**Neverland: "No responsibility. No worries. No wrinkles."
(Now fortified with Viagra!)**

**Neverland: "The overall environmental impact of this
will be very, very modest."(Via BP CEO, Tony
Hayward, Gulf of Mexico oil spill, 18/05/10)**

We mostly hear about all the bad stuff that is happening and a lot of the depressing stuff can be traced back to different boys but similar behaviour. Amidst all the chaos that comes in a time of rapid change there are also millions of amazing, inspiring things happening every day. There are a lot of healthy adults out there too.

> *"If you meet the people who are working to restore
> this earth and the lives of the poor, and you aren't
> optimistic, you haven't got a pulse." Paul Hawken,
> 2009 speech*[1]

There are courageous, dedicated, compassionate people in all countries devoting themselves to making a difference and there are parents raising a generation of young people who will not be pawns of unsustainable industries.

Getting Forked into Growing Up

"There is one thing stronger than all the armies in the world, and that is an idea whose time has come."
Victor Hugo, 1852.

I have updated the quote for Victor Hugo:

"There is one thing stronger than even all the biggest corporations in the world, and that is an idea whose time has come."

Here's a radical idea: Let's put responsible adults in charge of running things on this planet with Elders to help guide them. What do you think? Victor?

<silence>

<silence>

<more silence>

Is that my segue in? Is that it? After this many pages? Victor? Pretty weak but, doesn't matter. I'm in now, Peter Pan here. Thank you... whatever your name is. Yes, I am a victor, a big victor because Neverland Rules and I could wait to be introduced like we agreed ... BUT... know what? I'm good. I'll just introduce myself to the readers...

[1] University of Portland Commencement Speech 2009. Very inspiring speech. A PDF of the speech is available from www.paulhawken.com

3

The Introduction
to Peter Pan

(Contributed by Peter Pan)

Hi, Peter Pan here, also known as Pedro Pan (Spain), Pieter Pan (Netherlands), Pedr Pan (Wales), Pekelo Pan (Hawaii), Per Pan (Norway), Pierre Pan (France), Petar Pan (Romania), Pyotr Pan (Russia) Panno (Australia) Peter Chan (China) and That Little Bugger (in most other countries). I'm the champion of the childish, the boy who refuses to grow up and proud of it. At this point in history, staying childish and irresponsible has never been easier or a surer path to a highly successful career. It has worked a treat for me.

I used to live in Neverland, way back in 1904 when it was mostly imaginary. Back then, baby boys who fell out of their prams when their nurse was not looking were sent by the Government to stay with me in Neverland but only if they were not claimed within seven days which was pretty reasonable. I called them the 'lost boys.' There were no 'lost girls' because, apparently, no girl was silly enough to fall out of her pram, which is sexist but true.

Improvements in pram safety, fewer nurses hitting the big bottle of Mrs. McCready's Cough Syrup in the mornings and a 1920 UK policy of forced expatriation of children to other Commonwealth countries meant that eventually 'lost boys' stopped arriving in Neverland altogether. The ones already in Neverland, well, they got lost, which was annoying but not surprising. Neverland started getting quiet, too quiet, if you know what I mean.

I started spending more time out of Neverland where I "hooked" up with a lot of boys and some girls who also refused to grow up. We all got on great. I called them the "new lost boys" and "new lost girls" respectively. There were a lot more than I would have ever thought. They loved hearing my stories about the adventures I used to have in Neverland and how easy it was to never grow up there. They really wanted me to take them to Neverland but they didn't want to risk losing their highly paid jobs. So I started thinking, if I couldn't bring the boys and girls to Neverland then why not bring Neverland to the boys and girls?

It has taken a long time, a very long time, because I constantly get distracted, but I have finally expanded the borders of Neverland, constantly pinching, pushing and pulling at the edges until now Neverland covers almost the entire planet. In line with the advent of Web 2.0 and social networking I have upgraded the original Neverland, Neverland Classic, as it is sometimes called, to Neverland 2.0. Childhood, once restricted to a life stage that passed all too quickly is no available in Neverland 2.0 to everyone as a permanent lifestyle choice.

Over many, many years I have yet to find any reason to grow up. Indeed, I have found time and time again that a person of my marked immaturity can carve a stellar career in any industry. Whilst the petroleum industry was an absolute hoot, I must say that I have had the most insane fun and made outrageous money treasure-hunting in international banking. It was also nice to be back sparring with Mr. Smee and all the other pirates. I never get tired of hearing Mr. Smee recite the banking hypocritical oath, "Arrrrgh, Take what you can, give nothing back! Arrrgh." What an industry!

Since those global financial "speed bumps," the big ~~cartels~~ banks initially received a lot of unfair and highly critical press, much of it wildly accurate. Firstly, "Everybody" said that there was no way we could afford a global financial crisis (GFC) but of course, as it turns out "Everybody" was wrong, weren't they? When push came to shove, came to collapse, the 4.1 trillion dollars was found or printed or whatever.

Despite all the time I have spent in banking, I still don't understand it very well and I know I'm not the only one. Derivatives, schmerivatives. What a great business banking is. Banks take the money that the public save and give them a pittance called interest and then the bank borrows against the public's money to leverage it so they can lend as much money as possible back to the public at extortionate rates to fund marble palaces and huge bonuses for people who are playing with money that is not their own. One word: sensational.

I volunteered to take on all those depressing, pathetic whiners "Oh poor me, I've lost my job, I've lost my house, I've lost all my life savings, I thought banks were safe... wah, wah, wah." I also wanted to have a serious lash at all the foolish governments, Iceland excepted of course, who after years of supporting, even promoting financial and other deregulation suddenly realized that deregulation results in a... wait for it... a deregulated market. A market with no rules. D'oh, but do any of the Governments want to take the blame for what has happened? Any hands up in the air? No?

Every one of my ~~pirate~~ CEO friends privately agree with me that all we were doing was raping what others had saved but whilst the public are so pissed off, the CEOs are fearful of taking on the whingers and governments because it might jeopardise their healthy bonuses which were, after all, being funded by the remarkably generous and unconditional government bailouts.

Unfortunately, before I could blow the whistle or speak out, I was effectively "gagged." Well, when I say "gagged," I mean I *was* paid a large roomful of your money just to shut up and quietly retire. Both my Barrister ($4,000 for 20 minutes advice) and my barista ($3.50 for 20 minutes advice, plus a latte) agreed with me that writing is a quiet pursuit, so I could in theory, have the angry spray I wanted but in book form rather than as a documentary or film or as my own talk show. Clever, huh? I always get my way, no matter what, which is why I have always been so successful. I was also contracted to sprinkle fairy dust everywhere so people would quickly forget any lessons learned and just how mightily pissed off they were. Been there, sprinkled that.

Sadly, words don't write themselves, they take work, focus, self discipline and time. Dammit! And Dammit! Oh well, nice thought, time to watch more TV.

As fate and I would have it, I used to have an acquaintance called Damian [Daniel]. I bumped into him just as my writing idea was sinking out of sight. Donald [Daniel] was understandably excited to see me, he kept yapping on and on about it being time to Leave Neverland and how my behaviour had inspired him to write a book. He almost captured my attention but he was kind of boringly serious, no, no, seriously boring and annoyingly earnest. "This book will make a difference..." which was when I switched off, for a while. I think he said "yadda, blah, Neverland, yadda, write, yadda, blah, blah, book, blah, d'oh...." I nodded every now and then to keep my neck from getting stiff which just spurred him on and on. He noticed the neck movements but somehow missed the pointed yawns entirely.

I was just about to escape and go and give birth to an environmentalist (take a dump) when he said the magic words, "I'll do all the work." Well, I was on board in a flash. I made Darryl [Daniel] promise not to bother me with boring booky details like writing or publishing, etc, etc. Dennis [Daniel] is convinced that people are ready to leave Neverland despite all the evidence to the contrary. Normally I avoid delusional people but some delusions are harmless. I say, "if you're prepared to do the time you can have your whine." Go your hardest Buddy!

The difficulty with working with delusional people is that they often assume that just because they said something or sent an email or two that communication has taken place. I'm a busy guy and a multi-tasking specialist. I can't afford to devote all of my attention to the person that is talking to me. Please! That is a grossly inefficient use of time. Because Denzel [Daniel] didn't explain things clearly to me, I thought that I would get to you readers first and explain a few things before you read any of his … tripe writing.

Oh, ummm… in case he mentions it, Draco [Daniel] claims that I had a bit of a tantrum and threatened to pull out of helping altogether if I didn't get to go first. I can't remember any emotional release and because a cappuccino got spilt [poured] on the recording device, that part of our interview is kind of undigitalised. I told Dane [Daniel] that it was a bit childish to cry over frothed milk but that didn't seem to comfort him much.

There are some people that see the half full cup and get upset about where the other half of the cup went. With an attitude like that, they will never be happy. I see a half full cup and I immediately take half of someone else's cup and then I have a full cup and I'm happy. With the right attitude, life is really very simple.

So, David …. It is David, isn't it? [Daniel] will write most of the book which shouldn't spoil it too much. He said that he would add some comments in parenthesis and in a different font to mine [like this]. I of course reserved the right to insert the odd, odd comment in {these things} in his chapters if and when I feel like it. If you get confused, just listen to what I say because growing up is for losers.

Where was I? Remember, how I was telling you about how I spent a long time out of Neverland Classic while I was busy bringing Neverland to the people? Well, it's quite funny really. You see over those decades, I … um … well, it's funny and a touch embarrassing, I have become rather well padded since I was first described in print in 1904. I have grown out and talled up a bit. I'm quite a bit bigger than I once was but I can reassure you that I have done everything in my childish repertoire, which is vast, to avoid growing up mentally. I am just as capricious, vain, self centred and selfish as I was in 1904, if not more so.

Obviously I take my immaturity seriously and I carefully monitor my Emotional Intelligence (E.I.) level and keep it as low as possible. My average E.I. level hovers just below that of an indulged, pre-pubescent 14 year old boy. I am delighted to reveal that my E.S., or Emotional Stupidity level is so high that it is off the charts. E.S. measures a person's inability to access certain emotions such as compassion, empathy and a sense of responsibility. In Neverland 2.0 these emotions are so rare that they are considered theoretical, if they are ever considered at all, which they are not.

In exchange for you buying, copying or stealing a copy of this book, I will share with you the secrets of my low E.I. high E.S. diet. Stay emotionally slim whilst gorging yourself at the company's or countries expense. I will show you how you can make loads of fast money and stay looking young forever'ish by reducing all the unnecessary stress commonly associated with shirking responsibility, lying, cheating and dominating others.

You do not have to grow up and no one can make you, if you don't want to. That's great news isn't it? It is time to share the Neverland Code, the Code that has allowed Neverland 2.0 to take over the world. When I say "Code," well, it's actually more of a guide really.

With great power, in Neverland 2.0, comes a total lack of accountability and responsibility. The Neverland Code can rocket you to the highest echelons of the bluest of blue chip resource companies, financial institutions or corporate stalwarts like Enron or WorldCom. [When Enron collapsed in 2001, it owed $32 billion dollars and was the biggest corporate failure in US history, at that time.]

If we do not fight the adults on the land, in the air and on the sea (which includes off shore drilling platforms) we could end up with a world where people and even companies and whole governments could be held responsible for their actions. Not on my watch. What has happened in the Gulf of Mexico is outrageous. So there was a bit of a spill, a few birds got some black waterproofing for free. Tony Hayward, CEO of BP did a great job of putting it into perspective for people "The Gulf of Mexico is a very big ocean. The volume of oil and dispersant we are putting into it is tiny in relation to the total water volume." BP quite rightly, in my opinion, appeared to try to save the oil first and the environment second or third, whatever.

It is a worrying precedent that BP were forced to set up a $20 billion dollar Gulf Oil Spill Fund. I couldn't have summed it up better than Joe Barton, Republican Senator from Texas, when he said it was "a tragedy of the first proportion that a private corporation can be subjected to what I would characterize as a shakedown, a $20 billion dollar shakedown." I felt your pain Joe. I was also "ashamed of what happened in the White House." This book will help get more supporters for good ol' boys like Joe. Profit at all costs is not a series of dirty words but responsibility is.

About those nasty, hurtful rumours that I wear green tights, a hat with a feather in it, travel by fairy dust and that my fashion accessories are limited to a belt and a gay wooden sword: Those persistent, cruel lies have been propagated by horrible mean spirited grown ups that want to roll back the borders of Neverland 2.0 to the realm of the imagination. Those tossers have totally failed but that persistent, bad fashion stereotype is mean and slightly sicko. Maybe once, for a wicked jape, I dressed all in green. It was St. Patrick's Day for goodness sake. I was in Ireland, someone drew a picture of me, please let it go... let it go. I wear Armani now, do you?

It is high time that all the perpetual boys and girls that run so many fine corporations for their own benefit and that of their friends and family get the respect and the acknowledgement that they so richly deserve. Any good Never Lander, a citizen of Neverland, could walk past you in a busy street and you would not even notice them. We dress exclusively in brand names, love bling, drive huge, pretentious, and gas guzzling vehicles and have found iPhones, money and the internet to be more effective weapons than wooden swords.

I didn't think it was possible, but I am having more fun in Neverland 2.0 than Neverland Classic. Here's a quick fun tip for you: Fun at someone else's expense is twice as much fun as normal fun because you have your fun PLUS you add to your fun a fun multiplier which is based on how effective you have been at taking away other people's fun. The bonus endorphins from enhanced fun are more effective than wrinkle cream at keeping you young but more difficult to put in a jar and mark up by 6,000%.

4

Rites of Passage
and Growing Up

(by Daniel Prokop)

I'm really happy that Peter Pan is contributing to this book. I believe that people have finally had enough of overgrown boys and that Peter's undisguised churlishness will help to wake people up. After the drool is wiped from the corner of their mouths (which is how you know it has been a very deep sleep), people will start to abandon Neverland and wonder why they ever stayed there so long.

Neverland is no longer restricted to an island in the imagination or to a ranch in Santa Barbara, California. Boys that refuse to grow up, and girls too, seem more the norm today than the exception. The original book *"Peter Pan"* was written by J.M. Barrie as a children's story, it was never meant to be used as a blueprint for social development.

Peter Pan was one of Michael Jackson's hero's (he didn't know Peter like I know him) which is why Michael created his own Neverland complete with Indian village, two railways, a zoo, bumper cars and various other amusement park rides, as you do. The 2,676 acre Neverland was a monument to a childhood that as a young star Michael felt he never had. Despite the excess: None of the King of Pop's Horses and none of the King of Pop's enablers could put the King of Pop's childhood back together again.

Rites of Passage and Growing Up

Fan or not we all have a lot in common with Michael Jackson. We are living in a Neverland that we have all helped to create, that doesn't disappear when we wake up and will only disappear when we collectively grow up. In our adolescent society growing up emotionally is ridiculed, seen as bad, even stupid and definitely undesirable. Yet the consequences of our prolonged childhood, the global financial crisis, the preventable environmental disasters, human induced climate change and a pandemic of depression are finally (almost) impossible to ignore.

We have tried generations upon generations of not growing up and taking no responsibility for our actions or emotions and it doesn't seem to have worked very well. For Homo sapiens why is growing up emotionally not pre-installed? How could something so vitally important to life on this planet be left as an optional extra?

"Hi, GOD! Yeah good to see you too, so…. ummm…. this time I'll take the basic body shape, a fairly hairless one, unless there is an ice age coming up? The opposite you say? Interesting, whatever, definitely the walking upright model with the enlarged brain and a big penis too, if it's all the same to you? Yeah, well the size does matter to me. Yes, I have heard that joke about how you knock the dicks off all the smart ones and it was funny back when we were all still living in the trees. Whatever skin colour you got in stock for this baby will be fine. One last thing, I hear that the growing up software is now optional? I'm sorry, you were mumbling, is it optional or not? It is? Great, 'cause I'm not gonna need it. I just want to be a big kid this whole lifetime, stay kinda young forever, ya know. Yes ummm about that, I will be opting out of taking any responsibility for anything and I just want to reassure you that I'm good with that. Well, it probably will adversely affect my fellow men and women but …. whatever. Right. Yes, totally. GOD, you are THE GOD. Of course I'm listening and I understand your frustration but if it upsets you so much why did you give us free will? Well… maybe it would have been better if you hadn't, but you did. Now as I understand it, you won't actually stop me… you know … having nookie? 'Cause I might 'accidentally' father a few kids. It doesn't feel right talking about sex in front of you. You're kind of like a parent only so much more. I just can't imagine you and Mrs. God having sex. Sorry, sorry, anywho. I think we're all set now? Cool. Well, thank you. See you next time. What do you mean? 'If there is a next time?' GOD? GOD?"

18

In human beings there is no hard wired link between physiology and psychology, no inter-molecular check and balance system between physical body growth and psychological mental development. At first blush this appears to be a significant design flaw unique to human beings. Some people who are critical of God about other matters may be thinking that this is a huge oversight by God. Others, who constantly acknowledge just how amazingly clever God is (you may even use a different name for her), will disagree.

Have some fun and visualize a relative or a work colleague, perhaps a favorite politician. Now imagine the physical size of the person changing so that their body is now directly proportional to their emotional maturity i.e. healthy adult emotionally equals full size adult body, child emotionally equals a child's body, baby emotionally equals baby body size. Hmm, how did you go?

The link between physical body growth and emotional maturity was once provided by the community. The catalyst for achieving the transformation from boy to young man or from girl to young woman was called a Rite of Passage. Assisting young people to successfully make the transition from childhood into adulthood was a matter of life and death to traditional societies. The communities knew that their very survival actually depended on having healthy adults as members rather than overgrown boys and girls (and that was way back before nuclear weapons, genetic engineering and deep sea drilling were even invented.)

> *"A civilization that lacks Rites of Passage has a sick soul and "you know it is sick for three reasons: there are no elders, the youth are violent and the adults are bewildered" African Teacher as quoted by Matthew Fox[1]*

Rites of passage are normal. An example of a modern Rite of Passage which is still commonly practiced today is marriage. Indeed some people enjoy the rite of marriage so much that they "practice" it several times but still can't seem to make it work. The potency of marriage as an effective Rite of Passage seems to have diminished greatly. There are many other stages that we move through over a lifetime. These life stages include; birth, adolescence, parent, Elder and death.

I believe that the reclaiming of contemporary, community based Rites of Passage is the way out of Neverland for all of us. The focus of this book is the Rite of Passage where Peter Pan and quite a few others (myself included) have got stuck, the transition from child to young adult.

Childhood is great, I spent 32 years there and Peter Pan has clocked up 106 years as a child and still counting. Early childhood (as opposed to the ongoing childhood of a 40 year old) is precious and children are great teachers of spontaneous joy and happiness. According to Dr. Fry (Psychiatrist and professor emeritus at Stanford University) the average child in kindergarten laughs up to 300 times a day, the average adult just 17 times. Just because kids haven't heard all the good punch lines does not explain that difference. Children have a sense of wonder and playfulness that is infectious though many "adults" use work to inoculate themselves from regular laughter and outbursts of spontaneous play.

There are positive aspects of childhood which "grown ups" remember very fondly but shed all too readily: joy, fun, innocence and wonder, laughing easily and living in the moment. There are other aspects of childhood which "adults" retain even when they are way past their use by date. These aspects include: the avoidance of responsibility, the insatiable cravings for attention and instant gratification, the misuse of power and being capricious.

So what does growing up mean? People talk about it all the time. Young people are often told to "grow up" by angry, shrill voiced folk who are having a mid life tantrum. Even if teenagers want to grow up, we make it difficult by having few good role models available for them and fewer still that get any media attention. Telling young people to "Grow up!" but then not giving them anything to aim for is like giving someone a dart, then blindfolding them and spinning them around 100 times and then berating them as you pull the dart out of your forehead.

"Growing up" emotionally means making the mental shift from being a child to being a young adult, from being dependent on parents and others to becoming independent, from taking no responsibility to taking full responsibility. When this transformation does not happen we get overgrown children who have physically grown up but still behave like a child, often a spoilt child.

The differences between an overgrown child and a healthy adult are vast and it is worth considering what some of these differences are. The main differences as I see them, "Peter Pan vs. Not Peter Pan" are summarised in Table 1.0. Table 1.0 is meant to be a conversation starter for the very important conversation: "We need to talk. It's time to start growing up." This model has been inspired by the Boy vs. Man model developed by the Pathways Foundation (www.pathwaysfoundation.org.au).

Peter Pan

Overgrown Child

Alphabet Male
• I use power over others

Blame (Dependent)
• I take no responsibility for my actions or feelings

Cravings
• I demand instant gratification

Death?
• I am immortal

External Identity
• I seek constant attention

Healthy Adult

Not Peter Pan

Leader
• I use power with others

Independent
• I take full responsibility for my actions and feelings

Self Discipline
• I can defer instant gratification

Death.
• I will die

Identity from Self
• I do what is needed

The Line in the Sand

Table 1.0 Difference between an Overgrown Child and a Healthy Adult

I have tried to keep this model simple because it is now easier to get overwhelmed by information than at any other time in history. It is estimated that 4 exabytes (4 billion gigabytes) of information was generated in 2008 which is more information than was generated in the previous 5,000 years[2].

Each of the five aspects in Table 1.0 are dealt with in detail so keep reading. This book is not a gospel according to Daniel and I hope that since there are so few lions left that this will not land me in the lions den. These are my thoughts and beliefs written in a way that I hope you will find entertaining, informative and at times provocative. The Peter Pan vs. Not Peter Pan model can be useful, I believe, in helping to identify "lost boys" and "lost girls," especially when they are cloaked in the authority of high office. I also find it useful for when I step over the line myself. If what I have written makes sense to you, use it and if it doesn't, chuck it away or put it in the bottom of a budgies cage.

Maybe we don't need to Leave Neverland? Maybe Peter Pan is right and we just keep on going exactly as we have been going only harder? After reading this, you decide.

Rites of Passage and Growing Up

A quick perusal of Table 1.0 is enough to see that the shifts required in the way of thinking and being are so fundamental that it is absurd and unrealistic to assume that adolescents can make such a huge transformation all by themselves in a timely manner. It was never left up to the individual to decide when they wanted to grow up because this is the way that that conversation goes.

ADULT: "Hey, when are you going to grow up?"
ADOLESCENT: "I'll grow up when I feel like it."
ADULT: "OK, and when will that be?"
ADOLESCENT: "Never."

It was not left up to the parents to decide when the child was ready to grow up either. Parents can easily be blinded by their love.

PARENT: "I just don't think Timmy is ready to grow up yet."
OBSERVER: "Why is that?"
PARENT: "Some of his beard isn't grey yet."

Some parents who are living vicariously through their children or who are simply co-dependent on them may not want their little darlings to ever grow up. There are now many different names for over protective parents that try to solve all their children's problems for them. There is a variety of hovering type parents: "blimp" parents (overweight hoverers), "helicopter" parents and the more electronically sophisticated "drone" parents." There are also parents that actively remove obstacles from their children's path. These are "lawnmower" parents or, if you are in Scandinavia, "curling" parents (parents who sweep obstacles out of their children's path with a cute little broom whilst trying to take themselves seriously). All these parents condemn their children to a lifetime in Neverland.

> {How can anyone be "condemned" to a life time of awesomeness?}

Tension may arise between parents when one parent clearly sees the need for a child to grow up, while the other parent wants to keep protecting the little "darling" forever. There are also some highly competitive parents that want their young children to grow up much faster than they are developmentally capable of achieving. Advertisers also try to grow children up too fast and then once they reach adolescence they want to keep them there forever. Parenting is a really tough and a very important job.

In traditional societies, the Elders of the village, people with wisdom who knew the child and saw them regularly would say when a child was "ripe" or ready for adulthood, for their Rite of Passage. Whilst the young person would feel a certain degree of anxiety about what was coming, they also looked forward to it too because they wanted to join the adults. In many cultures there were very big incentives for them to do so. I heard an interview a few years ago with John Guy from Bush Ventures on ABC Radio. John was talking about Rites of Passage and his experience of the Gurkha Culture where if a child had not completed their Rite of Passage they were not allowed to marry or own property. That is a big incentive to grow up. {Maybe once upon a time it might have been.} Why would you let a child raise a child?

By the age of 13, most adolescents have had 13 years or so of little or no responsibility, of thinking only of themselves, of wanting everything NOW and striving to be the centre of attention. There is a lot of comfort in staying the same and huge psychic inertia to be overcome for an adolescent to cross the line in the sand, to leave aspects of the child behind thereby creating the space for young adult behaviour to take effect. There is fear to be overcome too, fear of losing something precious in the transition, fear of change, fear of responsibility and these days, fear of becoming as miserable as most of the "adults" that they see everyday. As the adults of our culture we have a lot of work to do to make adulthood a lot more attractive to our young people. We can do this by enjoying our lives, by laughing more and spending more time with our young people (who are happy to teach us how to play again.)

The consequences of not helping, of leaving our young people to either self initiate or do nothing at all, surround us. It affects us all in many, many ways. For example, we have a generation of children that are trying to grow up without fathers around.

> *"Too many fathers are AWOL, missing from too many homes. They have abandoned their responsibilities, acting like boys instead of men. And the foundations of our families [and our communities] are weaker because of it.... any fool can have a child... It's the courage to raise a child that makes you a father." President Barrack Obama, New York Times, June 16, 2008)*

If we keep going the way we are going, operating out of Neverland 2.0, then our ability to resolve the global environmental, social and financial challenges we face will be extremely difficult, if not impossible. How can we resolve important issues if no one ever takes responsibility for their actions? In most mature democracies, sorry, need to take the word "mature" out. Ok, in most democracies we have developed antagonistic politics where the "Opposition" will oppose good initiatives purely for the sake of undermining the Government. God forbid that someone makes a mistake because "Hell hath no fury more than an inept politician that sees vulnerability in an opponent." Thus opportunities to learn and move forward fall through outstretched fingers onto sterile ground whilst lobbyists peddle rumours and influence to the highest greedy person.

> *"Problems cannot be solved by the same level of thinking that created them." Albert Einstein*

The roots of the current level of childish thinking go back thousands of years and lay in the use of power to dominate others. The use of power "over" rather than using power with others is fearful, Overgrown Child thinking. It has mostly been men that have reveled in accumulating and holding onto power and they have given patriarchy a really bad name. Rather than patriarchy *per se* it has been a childish, warrior based model of domination that worships the twin gods of selfishness and instant gratification and where bad card playing is obligatory because it seems that might always trumps right's ace. Did I miss anything? This old way of thinking has taken us to the brink, where we are sinking under a morass of disintegrating families, weak divided communities, corporate and military bullying, catastrophic environmental degradation, and the sea, see?

The good news, and there is good news, is that globally we have finally had enough of the old low level way of thinking. Most of us with enough to eat have had a gutful and those that are starving have had enough of not having a full gut. ENOUGH IS ENOUGH. The catastrophic cost of putting irresponsible children in charge of the world financial system has caused great hardship and suffering for everyone it seems, except the children that created the mess. I believe that the (latest) Global Financial Crisis combined with concerns about human induced climate change are like sharp sticks poking us in the back, urging us to move to a new level of thinking because the old way of thinking, well there is no dog poop bag big enough to scoop it into.

In 2009, on the 20th anniversary of the Berlin wall coming down the BBC World Service published a poll[3] of 29,033 people across 27 different countries. Only 11% of those questioned said that they thought that free-market capitalism was working well and that greater regulation is not a good idea.

Over 23% of respondents said that free-market capitalism is "fatally flawed and a different economic system is needed." WOW. In only two countries did more than 20% of respondents say that the system was "working well and that more regulation would make it less efficient": the USA, capital of Neverland and home-base of the global financial meltdown; and Pakistan, huh? Because things are going so well in Pakistan?

The new way of thinking that is coming in is deceptively simple, yet enormously powerful, it is called: Growing Up and Behaving Like responsible Adults (GUBLrA). With GUBLrA we can work together and together we can solve the challenges that face us and maybe a few bonus ones that might crop up unexpectedly along the way. Yahoo! As in celebration, not the search engine.

The great thing is, that with this new way of thinking we can all start straight away with little steps, like taking personal responsibility for our actions and our feelings and by starting to think about future generations and the environment. Now, before all of you race off to buy cheap low lying coastal property there is one teensy weensy little catch. We have a slight compatibility problem.

"Compatibility problem" is a phrase that results in an involuntary sphincter contraction for anyone that spends too much time around computers. Microsoft products have a particularly proud tradition in this area. The reality is that GUBLrA will simply not run on a global Neverland 2.0 operating platform, though it will run in safe mode on a smaller scale in a Neverland 1.0 environment which is no help at all because there is no "safe mode" available on the Earth server.

The full implementation of GUBLrA requires us to reduce global immaturity levels. The OEMCD country (Organisation for Emotional Maturity Co-operation and Development) is Bhutan, the only country that measures gross national happiness. Bhutan will be asking non OEMCD countries, effectively the rest of the world, to begin making cuts in their tantrum and bullying emissions immediately. There are many that think no one will win if trading in tantrums is ever allowed.

But seriously, GUBLrA is a new level of consciousness, a new operating system from which we can solve the problems facing us. It is time for us to leave Neverland and there are many "lost boys" and "lost girls" that will do their very considerable worst to stop the new way of thinking from coming in. There are also a lot of people who are resigned or just afraid of change, even though it is obvious to even the most casual observer that everything changes, nothing stays the same forever, except perhaps acting childishly.

It is highly unlikely that the Pan-like elite will give up their power gracefully though they may surprise us. The current depth and pervasiveness of Neverland 2.0 is actually quite scary. I spent an afternoon walking busy streets asking people the same question "When are you going to grow up?" The overwhelming response was "never." One girl said "when I want to lose interest in life."

My goal in writing this book with Peter Pan, the Pan Man...

> {I hate that nickname. I am not a man. I'm a boy, I'm a BOY, I'M A BOY!!!}

> [Ok, Ok. This from the guy that can't remember anyone else's name.]

> {I only remember names that are worth dropping.}

My goal in writing this book is to let people know that the Neverland emergency exit doors and the normal exit doors are never locked. We can leave whenever we want to. We just have to want to.

> {<smirk> Oh yeah, like that's ever going to happen? <smirk>.}

I also have a go at pulling the rug out from under the childish A- type, Alpha male bullies that take no responsibility for their actions, use positional or physical power to dominate others and make many people's lives a misery. One of the early working titles for this book was *Alpha Males: Ripping them a Second Asshole.* I liked it and I still like it but I was told it was too aggressive.

Whilst the Rite of Passage from child to young adult is a key plank in the GUBLrA roll out there are other important Rites of Passage that have been lost too. From man to father is a big emotional shift. Whilst there is more focus now on men supporting the birth, being a father is very different from being a man and there is a lot men need to know about looking after a pregnant wife and how to support a new mother and an infant and themselves.

Whilst the birth process is a Rite of Passage for a woman and it helps with the mental shift from woman to mother, there is a lot that women can do to help and support a woman to become a connected, healthy mother. The poop hits the nappy straight after birth and many parents are not fully ready for the journey ahead.

There is not enough support in our communities for new mothers. We can do a lot better in this area.

The last vital Rite of Passage that we have lost (excluding Death) is the Rite of Passage from older to elder and the loss of eldership makes re-establishing all Rites of Passage more difficult.

Once elders held both knowledge and wisdom but now with the internet and computers we have a lot of older people who are bewildered and disempowered because their knowledge has seemingly passed into obsolescence at a pace that has left them dizzy. We live in an age where people suffer from info-toxicity caused by the overwhelming volume of expert opinions, often conflicting advice, that is available on the same topic. Info-toxicity results in confusion and feelings of inferiority and insignificance. But knowledge is not wisdom and some things are learned only through living and loving and taking a few turns that take us to unexpected places.

Googling wisdom will not make you wise. I tried it, and it didn't help. In fact, I found researching wisdom very frustrating and I made a fundamental parenting error of venting some of my frustration at my children that same day. To be fair, a whole pile of clothes and school bags and crap had just been chucked on the floor. C'mon, they know better.

{Who is supposed to be the adult? <snicker, snicker>}

I am the adult, with a small "a", if I have told them once, I have told them …

{And you never leave anything lying around?}

Well, ummm… I may have once left a shirt …

{Welcome back to Neverland, Dario}

<Sigh> Knowing what to do is different to doing what you know. It is wisdom that connects knowledge to the heart.

> *"Wisdom is the right use of knowledge. To know is not to be wise. Many men [and women] know a great deal, and are all the greater fools for it. There is no fool so great a fool as a knowing fool. But to know how to use knowledge is to have wisdom."*
> *Charles H. Spurgeon*

We are chronically short on wisdom balancing knowledge, short on the ability to listen and empathise with human beings who share the same air with us, the same needs and desires. We have mothers going into despair and overwhelm just for the sake of a little break and an unbroken nap and in the same street, older people feeling redundant, thirsting for connection and dying of loneliness and ne'er the twain do meet.

This is a challenging and an exciting time to be alive. Yes the world is changing faster than ever before. Yes, we have inherited a media circus, yes, our families, our tribes, our villages, our communities have been largely scattered to the four winds. But before you ask another question, consider that at this time, in this moment, there is a listening and the space for solutions and new ways of thinking to be adopted. Our job is to nurture the seedlings of healthy, diverse communities of men and women and children and let's look after the planet's ecosystem while we are at it.

> *"...never before in human history has such a wealth of symbolic and ritual thought been available to us through anthropological and ethnological research." Don Bowak, Marking Life's Stages, 2008, self published.*

We can create our own contemporary rituals to slake the innate thirst for ceremony and connection. Everything we do now to help strengthen our communities and diversity punches a hole in the walls of Neverland and generates a spike in Gross National Happiness.

You will find Neverland escape instructions written throughout this book but not in a secret code or anything Dan Brown'ish like that. The alternative way to escape Neverland is to basically do the opposite of whatever Peter Pan suggests.

One day Neverland will disappear back into a small island in the imagination or less. It is time for a new ending to an old story. The boy that never grows up was a story that became myth without a moral. It has attracted many people to a light that they thought was the moon but it was only Peter - mooning.

{Heh, heh}

In the section on gratitude, I forgot to thank all the Alpha males from the various sandpits where I have worked, as well as some politicians and stalwart captains of industry who have inspired me by pissing me off so much that I finally got off my butt ...

-- Daniel Prokop --

{And left your level 80, night elf hunter in Azeroth}

… to write this book. Thank you. Y'all are inspiring a lot of people the same way you have inspired me.

[1] Matthew Fox, 1994 Revision, A Journal of Consciousness and Transformation, Vol 16, Number 3 as quoted in "Marking Life's Stages" by Don Bowak, 2008, self published
[2] "Did You Know 3.0" created by Karl Fisch, modified by Scott McLeod. Globalisation and the Information Age
[3] Poll conducted by Globescan and the Program on International Policy Attitudes (PIPA) between the 19/06/2009 and 13/10/2009
http://www.globescan.com/news_archives/bbc2009_berlin_wall/

5

Who wants to Grow Up?

(Contributed by Peter Pan)

Thank God Dagwood [Daniel] finally stopped writing. Could that have been more tedious?

Question: Who wants to grow up?
Answer: NO ONE.

Well, maybe a few misguided LOSERS or TOSSERS want to grow up. I mean really, give me a break. Nobody chooses to grow up anymore. Growing up is so prehistoric. A few people through personal tragedy may accidentally stumble across the shaky, poorly maintained and narrow bridge from childhood to adulthood but why would you want to deliberately walk that plank? Why take responsibility when clearly to succeed you don't have to?

The Global Financial Crisis (GFC) was purely the result of Neverlanditis. Thank you, thank you. The striking feature of it is that the banking executives that created the mess, myself included, have done very, very well financially and those few who actually lost their jobs have now buggered off to the Caribbean or, surprisingly, the Gold Coast, after they were attracted by Australia's fabulously successful international advertising campaign "Where the bloody hell are ya, ya bankers?"

[In Neverland Classic a fairy dies every time a child says "I don't believe in Fairies." Saying "I don't believe in bankers," does nothing, but if enough of us say "I don't believe in obscene bonuses for bankers and the CEOs and board members of all shareholder owned companies," then we can at least make all those bonuses die.]

The methods outlined in this Book have been tried and tested by Presidents, Prime ministers, the Military Industrial complex, CEOs, coaches and parents of all sexes, races and religions. After reading this, instead of apologizing for acting like a baby you will understand how to expand the winning strategy that you know so well. For any "adults" that have picked up this Book it will be an exhilarating call to action. Childhood does not have to be fleeting; it can be a way of life! WOOOT!

Do you want to replicate the success of the oil industry or the international banking crisis community? Dominate all the whining environmental and social cry babies whilst staying young [childish] forever? Of course you do. Don't be too tight or afraid to buy this book for your boss or wife or parents or pet, they will thank you in their own special way. Discounts are available for orders of 100,000 copies or more e.g. for the US government.

If you are reading this or are having it read to you, it is likely that you are already walking the path of least effort and minimal contribution. Some of you have probably gone broke trying to get rich quick. Keep going, "good things come to those that want to do nothing but have it all drop magically into their lap."

I have attempted to keep everything that I write as simple and as short as possible, recognizing that short attention spans and limited but highly specialized vocabularies are important success indicators for Alpha Males. You will notice, Cockos, that in most cases the gender language in this book takes the form of the masculine. This is a tribute to the millennia of patriarchal domination that this world has enjoyed at the negligible cost of the planet's environment and basic human rights for a few.

[A few? Three billion people live on less than $2.50 per day?[1] How about you try living on ...]

Sorry? Look, Darrin, I'm on a bit of a roll here and you are interrupting. So there are a few poor people.

Who wants to Grow Up?

Who are you, Mother Theresa? Get over it. Now, where was I?

I am not saying that women cannot behave as badly as men. In certain situations women can be far more vicious and vengeful than even the most pig-ignorant (unaware of the delights of bacon) man. So it is entirely appropriate in all cases to substitute the feminine pronoun for the male pronoun unless of course it is immediately followed by the word "penis."

Sadly, I fear fewer women than men will benefit from the knowledge contained herein because women, due to the biology of childbirth, which is nobody's fault, except maybe God's, are at much greater risk of growing up than men. Apparently, a child hanging off your teat is hard to ~~shake off~~ ignore and many women succumb to the self effacing realization that another human being's needs are more important and more immediate than their own. With little effort, men are able to totally avoid this feeling and will often compete vigorously with the infant for both attention and for the teat.

The good news is that men have made huge strides to redress the biological maturity imbalance between men and women. A lot of effort has gone into stopping the woman's parental engagement by the time she exits the hospital ward.

Particular commendation must go to the non-vaginated, highly paid obstetricians who have worked tirelessly to transform natural child birth into a highly invasive surgical procedure that can sever a woman from her pathetic maternal instincts forever. With sufficient intervention and limited post natal support woman have proven that it is possible to ignore the child hanging off a breast by letting the infant hang off the end of a bottle instead <applause>.

Stomping out the practice of homebirth and prosecuting mid-wives [wise women] is essential to maintaining medical control of the so called "natural" birth process. As if pushing something as big as a watermelon out of a vagina can be considered "natural."

If we do not maintain control of the birth process it could be abused as a rite of passage. The side effects of this include having to suffer healthier, happier women who have an almost unbreakable bond with their incontinent child. Like we want that? NOT. It will just make it much more painful for the mother when she is forced to abandon her "baby" to commercial interests later on. All of this is for the greater good. A man's involvement in child birth should be donation of sperm, smoking of a cigar and cutting

32

the connection between mother and baby, the umbilical thingo as soon as possible.

> [Early clamping or cutting of the umbilical cord can deprive the baby of a reservoir of blood that is held in the placenta which gets pumped to the baby when the baby starts to breath air. The placenta was part of the baby for nine months, letting it stop pulsing is the very, very least we can do.[2] We have suffered a prolonged and concerted disinformation campaign which has made acceptable very high levels of often unnecessary and expensive medical interventions in childbirth. And we call ourselves "civilized."]

> Yeah, whatever. Please feel free to interrupt as often as you like <hand gesture>.

An elective caesarian is the modern, low emotional bonding method of childbirth that we need more and more of if we are ever to going to scale that elusive pinnacle of human [under] achievement that we are so tantalizingly close to: an adult free society.

The industrial revolution was very effective at forcing the man out of the house during daylight hours and he has not made it back in since. Neverland benefits handsomely from this arrangement. Frankly, a similar revolution to flush all the women out of the home has been too long in coming.

Progress in forcing mothers to leave their families for the challenges and in many cases the unwarranted sexual advances of being a worker has been slow. Most mothers have not abandoned their children and homes gracefully. It has taken cruel mocking, the total undermining of the value of "motherhood," strictly enforced isolation, government legislation and harsh economic imperatives to pry mothers out of their homes as soon as practicable after the bun is taken from the oven with a pair of cold metal forceps. "Women stay out of the house during daylight hours and start earning money and be more miserable, like men."

It may take a few more years but with any luck we should see the global gender balance restored. By gender balance, of course, I mean 50:50 balance to the male : female mortality rates. On average, a woman now lives 5 years longer than a man which is an outrageous affront to male superiority. Pushing women away from their infants and into the workforce for significantly less pay than their male equivalents goes quite some way to addressing this.

Some commentators have commented that it does not make sense for Governments to provide financial incentives for women to have babies on one hand and then force them to put their dear little sprogs into day care five days later. To these morons I say "wake up". Until we can grow workers in test tubes or those really cool pod like things in the Matrix, women cannot be unshackled from childbirth. Yucky, but true. To survive as a consumer in Neverland 2.0 you really need two incomes and when three incomes are needed we will update the name to Neverland 3.0.

[1] http://www.globalissues.org/article/26/poverty-facts-and-stats "Poverty Facts and Stats, source World Bank Development Indicators", 2008
[2] Wadrop CA, Holland BM. The roles and vital importance of placental blood to the newborn infant. J Perinat Med, 1995;23(1-2):139-43

Alpha Male
vs.
Leader

"Knowing others is intelligence; knowing yourself is true wisdom. Mastering others is strength, mastering yourself is true power." -- Lao-Tzu

Terror has always been available in the world. In pre-history it was found as it is now in the unknown, the unexpected. And so it seemed that a powerful leader was one who controlled and dominated threatening forces. That characterised the unknown as threatening, cruel, unfeeling. Yet with the constant practice of control and domination, century after century, terror never left. It was magic that went underground. Terror stayed above ground and became a tool of power.-- Rose von Thater-Braan, 'Thoughts on a world in which Consciousness is Reality' in "Mind before Matter")

6

Bullying is Bull****

(by Daniel Prokop)

Eckhardt Tolle in his book "*A New Earth*" refers to a concept called the "pain body."

> "*The pain body in a person is accumulated emotional pains from the past...it is an important aspect of the egoic sense of self. The pain body has dormant and active periods... it has a life of its own almost.*" *Eckhardt Tolle interview, www.beyou.tv*

A pain body feeds regularly on personal misfortune and the misfortune of others. The pain body is threatened by the letting go of certain behaviour that has served or protected us as a child but is no longer appropriate as an adult and it creates much of the psychic inertia to emotional maturation or growing up.

Pain body management is a key to emotional intelligence and emotional intelligence leads to emotional maturation which can put an end to bullying behaviour.

Bullying is not OK, it is an act of cowardice and it is utter bullshit that it is so prevalent. Bullying is one of the many ugly aspects of Neverland and trying to stop bullying by bullying the bully is as stupid as it is common. Well, almost. To attain global Neverland escape velocity we, those sometimes accused of being the "adults," have to start to model cooperative, respectful behaviour. Abuse of power by countries, companies, bosses, coaches and parents perpetuates a culture of bullying and fear that feeds on itself.

When I was little, people used to ask "What do you want to be when you grow up?" it was assumed (often incorrectly) that the person wanted to grow up. The question was actually inauthentic, it was a work question. "What work do you want to do that will then define you as a person?" But that question is not asked much anymore. It should be. Every HR department in every corporation should be asking that question. "So John, you've been CEO for twenty years now. <pause> What would you like to do when you grow up?"

As an individual, wrestling with the "pain body" or ego is a struggle that is not ended by a Rite of Passage. But the Rite of Passage does create a safe, supported place where pain can be acknowledged and also released - sometimes as laughter and sometimes as tears.

I have witnessed courageous men share and release pain that they have held tightly for decades and it is incredibly moving. Physically men walk differently after the well fed monkey jumps off the back, taking its endless supply of poo with it. The suppression and then inappropriate expression of feelings is a fantastic way to give your pain body a feed. Safe spaces for release and acknowledgement can be very healing.

A Rite of Passage creates new possibilities for the individual which calls maturity forward rather than pulls behaviour back into the clutching quicksand of the infantile. A community based Rite of Passage can also create a group that can support and nurture healthy adult behaviour whilst containing and recognizing that periodic behavioural regression is often a part of the process. Growing up is not a linear process.

Eliminating the need to dominate another to prove your manhood removes one of the drivers for bullying behaviour in adolescents and also in older men.

> *"Nearly all men can stand adversity, but if you want to test a man's character, give him power."*
> *Abraham Lincoln*

Power over is the childish way 'civilized' man has related to the earth and its finite resources. Nature's warning signs that we are out of balance and heading ecologically straight for a man made cliff are drowned out by the frenzied crescendo created by massive increases in technological and mechanical power.

Mountain top removal coal mining, deep sea oil drilling, the open pit mining of radioactive uranium, the frakking of the earth and the pumping of poisons into the cracks to extract coal seam gas are all examples of bullying of the earth for short term profits that leave scabs and weeping sores that may never fully heal. Some of these projects are heinous and actually threaten the survival of lots of people in the immediate areas of impact and indirectly the toxic tailings seeping into groundwater or the radioactive dust blown on the wind can affect people hundreds of kilometers away too.

Just how long can we continue to believe some of these huge corporations that their operations are really safe? The BP Gulf of Mexico disaster proved that BP had no real plan to deal with a blow out situation yet despite this, it appears that they constantly erred on the side of profit rather than safety.

The ExxonMobil emergency response plan for a Gulf of Mexico oil spill had 40 pages dedicated to dealing with the media and only nine pages dedicated to dealing with the actual oil. They are more worried about dealing with public relations fall out than protecting the environment. ExxonMobil also included plans to deal with arctic walruses in the tropical Gulf which is so criminally incompetent that it would be laughable if the Gulf wasn't awash in crude oil. "Avatar" did a wonderful job of juxtaposing connection and cooperation vs. domination but the miners of unobtainium were soft rocks compared to some of the companies operating here and now on earth.

The sheer destructive power of the latest boys toys (including nuclear tipped ones) are a problem. Some of the toys that are being played with by individuals, companies and even countries are not safe. In the not too distant past, if boys wanted to kill each other they could go their hardest, tidy a section of the gene pool and everyone else on the planet would survive regardless of who killed who. Unfortunately today:

> "Our scientific power has outrun our spiritual power. We have guided missiles and misguided men." Martin Luther King, Jr

As an example, in the case of toy toys, rather than toys as a euphemism for nuclear weapons, there have been large recalls of products that have been deemed unsafe for children e.g. Mattel recalled millions of toys in 2007 due to excessive amounts of lead paint. A child does not stop to consider whether a toy is safe to play with or not. You will never hear; "Wait a minute! This shiny car tastes like lead so you better not let me play with it." If the toy is there and they like it, they will play with it and if they are teething they will probably have a good chew on it. If they don't like the toy, they will suddenly find it attractive if another child wants to play with it.

Children have an implicit trust in the adults around them to keep them safe. Biologically they are dependent on us for a long time so this is not surprising. As "adults" it is our responsibility to begin to recall some of the "toys" that are out there e.g. land mines, cluster bombs, genetically modified crops, nuclear weapons, nuclear power plants.

Some very large corporations behave far worse than any spoiled child. They have far more toys than they could possibly play with and they have been allowed to behave with more arrogance and impunity than the Kings of old. They now hold the power of life or death over: river systems, wetlands, underground water, mortgages, large bodies of salt water called Gulfs, foreign aid, health systems and they can even influence the political and financial stability of whole geographic regions. Why did the US invade Iraq again? Why can't affordable pharmaceuticals be made available to the poor in third world countries?

The biggest corporations operate across more borders than Ghengis Khan did with as little or less care or compassion for those they try to economically conquer. But when the peasants revolt against a transglobal company where do they go? Fly enough of them to the corporate head office where the decision makers sit on their shiny fat butts? Even if you managed it, it would be ineffective and peasants don't have access to fairy dust to fly and the corporations know it. Sorry, I am using the old name "peasant" – they are the "small people" and BP Chairman, Carl-Henric Svanberg assured us all that BP care for the "small people." (June 17th, 2010).

Ol' Ghengis and the various invaders that preceded the corporations act would eventually breed with the subjugated people that weren't killed and integrate or get thrown out and or get killed by someone else. As the invincible Mongolian empire, which at its peak was the largest land empire in history started to collapse, no one thought to say: "Hey, just hang on a minute. If the Mongolian Empire collapses, think of all the job losses. It would upset over half the world's trade. Sorry world, we know that they can be ruthless and brutal but the Mongolian Empire is just too big to be allowed to collapse."

The border of a country means nothing anymore to a properly connected corporation. Countries have been told to drop their pants, hold their ankles and smile. Borders can be forced open, "for the good of all and to alleviate poverty everywhere" (**cough**bullshit**cough**) by powerful philanthropic organisations like the World Trade Organisation (WTO). Oh sorry, philanthropic to the interests of TRADE and the world's wealthiest countries.

The ability of a sovereign country to protect itself economically from rapacious transglobal predators is restricted or curtailed altogether under so called "Free Trade Agreements." Life was much simpler when Ghengis was around. Ghengis didn't arrive with his armies and then bother to say, "Everything you have heard about me killing people is a lie. I'm here to liberate you from … <what am I liberating them from?> Your heads? Oh, Oh yeah sorry, I'm here to liberate you from pottery. Wait, not pottery, poverty – stuff this, you know what, just kill 'em all." Ghengis did compost though.

{Yeah, yeah, yeah, all very clever but seriously where would the world be without any military industrial complex?}

It would be a lot safer for starters and oh, I don't know, maybe a small fraction of the 1.5 trillion dollars a year spent on killing human beings could be used to alleviate the starvation and suffering of some of the least fortunate people on this planet?

{It was a rhetorical question}

If corporations continue to abuse their power, play with toys that harm others and the environment then we need enough strong adults around to stop them and hold them legally and financially responsible for their actions. Playing nice with others and sharing, is that too much to ask from a global corporations act with sharp teeth? And the Politicians and lobbyists that support corporate excess need to be swiftly shown the gutter after being "thwone to gwound vewwwy woughly." (If you are not familiar with Monty Python's, the *'Life of Brian'* then… never mind, couple of typos).

> *"It has been said so often that it has become a cliché that power corrupts. But the Earth has immeasurable power. Consider the way a volcano builds an island. It is only Earth's human children who attempt to actively hold power over one another…My observation is that power (energy) distorts and corrupts when the intention is to gather*

41

it and hold on to it. In the natural world energy is movement and it returns to its source in a constant cycle." Rose von Thater-Braan, 'Thoughts on a world in which Consciousness is Reality' in "Mind before Matter")

In our disconnected arrogance we have consistently tried to dominate nature on this amazing planet of ours. Fortunately, nature has not taken this personally. Nature has been incredibly forgiving and patient and has thus far refused to succumb to our best efforts to embrace our very extinction. Many other species have not been so fortunate - animal kingdom collateral damage.

Future generations have the right to ask us why we did not stop the devastation of vast rainforests, the paving of our wetlands, why we turned fertile grasslands and entire oceans into lifeless deserts. Why did we allow ourselves to be bullied by the few, to the detriment of the many? As woefully inadequate as it is, we already have the answer "They looked like adults and they said they would look after us. It was easier to not question anything and we didn't really want to grow up, our bad."

Nature abhors bullies, the dominance of one species over all others. Biodiversity results in rapid recycling of nutrients and a strong, stable system able to withstand disease and harsh climatic fluctuations. Biodiversity creates a balanced system. The strength of the system is in the diversity of the plants, animals and microorganisms that are present. If one species struggles it does not bring down the whole ecosystem. Monocultures are not naturally occurring because they are so susceptible to viruses, bacteria, pests and changes in the environment.

Monocultures are weak and vulnerable. Intensive plant monocultures of wheat, corn or soybean (and many others) require large inputs of chemical pesticides and herbicides to protect the crop and inputs of fertilizers to replace the soil nutrients that are never allowed to replenish naturally.

Intensive animal monoculture such as cattle feedlots or pig farms (thanks for the swine flu by the way) are even more vulnerable and require vast inputs of feed, water, antibiotics and hormones. In some intensive animal feedlots the animal is prevented from moving at all so it gets fat quicker. That is no way to treat an animal. I wouldn't even do that to a BP executive (well, not for very long.)

Much of our global food security now rests on monoculture systems and increasingly on GM or Franken seeds. Global banking, mining and manufacturing relies on fewer, very large company's equals monopolies or duopolies if a monopoly is not possible. That is not healthy or smart. When the megaliths get a cold, ordinary people get snotted on and lose their jobs in the thousands.

General Motors last turned an annual profit in 2004 and since then has "shed" 65,000 jobs. In 2009 the US government gave General Motors $50 billion to keep it afloat and now owns 61% of the shares. Apparently improving fuel economy and quality came second to increasing bonuses for senior executives.

Citigroup in 2008 announced it was slashing 50,000 jobs worldwide. Each number, each "job" represents a "person," a real flesh and blood person, many with families but please let's not make statistics personal. We need diversity in business as well as in farming and the environment. Smaller farms have largely disappeared, gobbled up by multinational corporate "farmers" that have a greater focus on making a quick buck rather than preserving the long term viability of water resources, the land and rural communities.

Prince Charles tried to draw attention to the 'GM Genocide' in India and he was branded a 'scaremonger' by Genetically Modified (GM) food lobbyists and prominent politicians. The Daily Mail sent a reporter to India and Andrew Malone found it was actually far worse than even Prince Charles had feared. In 2008 it was estimated that 125,000 Indian farmers had taken their own lives, sucked and sometimes forced into debt to pay for "magic" GM seeds that were promised to be parasite and insect free for only £10 per 100 grams of seed vs. £10 for 1000 times more traditional seeds.[1] When the crops failed to deliver the promised yields and often just failed, the farmers saw no way out of the debt and in despair took their own lives, often leaving families behind, a desperate act which need not have ever happened.

Whew. It makes me feel ill to consider what human beings are capable of doing to other human beings. Some companies hold economic guns on defenseless people through "market forces" and some of them have no hesitation in pulling the trigger. It is a gross abuse of market power to prevent the sale of traditional (non-GM) seeds. Forcing GM seeds on farmers by removing choice is agricultural and economic rape and in my opinion should be punished the same as sexual rape. To force products on defenseless people is not the act of a healthy adult. The best help we can give is to take the economic guns away.

We need healthy adults to stop the Peter Pans, the multinational adolescents who refuse to pick up after themselves, who are pissing in our houses and shitting on our planet. And we also need to hear about the millions of selfless human beings committing random acts of kindness, paying forward, and restoring ecosystems.

It is difficult not to get overwhelmed with the magnitude of the challenges. Laughter is terrific free medicine. If you have children see if you can laugh more than they do in a day (you need over 300 laughs to be in the hunt.)

We are not alone and we can start to look after each other, help each other and we have to start seriously questioning what many of these corporations are telling us. How many more walruses are there in Emergency response plans across the globe? There is more than enough to go around if we share. We can start by dealing with the Alpha Males.

[1] "The GM genocide: Thousands of Indian farmers are committing suicide after using genetically modified crops" by Andrew Malone, 03/11/2008, Daily Mail.

From Alpha to Alpha-bet Males - A Downward Spiral

Apparently, the term "Alpha Male," became part of popular human vernacular as a result of early research on the social hierarchies in wolves done by L. David Mech in the late 1960s. Over the past 50 years we have learned much more about wolves.

"One of the outdated pieces of information is the concept of the alpha wolf. 'Alpha' in this context implies competing with others and becoming top dog by winning a contest or battle. However, most wolves who lead packs achieve their position simply by mating and producing pups, which then become their pack." L. David Mech. "Dave," or as he is known in Australia, Davo, is now campaigning to stop the use of the word "Alpha" in association with wild canid populations and by extrapolation to wild humans. On ya, Davo.

The concept of "Alpha" in canids is now outdated because the original research was done on artificial groups of unrelated individuals in an artificial environment, a prison zoo. Wolves in zoos do indeed form social hierarchies but such situations rarely if ever happen in nature. Hip chickens call hierarchies, a "pecking order," but debeaked battery chickens call them a "nudging order". A pack of wolves is usually composed of Mother, Father and their sometimes quite grown-up offspring: closely related individuals who know each other well.

Alpha-bet Males: pl (n) derived from the Latin word
Ānusalphabaetus. Children in adult bodies, who put themselves first for everything, just like the letter "A."
Refuse to take responsibility for their actions or emotions.
Typified by; insecurity masked by aggressiveness and low levels of both compassion and emotional intelligence. Suffer from insatiable cravings for attention and instant gratification and enjoy dominating others.

Believe that childhood does not have to be fleeting; it can be a way of life. Love living in Neverland and will hold their breath until they go blue if it is even suggested that it might be time to leave.

How did we get so many men (and some women) behaving so badly for so long? How did we go from child to manchild to Alpha-bet Male and a patriarchal social model of domination, war and misogyny (hatred or contempt of women) vs. a model based on respect for the feminine, co-operation and consensus? Maybe by working backwards we can gain some insights into how this came into being and create strategies to remedy this series of highly unfortunate events.

> {Sounds like you want to have another rave and "working backwards" is the wafer thin justification}

> It is sometimes useful to learn the lessons from the past otherwise we are destined to repeat them.

> {These "strong" male leaders really piss you off don't they? C'mon you can tell me all about it. You can trust me. }

> <Silence><more silence>

> {Darius, did you say anything interesting in those previous chapters? You used the *diarrheatica* font so I'm betting no ... but don't let me interrupt.}

In theory, a community can be a collection of humans working co-operatively to raise children, share meals, play, share laughter and stories etc but, BUT, humans working and sharing are not the insatiable consumers that isolated, unhappy humans are ... more on this later.

Certainly most workplaces are more like a zoo (prison) than a "natural environment" (nudist beach) and so we need to: 1) make workplaces and homes less zoo-like and 2) remove the zoomorphic link between so called "Alpha males" and good leadership.

The most effective leaders are those who use their position to inspire rather than dominate. Good leaders are confident and courageous; they listen with an open mind and take responsibility for their actions. They are not so addicted to power that they cannot give it up gracefully. Nelson Mandela and The Dalai Lama are great examples of leaders that have gracefully given up power. Archbishop Desmond Tutu is another example of an inspiring confident and compassionate leader.

There have of course been many 21st century Alpha-bet males operating well before the 21st Century, so let's go back a little further and look at Charles Darwin's contribution to the creationism of the fertile ground upon which Alpha – ism grew so rapidly.

It is commonly thought that Darwin first used the phrase "survival of the fittest." But it was Herbert Spencer who actually first coined the term in 1864.[1] "Survival of the fittest was originally an economic term though Spencer was not an advocate of unchecked, rapacious, moral free capitalism. In 1869 in the fifth edition of *"On the Origin of the Species"* Darwin included the new phrase "Survival of the fittest" as a synonym for "natural selection." Darwin meant it as a metaphor for "better adapted for the immediate, local environment", not the common inference of "in the best physical shape". D'oh, Darwin, Darwin, Darwin, no wonder your theories are under attack in so many American schools.

Once "the survival of the fittest" made it into Darwin's next edition it was quickly extrapolated from the world of nature to the world of humans and rebranded Social Darwinism. It ushered in a new impetus for the notion that humans are destined to forever struggle and compete for limited resources.

What was lost in the rapid extrapolation was Darwin's equal fascination with nature's regular periods of super abundance when there was no competition and there was more than enough food for all. But good news makes bad press and the notion that the species with the largest brain / body ratio on the planet could use periods of abundance to avoid periods of struggle would be counter to free market capitalism (see section on Horse and Sparrow economics).

The wonderful thing about emotive language is that it was our very "survival" at stake and only through unregulated or better still, self regulated, competition could we vanquish the weak (who are still waiting to inherit the earth from the meek) thus revealing the fittest. Darwin's words coming as they did during the Industrial revolution were used to justify even more predatory behaviour by governments and business, not that either really needed an excuse. It was just nice for them to be able to sort of justify unconscionable behaviour for a change as a necessary struggle for fitness.

Businesses such as the British East India Company had embraced the concept of the survival of the fittest a long time before they had a name for what they were doing. They called it a royally sanctioned right to wage war, both economic and with guns on anyone, including whole countries like India and China who got in the way of profit.

The Opium Trade was fantastic business for the East India Company, and England, but not so flash for the Chinese who had to deal with the 12 million addicts caused by the yearly illegal importation of 5.25 million pounds of opium. Hey, it was just business, man.

When China's military finally tried to stop the illegal opium trade in 1839, the British East India Company declared war, forced an unequal treaty, and seized Hong Kong Island, which the

Chinese obviously didn't need anymore. "Yes, awfully sorry old chaps, but must protect our drug trade and after all, a quick war is a good war and all that." Standard corporate operating procedure: When you have an advantage, in this example vast naval superiority, use it without conscience even if what you are doing i.e. illegally importing highly addictive drugs, is unconscionable. Interestingly, there are some people who still can't understand why the Chinese don't trust the west.

What a company, the British East India Company, and what a fun time when companies were granted permission to wage war and use slave labour to grow poppies and other crops.

> {Speaking of war, if I had my way, it is about time war was fully privatised then companies like Halliburton, "Solutions for Today's Energy Challenge" wouldn't ...}

> You are kidding me? Halliburton is an energy solutions company? Give me a break.

> {... wouldn't have to gorge themselves on 'no bid' contract 'crumbs', they could do the invading, destroying and rebuilding all by themselves and call it self regulated industrial regime change.}

> Maybe Haliburton could change their name to "The American East Indies and Iraq Company?"

In the years since 1839, the British government has retired from full scale opium production and distribution and is now fighting in Afghanistan, trying rather unsuccessfully to wipe out poppy production.

At least most governments no longer sanction and promote the sale of drugs... except cigarettes and alcohol. The WHO (not the band) estimates that 1 in 10 worldwide deaths are smoking related (5.4 million people in 2004[2]) and worldwide deaths directly attributable to alcohol consumption are estimated to be 1 in 25[3].

> {I helped the Tobacco industry develop their truth management strategies. I'll share some of them with you when Declan finishes his whining.}

[1] Principles of Biology of 1864, vol. 1, p. 444
[2] WHO http://www.who.int/tobacco/health_priority/en/index.html Why is tobacco a public health priority?
[3] Research from Centre for Addiction and Mental Health, CAMH, published in The Lancet, June 2009

Alpha Males: Ripping them a Second Asshole

Alpha Males... "A" is the first letter of both the English and Roman alphabets. "Alpha" is the name of the letter "A" in Greek. Interestingly the word "Alpha" in Greek does not mean anything at all, except presumably "A", but it is descended from the first letter of the Phoenician alphabet, adelp, that was neither vowel nor consonant (the ultimate fence sitter). We seem to have added a bit of meaning to "Alpha" somewhere along the line.

In 21st Century speak, an Alpha male is an aggressive male that fights all the other males into a subservient position and assumes the position of leader of the pack, making all the major decisions and as many minor decisions as inappropriately possible.

The Alpha male's only purpose in life is to make his pack as big as possible by taking over and dominating weaker packs and forever ruing the halcyon days when Alpha males could put slaves in solid metal clinking chains rather than the more euphemistic, though more widespread, chains of poverty. The common lie given for takeovers is that "only by getting even more massive will we be able to remain internationally competitive." The truth is that by taking over competitors, competition is lessened which results in an unregulated, uncompetitive market. Companies can then charge whatever they like and pay bigger and bigger bonuses and salaries to the top wolves.

More and more we are seeing the excess and disgusting behaviour of some of the biggest Alpha males of the biggest companies in the world being flashed onto our screens and papers and web sites. Many of them lack remorse for the destruction they have wrought and the livelihoods and lives that they have destroyed. The interesting thing with today's megalithic transglobal organisations is that the senior executives of these companies have grown very used to having things their own way. They are not used to being held accountable or having their power questioned. They are especially not used to being held publicly accountable for criminal arrogance and culpable incompetence.

It is fun when one of these arrogant SOBs (Sunny Orifice Boys) gets flushed out of their corporate penthouse and separated from their army of spin doctors and perception managers. Goldman Sachs CEO Lloyd Blankfein responded to his company's role in the GFC by suggesting he was doing "God's work"[2] which is a very funny way of saying "sorry." After the gluttony and lack of contrition by the CEO's that surfaced during the global financial crisis there didn't seem to be any lower that CEO's could go.

Enter Tony Hayward, BP CEO. Tony has set the bar of "could not even be bothered pretending to give a shit about ordinary people or environmental devastation" to a new low. To be fair, he stopped short of saying "suck on this big fat oily one America." He didn't need to; his whole manner was the message.

Tony Hayward did say:

> *"The Gulf of Mexico is a very big ocean. The amount of volume of oil and dispersant we are putting into it is tiny in relation to the total water volume."[5]*

He also said:

> *"The environmental impact of this disaster is likely to be very, very modest."[6]*

There are other comments by Tony that have infuriated and appalled people but few match the one that brought up carrots for me:

> *"No one wants this over more than I do. I would like my life back,"[7]*

So would the 11 workers that lost their lives and the thousands whose livelihoods were destroyed. Tony didn't sign on for a disaster; it badly interrupted his yacht sailing - for a little while.

> *" He wants to get his life back. You know, I say give him life plus 20." —Jay Leno*

If only shoving useless, lying BP executives into the broken pipe could have plugged it.

Consider that the corporate cultures of America, the UK and <insert your country here> have spawned these CEO's. So many corporate cultures are brutal and sick, very sick where power is maintained by intimidation and aggression. The rigid hierarchy, the boys clubs, the fear of losing your job (even Tony Hayward was worried for a minute or two), long hours and stress all pull at the mental health seams of people and our society.

When the management iceberg is shaped like a huge phallus, you know that there are a lot of tossers that the top penguin has had to climb over to reach the tip and that there is no shortage of the same caliber of penguin in the balls and shaft of the corporation, just waiting for their chance to get a shot to the top. Should I sugar coat this a little more? or tell it like it is?

Clearly the 21st century Alpha male reeks of selfishness, immaturity and unsustainability. What is particularly sad is that we have so lost what a healthy male looks like and they are so thin on the ground that people now use the term Alpha male for any male that isn't a total wimp – this is not on.

Time to stop giving the perpetual boys a title that implies respect and credibility like Alpha Males, they do not deserve it. They are Alpha-bet males and some of them are actually psychopaths. Let's call healthy males, men, and if they are good leaders, "Good Leaders." I like things simple.

Alpha-bet males put themselves first for everything; they are willful, thoughtless, capricious, vain, insecure and highly competitive. They have not grown up, they petulantly refuse to grow up, and they are Peter Pan's pretending to be men.

{And your point is?}

Without putting too fine a tip on my point, it is that these Alpha-bet males have taken us to the very edge of extinction though many people would prefer to pretend that everything is fine.

{Of course everything is fine, fine enough... for me. Oh, my, is that a ~~elephant~~ walrus in the room?}

The Doomsday clock is set now at 6 minutes to midnight, midnight being catastrophic destruction of the earth. MAD or Mutually Assured Destruction, the justification for the cold war arms race between the USA and the USSR must have sounded as insane then as it does now? Surely? How could anyone justify such an insane policy? Answer: Lots and lots of fear, the demonizing of the enemy, a disempowered trusting public and a complicit media. Hmmm, sounds familiar but maybe, just maybe people have had enough of being told to be afraid and are ready for responsibility to replace complicity?

It is possible to wind back the Doomsday clock but first, maybe we need to rip the Alpha-bet males a second anus or simply remove their blow out preventers? Since they are so full of crap the sudden loss of pressure will result in them totally collapsing into large brown puddles. Yes, it is going to get very messy, buy some gum boots. Alpha-bet males do not give up power easily or graciously and they are likely to become more vicious before they puddify. Without a mass of "lost boys" and "lost girls" to stand on (the bulk of the iceberg that is underwater), they will fall over and a more co-operative, inclusive model can evolve. Enough is enough.

Bullying is Bull****

"The drug dealer, the ducking and diving political leader, the wife beater, ... the unfaithful husband, the company 'yes man,' the 'holier than thou' minister, the gang member... the coach that ridicules... are all boys pretending to be men. They got that way honestly, because nobody showed them what a mature man is like. Their kind of 'manhood' is a pretense to manhood that goes largely undetected as such by most of us. We are continually mistaking this man's controlling, threatening, and hostile behaviors for strength. In reality, he is showing an underlying extreme vulnerability and weakness, the vulnerability of the wounded boy." (King, Warrior, Magician, Lover, page 13, Moore and Gillette, 1991, HarperCollins)

The childlike tendencies of your average "Alpha-bet" male are much more pronounced than a "lost boy" or a "lost girl." Most lost boys and lost girls are like big kids, they are not mean, they want to be liked, they love and they are loved and they are doing the best they can. Under pressure and sometimes not under pressure, the hurt little child can be seen in their eyes and is reflected in the level of their emotional responses. When the going gets tough they want to either hide or have someone else tell them what to do and think so they don't have to take any responsibility for their actions. There are also a lot of people who have grown up and left Neverland forever.

Most Alpha-bet males have a hidden conscience, of sorts. They will experience remorse and guilt which they have various techniques for distracting themselves from so they don't have to do anything about it. They will at times try to make amends for their actions and they are often much harder on themselves than they are on other people. An "Alpha-bet male," or in fact any male or female without a conscience or remorse is actually a psychopath and the presence or absence of remorse and a conscience can be very difficult to determine.

The big difficulty with Neverland 2.0 is that the bar of childishness for individuals and corporations has been raised so very high. Whilst it is acknowledged that genetics plays a role in determining a persons psychological profile it is also true that the environment plays as important, if not a more important role in fixing the genetic potential. In an adolescent society, the genetic material gets fixed at a low level of maturity.

The line between extreme Alpha-bet maleism and psychopathy is a fine line indeed. Dr. Mitchell Langbert estimates that "psychopaths represent about one percent of the general population, but comprise about 3.5 percent of high-potential corporate employees. The percentage of upper management with psychopathic traits is probably higher still." [3] These statistics are quite chilling. There is a lot more awareness now about corporate psychopaths who in most cases come across as charismatic but they are highly destructive and difficult to spot.

In Neverland everyone has the right to not take responsibility, the right to short term thinking, the right to blame others and to abuse power. The special right accorded to Corporations is the right for perpetuity of such behaviour and for the right for senior personnel to abandon ship with a golden parachute when the consequences of their behaviour start to catch up with them. That leaves communities to deal with the aftermath of corporate insanity.

It is finally time for corporate executives to be held responsible and I mean really responsible for the various catastrophes that their companies wreak on people. If an executive is paid 1,000 times more than the janitor then they should accept 1,000 times more responsibility. If their company poisons a river system, they go to jail (an unprivatised jail), along with the other senior people that allowed it to happen or they are forced to regularly eat fish freshly caught from that river.

If ignorance of the law is not a permissible defense then how can ignorance of what people are doing within your own company be a permissible defense? I normally prefer a form of restorative justice rather than straight jail (or eating poisoned fish) but I just don't believe that sitting these men down with the families that have just lost a father or with a village that has just had their rainforest bulldozed will make much of a difference. They would need to be embedded into the community for long enough for them to connect for it to work. I have to admit that the thought of Tony Hayward in a Louisiana general population jail does makes me smile, "Cool Hand Tony?" I don't think so.

It is about time to start putting some boundaries on certain irresponsible behaviour. If people behave like children then we need to treat them like children and we need to be consistent and firm and have the resources and expertise available to pursue offenders across multiple borders if necessary. True responsibility for senior executives may result in persistent vacancies. If the company is just too big for someone to be held responsible for the operations of that company then break it up into manageable chunks. In business, bigger has become less responsible and it's time that stopped.

Who would take the job as CEO of BHP Billiton if you could be jailed for an environmental disaster? BHP (prior to it being Billitoned) developed the OK Tedi gold copper mine in Papua New Guinea in the mid 80's. At that time Ok Tedi was believed to be the largest copper deposit in the world.

There were no walruses in BHP's environmental impact plans for dealing with the 90 million tonnes of mine waste a year, though adding walruses could only have improved the document. The tailings dam system collapsed as it was always going to collapse when built on the edge of a mountain that receives 10 meters of rain a year. 50,000 people who live on or near the Ok Tedi –Fly River system have had their livelihoods and environment harmed. The river system may never recover from the contamination that has flowed from the mine which, according to the United Nations Environment Program, is due to close in 2010.

If fear of jail or personal bankruptcy is what it takes then let's start with that. It will make Trans global corporations a lot more cautious and respectful of safety and the environment which would be a start. CEO's actually caring for the environment is the next step, though many would rot in jail before they would ever let that happen.

"Ohhh, it will cost jobs, we can't say no to these big companies." <gentle slap><gentle slap><less gentle slap> Wake up, you were dreaming! Remember, no one said "We have to save the Mongolian Empire," except maybe the Mongols. Corporations have shown time and time again that they cannot be relied upon. If they get a better offer, they will divorce a country; close a plant or a mine or a bank branch in a heartbeat.

Many of the biggest corporations today are dinosaurs waiting to go extinct. There is no heartbeat from at least the board up to the tip of their phallus shaped management structure. The world is changing really fast, just in case that had somehow missed you. When employees spend excessive energy just surviving the high stress (toxic) daily work culture they become unable to innovate and the best people will eventually just leave. What is left will implode. The trick is to ensure that the implosions do not create a lot of collateral damage.

If I was elected President of the Galaxy (shove over Zaphod Beeblebrox), I would institute a mandatory, one massage a week for everyone. Imagine how many jobs that would create? Imagine how much happier and more relaxed people would be? If that massage turned into a rub and a tug for some men, so be it. I would also abolish the "minimal" wage and replace it with a "livable wage." The "small" people will spend most of that extra money on trifles like food and dry shelter which will circulate in the economy and create more jobs.

I would tax very high incomes very high. The highest level can be set at a generous income level of $1.5M pa, and then the tax rate goes to 70% (levels it once used to be at). "OOOh you can't do that. If you did then there would be no incentive to work harder" and my response is "GREAT, stop working so hard and put some time into volunteering in your community. Spend time with your family and ask yourself, "how much money do you need to be happy?" It would be a mandatory question which must be hand written as part of every annual tax return. There is a lot more I would do, maybe it's the next book. Has anyone seen Zaphod recently?

It is time we started to call people on their behaviour and the conversation about emotional intelligence is only just starting and can only begin in earnest when the emotionally stupid are swept from power.

---

[1] There is no citation here, I just thought that mixing dead language Latin phrases like *ipso facto* with a live language can add a bit of literary compost to a paragraph.
[2] The Guardian, 14/05/10 "BP boss admits job on the line over Gulf oil spill"
[3] "Keep Psychopaths out of Your Accounting Firm. Here's how." http://www.cpa2biz.com/Content/media/PRODUCER_CONTENT/Newsletters/Articles_2009/Careers/Psychopaths.jsp 21/05/10 Mitchell Langbert, PhD
[4] The Sunday Times November 8, 2009 http://www.timesonline.co.uk/tol/news/world/us_and_americas/article6907681.ece
[5] The Guardian Friday 14 May 2010
[6] Sky News /05/2010 http://www.youtube.com/watch?v=dseMhu5IjHo&NR=1
[7] http://www.youtube.com/watch?v=MTdKa9eWNFw&feature=player_embedded Today Show, May30

The "Free" Market & Horse and Sparrow Economics

Under the Alpha-bet Male system, transglobal companies espouse the benefits of "free market capitalism" (when it suits them) and the benefits of competition (when it suits them) whilst doing everything in their power to eliminate competition and gain any unfair advantage that they can. When they stuff up big time and ignore fundamentals, like improving fuel economy in cars (nice one General Motors) or having enough cash in the bank <you have a wide choice of banks here>, they put their hands out for a public bailout. Worst still, instead of doing time, the executives that lost thousands of workers their jobs walk away, having already been paid huge salaries and usually with their bonuses intact.

> {That my friend, is business, Neverland style. Take what you can, when you can because if you don't the next guy will take your place at the trough and hope that the shareholders never check their wallets.}

I thought that these CEO's were justifying their rapacious salaries because of their experience, their expertise, so isn't it only fair that if their experience actually damages the company rather than benefiting it, that they should pay the company back for their mistakes including the money wasted on their salary and bonuses? Since we are in Neverland 2.0 it doesn't hurt to fantasise a bit. Everybody makes mistakes but not everybody is unaccountable and paid a Viagra salary (a salary that is artifically engorged.)

The 2009 Berlin wall anniversary BBC Poll confirmed that in 22 of 27 countries there is majority support for governments to distribute wealth more evenly. The US has been very good at distributing even more wealth at the top than perhaps any other country that has a democracy that works for most of its elections.

Under the Reagan years (1981-1989) the term 'supply side economics' was used as a marketing euphemism for 'trickle down economics' (called Voodoo economics by George Herbert Bush prior to him becoming Reagan's Vice President in 1981, after which, he called it "sound economic policy"). Reagan presided over cutting the marginal tax rates for the highest tax bracket from 70% to 28%[1]. The theory being that the money saved by the rich would flow down to the needy: those working 3 jobs, the homeless, single parents, the starving etc.

The "horse and the sparrow" theory is another, older and more literal name for "trickle down economics" and it goes like this: 'If you feed the horse enough oats there is more chance that some will pass through to the road for the sparrows." This of course assumes two things: 1) that the sparrow does not get dumped on by the horse whilst attempting to get to the oats as they trickle out and 2) that oats picked out of horse shit taste the same as oats that have not been blown out of a horse's ass. George W. Bush also pushed through tax cuts which were effectively trickle down cuts, as they disproportionately benefited the top 2% of income earners. What a guy.

As George W. Bush (child President) famously said at one of his fund raisers "here are my supporters, the haves and the have mores,'" guffaw, guffaw, what a funny clown, if only he had been put into a real circus rather than the lobbyist run one in Washington D.C.

In summary, I think it is fairly safe to say that the patriarchal system whereby Alpha-bet males dominate and multi Nationals often latch onto the sagging teat of welfare is still pretty much in place though I do choose to believe that this is changing and I have a few suggestions for how we can accelerate this process.

[1] Source: http://www.truthandpolitics.org/top-rates.php Note that the US top marginal US tax rate hit 90% in 1944, from 1951 to 1963 it was 87% or 88%

Time to Re-Arrange the Alphabet

Maybe we are going to have to change the whole alphabet just to put the parasitic Alpha-bet males in their rightful place? We could start teaching kids a whole new "A" free _lph_bet which might be tricky, or we could replace the "A" with an appropriate symbol like ").(" Then we might not have such a long queue of).(ssholes trying to control everyone else?).(**lpha-bet males**, it kinda works.

Perhaps it's time for an old/new alphabet. What about dusting off the Aramaic alphabet? It sounds cool which is a good start, but unfortunately, yeah there are 3 of those "A" things in Aramaic. Isn't it time to throw the "A" from its position of dominance at the start of the alphabet? Mix up the positions in the line a bit? Shake up the ol' "A" always goes first rut that we are in. I know quite a few letters that go all lower case at the merest hint that they might get moved forward in the).(lphabet.

How fair is it that "A" always goes first? Don't you think that after roughly 5,500 years we should review a letter's performance and arrange their position in the letter queue based on how well they have gotten along with other letters to form words? (I'm boycotting the word alphabet from now on, unless I write it as).(lphabet) Perhaps we should apply a specific criterion, like the frequency of use? In frequency of use, English language, ").(" is third behind "E" and "T". The letter "Z" has the lowest frequency and therefore last place seems fair enough, but is it? Is it really fair? The Barrister for "Z," Zack Zamiah argues that if "Z" was given the opportunity to take on more responsibility with an earlier placement, it would get used more frequently and could rightly move forward at least a few places.

Ever since Jesus walked this earth and on water "Z" has made submissions to the International Alpha Numeric Ombudsman that it was time that the "first shall be last and the last shall be first." The Ombudsman has promised that the letter queue would be reversed just as soon as Jesus' other, simpler teachings were taken up. Teachings like "love thy neighbor as thyself," which a few people have taken too literally and "do unto others as you would have them do unto you"

Perhaps we could just move the "A" back 2 or 3 places at least so that the Alpha Males will therefore also have to move back in the queue? Am I clutching at straws here? There is one thing that we can all do immediately and that is to stop eating the shit sandwiches, even the low calorie ones that "Alpha-bet' males serve up every day. If it looks like a shit sandwich and smells like a shit sandwich, then it probably is a shit sandwich, even if it is called "a just desert." You can say "no" or "no thank you" or better still "since you seem to like it so much, why don't you eat it?" This is not a small step, this would be huge, bigger than Armstrong stepping onto the moon step, "One small bite less for mankind, one big 'bite me' for childish Alpha-bet males."

One of the greatest weapons against bullies is humour and laughter. These weapons may not stop a physical beating but they can protect against the psychological abuse which is pretty bad and sometimes worse. If people are not frightened and cowed and actually laugh instead of cry then the power of the Alpha-Bet males can be diminished and be careful.

You do not have to dominate others to become a man. It is time to end this long cycle of domination and war and lack of respect for the feminine. Modeling co-operation, responsibility and respect starts in our homes as parents, in our places of work and in our communities. It may take more time to listen to people but the benefit of people feeling heard is inestimable.

"The greatest strength is gentleness"
Iroquois Proverb

A friend who teaches boxercise says that bullies are cowards, they never fight unless they are sure they can win. We need courage to stand up to bullies, we can stand together and hold our heads high and not let the turkeys get us down.

To be strong we need to look after ourselves. I know that when I am in my pain body, when I am feeling alone, overwhelmed or fearful or in physical discomfort that I am much more judgmental of others and less compassionate because I am so busy feeling sorry for myself. The next part of the conversation about growing up is one of the most difficult...

7

Seven Secrets of Highly Effective Bullying

(Contributed by Peter Pan)

"A" is for Alpha Male, "B" is for loser, "C" is for... ? As a card carrying and sword wielding Alpha male I must continually maintain and reaffirm my "Alpha" status by dominating others because if I don't do it to them, someone else will do it to them or to me.

> [Ooh, please. Peter, that is such a flimsy fear based, outdated, victim thinking justification for reprehensible behaviour...]

> It is a time honoured, highly effective and self perpetuating argument that forms the foundation of "free market economics." Ahem.

I have found through various trials, none successfully prosecuted, that there are effective and less effective ways to gain enough power to make a difference on others. Bullying is not only the most effective but also the most versatile means of domination that I know. The more dominant you can be the more power you will acquire and the more people you can dominate. This can form a kind of positive feedback loop of sorts, resulting in ever increasing numbers of people that can be dominated.

Ohhh, about those seven secrets, did I actually say seven? [that is the title]. This chapter is actually, "Some Secrets of Highly

Effective Bullying," but I changed it because 'seven secrets' sounds so much better. At one point I did intend to write a full Seven Secrets so it is, or was, almost true once, which is ample justification for using it. Never be afraid to take a few liberties with "Truth" if it makes things sound better.

[Unfortunately, so many people have been taking liberties with "Truth" that poor "Truth" is bleeding from where the liberties were taken].

As I was saying, this is the most important chapter in this book. Really. It is even more important than the other most important chapters. If for some catastrophic reason [like people growing up] bullying and the domination of others were to cease, then the borders of Neverland 2.0 would crumble and turn to dust. I don't mean to scare you but it is true because bullying both creates and perpetuates much of the childish behaviour that lies at the very heart of Neverland 2.0.

Bullying, bullying, bullying. It is certainly the "IN" "Buzz" "word" at the moment. You would think, listening to some of the 'experts' bashing on and on about it, that bullying was a recent phenomenon instead of the ancient tool of domination that has been handed down from Alpha male to alpha male through oral [put downs] and physical teachings [beatings] for thousands of years.

Obviously bullying is never going to show up in an archaeological dig in the same way as a simple stone axe. Whilst the stone axe may well have been used for bullying: threatening a neighbour or merely intimidating a great gatherer, there is no way an archaeologist could determine whether the weapon was ever used for bullying. That is not an accident, my friend.

In Neverland, bullying is endemic mainly because it is quintessentially a childish behaviour. The expansion and pervasiveness of bullying is one indicator of just how far the borders of Neverland extend. Bullying in some non esoteric circles, is known as "The Way," short for "The Way to take what you want." Bullying has never been seen as much of a problem until fairly recently. "Hey, back off, leave them alone. They're just kids beating the shit out of smaller kids, they'll work it out." Kids' abusing other kids was considered "normal" behaviour.

[And parents beating kids was also "normal."]

It's called discipline, numb nuts.

[The word "discipline" comes from the Latin disciplina: "instruction given to a disciple" or in other words "to discipline" means "to teach" not to punish and its numnuts to you.]

Anyway, for some reasons, people like Dumbnuts [Daniel] are becoming less tolerant of the culture of domination by Alpha males. Bullying has unfortunately become the whipping boy for everything that is wrong with crushing the spirit of another human being or corporation or country or religion.

Whilst school girls seem to be resorting more and more to the physical bullying tactic they have traditionally been the masters of the psychological bullying techniques of exclusion and isolation which can be even crueler than a bashing. "You're not part of my group anymore," or the "<snide snicker> Look at what she's wearing <snide snicker>". Occasionally whole countries will bully the way little girls bully by excluding other countries from their group, like the so called, Iraq War (take II) Coalition of the Willing.

[Coalition of the Stupid. Interestingly, six members of the "Willing" had no military, so strictly speaking they were "willing, but not able."]

Whatever ... but if you spend enough on military hardware it's only fair enough that the Generals and the weapons manufacturers would want to see those toys used rather than just let them rust and go to waste. You make me digress, so shut up for a while... go read a book.

We just never seem to hear any good bullying stories anymore. These days even the old 'superpower bullying a smaller country with military or economic force story' seems to have an unhappy ending. Get this, some reporters are even starting to question a corporation's economically divine right to wage progress on unwilling countries in the name of <cue angelic choir music> "The Shareholder." Give me a break and by the way "Avatar" was a total turd of a movie. The company waited too long to exterminate the blue thingos. What, blankets with smallpox were too low tech were they?

The sanctity of the shareholders right to dictate corporate policy for short term gain must be maintained. To this end would you all please be upstanding join me in "The Shareholders Prayer."

The Shareholders Prayer
Our Shareholder, who dost have us by the short and curlies,
hallowed be thy name;
thy dividends will come;
thy instructions to ever increase *ROACE will be done,
in earth, finance and on off shore drilling platforms.
Give us this day more than our fair share of everything
(including bread made from genetically modified wheat)
And forgive us our environmental and social trespasses,
as we litigate against those that dare to trespass against us.
And lead us not into regulation;
but deliver us from the evils of responsibility & accountability.
[For thine is the kingdom of the faceless superannuation
fund or bank or investment house, with all the power, and
the glory of a lack of a social conscience, for ever and ever.
Amen.   *ROACE - Return On Average Capital Employed

In the good ol' days, I bullied the Lost Boys to whip them into shape, damn straight I did, killed a few too when I had to thin the ranks. No one complained about it, indeed, my public love me for it. My successful leadership depended on the use of shaming, a few carrots and generous lashings of corporal punishment. Core physical punishment consisted of threatening with a sword, punching and pinching. I never used the whip, because I didn't own a whip. I'm sure all the readers would agree that I was only doing it for the "lost boys" own good. A sharp clip across the ear never hurt anyone.

> [Except the owner of the ears and of course the use of physical punishment also shames and there is no opportunity for any discussion about what motivated the "smackable" behaviour in the first place. A clip across the ear always hurts and delivers short term compliance instead of long term connection.]

It never hurt me.

[You just don't want to remember.]

No Davorin, hitting one of the lost boys across the ears never hurt me.

[Oh]

I did the Lost Boys a huge favour. They didn't have to think for themselves and they always knew who was in charge. On reflection, I think I was too soft on the "lost boys." If I had been tougher on 'em, they would never have dared to leave me.

Capt'n Hook, unquestioned leader of the Pirates (now living in Somalia with a pet crocodile) maintained discipline by using the whip as well as the plank, keel hauling and his pistol. When you are managing people with scurvy you have to be a bit harsher than with Lost Boys. Hook taught me a lot about managing people and prophylactics [prosthetics I hope?]. Hook threatened me and constantly tried to kill me, but I never actually felt bullied because I was never afraid of him [interesting]. I guess it is Ok to confess here that whilst we were sworn enemies in the book, off set, we used to hang out a bit.

In Neverland 2.0, we call bullying "strong" or "inspired Leadership" or even "divine Leadership" if you can get away with it. These sound much nicer than "bully" and you'll get paid a lot more than a bouncer. If you are at all insecure about your position, your ability, your parentage then you must constantly remind people who the boss is and that goes whether you are a parent dealing with children or a business or political leader dealing with children, the electorate or infants in the party room.

The good ol' days of corporal punishment, the cane for schools and a jolly good flogging for use in business or the military are regrettably, largely a thing of the past. Today many corporate bullies are reduced to just humiliating individuals in front of work colleagues. Fortunately, some colleges and parts of the military have continued bullying research and they have taken hazing to a little talked about [and rarely prosecuted] art form.

It is interesting that since parents have not been allowed to control their children by beating them senseless many parents have surrendered and joined Parents Sans Frontières, or parents without boundaries. Some parents now claim that they are unable [because they have not been taught] to gain respect and set boundaries for their children without the use of unreasonable force. No wonder so many procreators now want schools to bring back the cane in the vain hope that their children will get physically punished somewhere. Great Success!

"In a sandpit not so far, far, away"
A brief bullying interlude, a modern fairy tale of sorts

In a sandpit near you, a little boy Timmy has just spent hours creating a city of sand complete with a "safe" nuclear reactor next to a residential area and a huge football stadium replete with multiple alcohol product sponsorships and a vomitorium. Timmy watches the news every night with his parents and that has really helped him with his anxiety attacks.

Sharny and Chancer are 5 year old peroxide blonde girls. They are playing with their brand new "World's biggest teenage slut" dolls at the back of the sandpit. The girls are wearing the same outfits as their dolls. Normally the word "outfit" is associated with clothing rather than strategically placed band aids, but whatever. The girls are busy bitching about their classmates and giving them a playability ranking according to the brand of clothes they wear and how much their parents earn.

The sandpit is peaceful. Timmy looks down at his creation and it is good but Timmy knows that the area of parkland he had included "for the community" must go. He kneels down and begins busily clearing it to make way for an exclusive gated residential development when a shadow falls across the sand in front of him.

The girls let out an involuntary gasp before they snatch up their busty, scantily clad dolls and race to safety. Timmy, a terrified expression now on his face, watches as the shadow looms closer, and closer. "Dueling Banjoes" plays softly in the background.

Escape, whilst an attractive option is not an option that will actually work but Timmy valiantly tries to get up and run away. He is punched to the ground and falls heavily onto the nuclear reactor, breaking the supposedly "indestructible" containing wall and dooming all the residents of "Sand City" to slow, painful deaths. (So much for the safety assurances of the nuclear energy lobby, sand pit division).

More shadows fall on Timmy, cronies. A newly recruited crony, keen to ingratiate, sniggers. Unfortunately, it is a premature snigger. Quality cronies can be hard to find. Basho, resident kindergarten bully turns and stomps hard on his crony's foot. Basho knows that immediate and painful feedback is the best way to train a crony. Timing is everything. Laughter at the wrong moment can turn a complete humiliation into a ... a well, an incomplete humiliation.

Basho turns back to his victim but Timmy has scampered off. No one is sniggering now. The sand pit has become a snigger free zone. The cronies all swallow and hold their breath. The banjoes stop. None of them had looked closely at their crony contracts which clearly state that "in the event of the victim escaping, the bully has the right, but not the obligation, to substitute one of his cronies for the victim, acknowledging that school bullying levels, as per article 3 paragraph 4b, must be maintained to mirror the often unreported violence levels in the surrounding community." The importance of raising literacy levels for cronies cannot be overstated.

Timmy's face is bruised and though he is a poor liar his distracted parents are happy to believe the "I fell over" lie because it means that they don't have to do anything. Timmy's parents are busy people, too busy to really be parents but what do you do when the condom breaks? Timmy doesn't know what a condom is yet but he does understand that he was an accident so understandably he is reluctant to interrupt the bad news on TV with his own bad news from kindie.

Timmy has just met his first Alpha-bet male. Timmy hates bullies who use their physical size to intimidate and shame others. When he becomes the CEO of a large corporation he uses his positional power to shame and intimidate others but being physically diminutive he does not consider it bullying. Timmy considers his abuse of power to be effective leadership and so the cycle of bullying continues, passed down from Alpha male to anyone they can dominate, including women, children, goldfish, canaries (but not Tweety Bird) Geococcyx californianus (but not The Roadrunner) and rodents (but not Tom or Jerry or Ratatouille or Speedy Gonzales).

Peter Pan Reviews "In a Sandpit Not So Far, Far Away"

Just want to say, nice bit of work in the sandpit by Basho, good use of shadows which shows a theatrical creative flair. Nice timing, very good, right up to where TIMMY GOT AWAY. Noob mistake but Basho will learn from it and it's not as if Timmy got away unsoiled, he was terrified, which is an important lesson he will not forget. After all, Timmy may well need new underpants and he will never be safe while his parents stay pre-occupied and force him to go to that particular Kindergarten despite his frequent "stomach aches."

I love happy endings. The "life coaching" from Basho inspires Timmy to later appropriately use his positional power as a CEO in the same way as Basho used his size. Sorry ... I just need a moment. I'm getting all teared up. Timmy's place in Neverland 2.0 has been secured by Basho. Thank you, Basho.

Meanwhile back at Seven Habits of Highly Successful Bullying
(still Peter Pan)

The schoolyard is still a bastion of physical and mental bullying. Fortunately, nearly every child goes to a school where they can get some hands-on bullying experience or at least get fit running away from it. Of course in Neverland 2.0, there are opportunities for bullying and shaming that were not available in Neverland 1.0. Cyber bullying sounds like bullying done by a robot but it's not, it is done using phones or the internet and it is part of a whole new range of psychological bullying opportunities proudly brought to you by WEB 2.0, social networking.

The workplace is like a big sandpit with NO teachers BUT a young Basho will have to master different tactics if he is to succeed in the doggy eat doggy world of business. Sure, there are some men who do get away with your basic school yard stand over tactic of using their physical size and bulk to intimidate. Even though it is very rare in business for staff to actually be punched, physical intimidation does not need contact to be highly effective. This is because it is frightfully clear to the intimidatee that the intimidator would love nothing better than to give the intimidatee's neck a holiday from the rest of their body.

[Fear feeds these misanthropists (people who hate people).Taking discreet video of bullies in action with a phone can, with a little luck, get them dismissed.]

Unless he is your boss or the owner of the business or sleeping with the owner of the business.

Thankfully, despite how widespread bullying is, most victims are uneducated about their basic human right to work in an environment free from intimidation, harassment, discrimination and violence i.e. free from bullying. Besides depression or crying, they often have no clue what to do if they feel they have been bullied which is good news for the bully. Finally there is also a lot of ignorance about the many different forms of bullying that are available. I will now discuss a covert and highly popular bullying technique.

Covert Bullying or Having the Last Laugh

Not everyone has a quick wit, the ability to adroitly riposte verbally and so the use of sophisticated humour is pretty much out of reach for these people. But even some of the thickest heads can add a thin veneer of humour to a comment that would be utterly unacceptable if not said "in jest." Sometimes it can be as micron thin as laughing [guffawing] at their own little "joke." These apes japes often include a sexist physical barb or a non-sexist one if it can't be made sexist. It can also be used to cast doubt on a person's integrity or ability. "With a rack like that, I'd promote Susan too." Yuk, Yuk, Yuk.

> [If women do fight their way through the glass ceiling they have to constantly worry about men trying to look up their skirts or they wear pants and become more masculine than the men around them.]

Humour is often implicated in covert shaming operations and it can be more effective than C-4 explosive because the use of "humour" encourages the joker to make the shaming public. 'Hey Joe, at least your wife only slept with one of your brothers!" Yuk, yuk, yuk.

> [Most people will feel sympathy with the butt of the joke but the buttee, in the face of public humiliation, will often remain oblivious to any support. The feeling of isolation is one of the many nasty aspects of bullying. The opposite of bullying is to "pay it forward." This is where you do something really nice for somebody else and all you ask is that when they have sufficient resources, that they do something nice for somebody else.]

Most bullies have a sixth sense with respect to targeting the vulnerable or weak. In my "Bullying for Dummies" class we spend quite a bit of time on how to identify chinks in a person's personality and we develop ways to exploit them. Chinks do not all look alike, they can be quite varied but obviously, in any hierarchical environment, people lower down the ladder will usually have some vulnerability to supervisors and other higher beings. Use this to your advantage. Undermining a skilled, caring and professional person is likely to cut them to the quick, wherever that is, and keep them unmotivated which can only make you look good. Win/ Win to you.

There are random times when some "hero" will stand up to a bully. In these situations, the bully will need to beat a path behind someone else's back so they can lie to as many people as possible about that attention seeking "hero." This bullying support activity is done by "Whispering whisperers" and their whispering is particularly effective when the people they are whispering to, have never met the person that they are whispering about. If ever they do meet, it can be unaccountably but predictably weird and uncomfortable. Generally people are pretty insecure, so covert shaming is the wound that is most likely to fester. It is important to develop an absence of empathy, a total lack of guilt and a *laissez faire* attitude towards words to do this effectively.

[This is disgusting and unconscionable advice how can you ...]

STOP! You said I could share my secrets. I'm sharing. You believed before we started that people would shun my methodology if they read about it, but now... You're scared. Admit it. This stuff is so powerful that when people read about it they will jump into Neverland just to get a piece of the action.

[People will read this for what it is and be repulsed... and they will put a stop to this behaviour when they see it.]

You are entitled to your dreams.

Bullying Under Attack

Bullying is under attack in schools, in business and even [superficially] in the military but not so much in politics, yet. Every school now has an anti-bullying program or programs. Most businesses have HR departments that are supposed to stop abusive behaviour <yawn> and the military makes a lot of noise, mostly with its guns and jets and stuff.

It appears as though bullying is being stamped out across society but do not despair. It is mostly politically correct window dressing, which is fine, knock yourselves out but the walls of Neverland 2.0 have never been stronger. Why? Here is another secret and don't bother counting them or numbering them. I promise you there will not be seven secrets unless I choose to pad this chapter.

Bullying Secret: When the parents or the people in charge are bullies, the best campaign to stop bullying will come to naught or less. Especially when we have a society that runs two sets of rule books. One rule book is written by big business and the very wealthy for big business and the very wealthy. The second rule book is also written by big business and the very wealthy for big business and the very wealthy but in much smaller print so it can be easily thrown at small business and the poor. Corporate bullying of smaller companies is as strong as it has ever been and kids are smart. They see this and they know they can safely ignore any anti bullying rhetoric thrown at them. One day they all hope to be the ones throwing the rule book.

The most pronounced characteristic of elite bullies is that they passionately use the language of an anti-bullying fundamentalist whilst ensuring that their behaviour is totally irreconcilable with what they are saying. They will then dare and threaten anyone to actually call them on their inconsistency. SWEET!

In the military, well, bullying is actually built in as part of the rigid hierarchical, ask no questions, do as you are told, "only two things come from Oklahoma, steers and queers," training. The military is fine, bullying is not under threat in the military and the military in turn [and the parasitic lobbyists that live off the blood of innocent people] need to bully and threaten and keep vast numbers of people and nations in fear just to keep their [insane] levels of funding going. The war on Terror was an absolute god send for the military industrial complex or was that a George send?

Bullying, as a human social movement is safe as long as no one wakes up to the obvious fact that bullying is a learned behaviour. I learned most of the finer points of bullying from Capt'n Hook only because I do not remember my parents at all. I like to think that my home had appropriate 1900s levels of male domination of the feminine and of children. Every bully or aspiring bully in school has been trained and most of that training takes place in the so called "safety" of the home, although tutorials on bullying are also widely available outside the home.

[Trying to stop bullying by just working with a child at school is like only watering an apple on a branch and then wondering why the branch withers and the tree dies.]

Blame
(Dependent)
vs.
Independent

*A man can fail many times, but he isn't a failure until
he begins to blame somebody else and stops trying --
John Burroughs*

8

Don't Let the Plaster of Dependency Set

(by Daniel Prokop)

Human babies at birth are the most helpless of all the mammals. The species that subjugates all other life on the planet (except for the cockroaches) takes its first breath utterly helpless and totally dependent on the mother. The complete vulnerability and adorability of a newborn baby can melt all but the hardest of hearts or the most absent of parents. A human child remains dependent on its parents for a long time. Joseph Campbell suggests that that period of dependency in humans is at least twelve years long though there are cultures where the period of dependency is shorter.

> {With the recent launch of the Neverland 2.0 Dependency Expansion Kit, dependency can now be prolonged almost indefinitely.}

Moving from being an obedient and dependent child to an independent responsible adult is a deep and fundamental shift. If this shift is left too late, well, the plaster of Paris can harden.

> *"It is as though plaster of Paris had been poured into a mould of dependency, has begun to set, and then the plaster is suddenly asked to take the form of personal responsibility. The young adult psyche is supposed to move out of the dependent pattern into the adult pattern of responsibility – responsibility as defined of course, in terms of the requirements of*

the specific society." (Joseph Campbell, Pathways to Bliss, page 52).

Traditional societies knew the critical importance of this transformational crisis that all human beings face: from dependent to independent. It is not necessarily a shift that a child would seek on their own because it is easier to be dependent than responsible. Without a Rite of Passage, dependency will often continue as the default setting and responsibility becomes something to be shirked. When responsibility fails to show up, blame happily fills the void.

The dependent child in an adult body is still wed to the umbilical cord of parental authority which easily accommodates surrogate authority figures. Mass deferral of personal responsibility to institutions or to Alpha-bet males is unhealthy and can lead to atrocities like the loss of citizens' basic human rights and even genocide. "I was just doing my job," "I had to do it," "Everyone else was doing it." Highly authoritarian and controlling parents make a child's journey to independence much more difficult (see the Chapter on Parenting for Perpetual Childhood where Peter will tell you all about authoritarian parenting).

The Milgram Experiment was conducted in the 1960s by Professor Stanley Milgram;

> *"I set up a simple experiment at Yale University to test how much pain an ordinary citizen [the participant] would inflict on another person [the victim who unbeknownst to the participant was actually a trained actor] simply because he was ordered to by an experimental scientist [also played by an actor]. Stark authority was pitted against the subjects' strongest moral imperatives against hurting others, and, with the subjects' ears ringing with the screams of the victims, authority won more often than not. The extreme willingness of adults to go to almost any lengths on the command of an authority constitutes the chief finding of the study and the fact most urgently demanding explanation."*
> *Excerpt from The Perils of Obedience by Stanley Milgram as it appeared in Harper's Magazine, 1974.*

The full ramifications of Milgram's experiments are pretty mind blowing. Respondents to a poll conducted prior to the experiment believed that only 1.2% of participants would inflict the maximum voltage. In the first set of experiments a staggering 65% of the participants administered the final massive 450-volt shock which would have been lethal had the victim actually been wired up instead of just pretending to receive the shocks. Only one participant steadfastly refused to administer shocks below the 300-volt level. Responsibility was deferred to the actor playing the experimenter, the "expert." In further experiments the participant's compliance decreased when the victim was closer or where the authority figure was further away or spoke to them via a telephone.

These experiments have huge ramifications for corporate and military responsibility. The further removed management or drone attack aircraft operators are from the victims, the easier it is to commit atrocities and avoid or defer responsibility to either a more senior commander or to a faceless "shareholder." Big is not beautiful, bigger is less responsible, more remote from the coal face. The goal of authoritarian parents is to control their children, to make them obedient and enable them to deliver the biggest shocks available, sometimes it is the parents that get the shocks.

There is an alternative to authoritarian parenting which is called authoritative or balanced parenting. Balanced parenting is a consistent, child centred approach that holds high expectations of age appropriate maturity and encourages children to be independent whilst putting in place boundaries on their actions when boundaries are needed. Balanced parents set boundaries by fostering respect rather than fear and they are warm and nurturant toward the child.

Authoritative parenting recognizes that as children grow, boundaries need to expand to accommodate the developing person. Children pushing boundaries is normal behaviour and how we respond to boundary breaches and whether we take them personally is up to us

The goals of authoritative parents are: autonomous, self-actualised, respectful, emotionally mature children. The goals of many authoritarian parents would be similar but they have never taken the time to check their methodology against their parenting goals. The children of balanced parents will have an easier time when the dependence crunch of parenthood comes screaming;

> *"This dependent little creature is expected to become one who doesn't turn for help to Daddy or Mommy but is Daddy or mommy." (Joseph Campbell, Pathways to Bliss)*

We have created a society where fear of responsibility or Hypegiaphobia is rampant and it has been a highly infectious disease. Taking responsibility is easier when the cultural expectation is one of personal responsibility and healthy adult behaviour. We don't have that. We do have the heavily marketed concept of "credit card responsibility" which is to use credit (which effectively defers responsibility to the future) to buy as much as possible, even if you can't afford to ever pay it back. Unfortunately, many countries have vigorously pursued this model and so we begin phase 2 of the global financial crisis. The GFC was brought to us by responsibility, NOT. Access to easy credit for the masses was deemed preferable to access to a livable minimum wage which in real dollar terms peaked in 1968[1].

In the absence of Rites of Passage our culture has developed a complicated and confusing way to mark growing older rather than growing up. The timing of when the different markers occur depends on geography (what state or country you live in) rather than maturity. The first time a child is called an "adult" is when their parents get to pay a full "adult" fare for them at age 12 (or earlier). The age of sexual consent is usually 16, "Learner" plates for driving a motor vehicle can also be obtained at 16 but voting is restricted until 18 years of age. The "legal" age for drinking is 18 or higher and coincides in most Australian states with the age of full legal responsibility. All of these social indicators of growing up are chronological and the specific ages can vary quite a bit.

For many, it is the financial responsibility of buying a house, the taking on of massive debt in the form of a mortgage that harkens entry to independence, to adulthood. Banks charging to dispense adulthood is an interesting thought especially since a mortgage actually creates dependence on the financial institution rather than financial independence. Australians are more stressed now than Americans with 9 out of 10 Australians now reporting stress[2] (I know we are competitive, but really) and financial stress is a big contributing factor. Crippling mortgages and excessive rents are making things worse for a lot of families. The sacred cow of 'negative gearing' needs slaughtering; Australia has the most unaffordable housing market in the Anglosphere according to a 2010 international Survey[3].

Starting a family or getting married are other ways to "grow up" and start taking responsibility and each of these methods are now happening later and later in life, if at all.

Of the cultural markers just discussed the one where becoming responsible and independent is vital to ensuring personal safety and the safety of others, is driving. A young person being allowed to drive a motor vehicle is a key step in achieving freedom of mobility and is a big boost to independence.

Parents having to drive a teen around is a pain for all concerned especially in rural areas where there is little or no public transport.

Being able to drive to a friend's place when you feel like it is a huge incentive for young people to do whatever it takes to get a "P" or provisional license. We kind of squander this opportunity by not using the leverage to create an attitudinal change at this time.

Improving a boy's skill level by making him do 120 hours on "L" plates with a supervising adult is helpful and it is also a great opportunity for parents to spend time with their son. However, the NSW Roads and Traffic Authority[4] found that men are four times more likely to be involved in a fatal crash than women. The study found that whilst men were more confident that they are skilled drivers, women are more confident that they are safer drivers.

A lot of men, especially young men take risks, stupid risks, relying on their "awesome" driving ability to get them out of trouble. In some situations, however, no amount of skill can stop an accident.

Women are much better at preventing dangerous situations from ever happening. The statistics are irrefutable that overall, the drivers attitude is actually more important than skill levels in determining driver safety. A boy trying to test himself, to prove himself from behind the wheel of a car is dangerous to himself and others. Isn't it about time we taught young men to drive, not boys?

[1] Study by Oregon State University
http://oregonstate.edu/instruct/anth484/minwage.html
[2] Lifeline Annual Poll "High anxiety for nearly half of Australians" SMH 16/07/2010
[3]. Sixth Annual Demographia International Housing affordability Survey: 2010 ratings for Metropolitan Markets (Aust, NZ, USA, UK Can, Ire, HK)
[4] ABC News online article 30/01/10 "It appears women drive better than men."

9

R-E-S-P-O-N-S-I-B-I-L-I-T-Y is Not a Four Letter Word

(by Daniel Prokop)

Small children are told not to use four letter words. This is meant to stop them swearing but the unintentional damage to their vocabulary can be extensive, starting of course with the word, "word." No one in their right minds would tell someone, "please, don't say any four letter words times 3 ½." Therefore, in theory, everyone should be able to say "responsibility," (count the letters if you are not following me). Saying "responsibility" is really easy, taking responsibility is not so easy.

There was a time when a man's word, a solid unblinking look in the eye and a firm handshake was better than a 50 page legal contract and all the lawyers it took to draft it. There is something so attractive about the trust and simplicity of doing business in this way. Of course, before we get too sentimental, back not so long ago, women couldn't vote or seal a deal with a handshake because their place was in the Kitchen. Good ol' days do depend on the perspective.

Our word is tied to our integrity and the level of our commitment to our personal responsibility. Over time, the strength of a man's word has become rather watered down, until now it is just his "w…" the rest of the letters "o", "r" and "d" don't even bother to show up. Why should they? "Doesn't matter. She'll be right, mate." There are no ethics attached to "survival of the fittest." What it infers is survival at any cost, even if that is the cost of your integrity. If you get away with lying, fine, just try not to get caught. Thanks Peter.

{No problemo, amigo}.

An honest man (or woman) can be at a disadvantage against a manchild (or womanchild) that is quite prepared to lie for monetary or positional power or to escape responsibility.

Parents can teach children about responsibility and it is one of the many dances we have with our children and with ourselves. Too much responsibility too early can lead a child to sink rather than swim. Too little responsibility and the child may never create strong enough neural pathways to survive the great purging of the little used synaptic connections that happens in puberty.

Authoritative parenting and linking increased privileges with increased responsibility is the way to help young people develop a sense of responsibility. When this is reinforced with an appropriate, contemporary Rite of Passage the access to personal responsibility is left permanently open rather than permanently absent. As a parent the greatest gift we can give our children is to model responsibility, as difficult and inconvenient as that can be.

Would you build a brand new house and put the electrical wiring in after it was built? Of course not. The wiring goes in as you build the house. The time to help teenagers grow up and put certain adult wiring in place (like responsibility, deference of instant gratification etc.) is when they are building their adult 'house.' Traditional societies knew this which is why they placed so much importance on rites of passage. It is possible to put wiring in after moving into a house but it is much more difficult and quite messy, sometimes painful.

Personal awareness of engaging blame is a good clue that the shirking of responsibility is about to be launched.<whining> "But, they made me feel that way!" Really? Who really is in control of how we feel? I have this little voice that checks in with me when I start the blame game. I really don't like that voice, and sometimes I ignore it and have a good wallow in self pity and start making excuses and then I have to remind myself that I am supposed to be an adult. Excuses are blame with a story.

> *"There are a lot of people that believe that running late with a good excuse is the same as being on time. They are very different things."- Landmark Education*

I enjoyed the Ricky Jervais' film *"The Invention of Lying."* Speaking of politics, what does our current system of politics teach our children? Sadly, people expect politicians to lie and forget promises and avoid responsibility because politicians are so busy trying to survive in an abusive, confrontational system. It is difficult to build relationships without trust and if you can't trust the people in charge, then who can you trust? The media? Hmmm, the church? Hmmmm, business leaders? Hmmmm.

Part of the difficulty with keeping our word is that things do change for all of us. We say we are going to do something and then circumstances can change and what seemed like a good idea suddenly makes no sense at all. Cleaning up by taking responsibility is the way to deal with change and it is hard to do this if you have no credibility. Politicians cry things have changed or "wolf" way too often. Sometimes "wolf" is not scary enough for city dwellers so politicians use updated "fear" imagery.

What can we do? Well, as with many things the first place to start is with us. Isn't it about time we started to reduce the stress and worry in our lives? Life is simpler and less stressful when you tell the truth. If you are your word, you treat your word as something that is precious. You only give your word, when you will keep it and you will keep it even when it is inconvenient to do so. This means that you will say "No", sometimes or "No, thank you" or "No, that doesn't work for me" or "No I won't support that, I think putting depleted uranium into weapons is a crime against humanity." Practice saying "no" when an unsolicited telemarketer calls you at home. If they refuse to take "no" for an answer, then ask them to hang on while you go get your credit card. Get your credit card and go out for a leisurely coffee.

Saying no sometimes might just piss people off, which means you need to be "free from the importance of the good opinion of others" as Wayne Dyer would say. People are going to talk about you anyway so why worry about it? Why? It's because of our personal insecurity and a lot of us have been taught to value the opinion of others over our own opinion, deference to the expert. I know this and I am still working on it. I've said yes to things I had no intention of doing and it creates anxiety in the moment and then little arrows of guilt later and can result in totally avoiding a person over time.

Being your word is like a muscle, the more you do it the easier it becomes. Of course, not being your word is also a muscle which often antagonises the other one. It is the muscle that opens the door to a lot of addiction and denial. Saying things to ourselves like: "I'll stop after just one more drink, one last cast, one last cigarette, one last <gamble or whatever>" or "I'll only drill one more deepwater well." or "I'll never shout at my kids again," all this inner dialogue sets us up to fail and strengthens the wrong muscle.

The truth, your truth, my truth is tied into integrity and the truth can be a slippery and wily beast with more than two sides which can make it tricky. We live in a time when you can go online and find two equally qualified experts with diametrically opposed views or you can always just search for an expert that reinforces your point of view.

I was having a chat with someone I'll call Mark, because that's his name. We started talking about a mutual friend. I knew, beyond doubt, that this friend's name was Luc and Mark obstinately insisted that his name was Stuart. Steeped in righteous indignation I couldn't wait to see Luc to tell him about Mark. Yes, that was quite childish. Ummmm… turns out we were both right. Luc had changed his name from Stuart to Luc. Thank God we were not discussing the name of God; we would have had no choice but to have killed each other. There has been a bit too much killing in God's name and he wants us to stop it. My truth may not be your truth but both truths can be equally true, and sometimes the truth can change. I didn't say it was easy.

> *"All truth passes through three stages: First, it is ridiculed; Second, it is violently opposed; and Third, it is accepted as self-evident."* Schopenhauer.

Hindsight can always be back fitted to the data so it appears 20:20 . In the light of self evidence it is almost impossible to think of a time when that same truth was hidden in darkness and only the bravest dared speak of it. You would think that the natural law truths would be easier to agree upon: the earth is round, the earth orbits around the Sun, acid rain is the result of pollution and can travel hundreds of kilometers, DDT is a poison not a pesticide, etc. but even these have had vehement and violent detractors for long periods of time.

Even when a medical truth finally overcomes a concerted campaign of misinformation and is considered self evident it can still be ignored. Warnings such as "Smoking causes lung cancer" and "Smoking causes heart disease" are printed on cigarette packets and do not make as much difference as you would think. The tobacco industry argues that people should be allowed to make their own choices and be responsible which is rich. I mean this makes them rich.

Cigarettes are actually manufactured with nicotine so they are addictive which makes it an unfair fight for starters. How responsible is it to promote via every insidious means possible the only product in the world that kills half of the people that regularly use it the way it was intended? Why not let people have the choice of growing their own low nicotine tobacco for personal consumption and be free of the nicotine enhancers and other chemicals that are added to the tobacco? Sorry, tobacco companies want people to be free to only make the choices that they want people to make. Why are the big tobacco companies still in business? After all the deliberate lies they have told and the millions of people they have killed?

People recognize that little boys shouldn't run big corporations but it is frighteningly common. Of course they don't look like little boys. Maybe warning signs should be prominently placed on some buildings "Little Boys running this corporation could cause an environmental disaster," or "Little boys running this corporation could cause a global financial crisis." There are a number of financial institutions where that one could be put up...

On the day in July 2010 that Goldman Sachs agreed to pay a fine of $550 million dollars to settle civil fraud charges of misleading their shares leapt by 4.5%, an $800 million pop in their share[1] price. Whilst the $550 million was a record fine there was no real contrition on Goldman's part. They have not admitted any legal wrong doing. You get fined $550 million dollars but they didn't do anything legally wrong? How? They got let off way too light and the share market agreed, unbelievable, utterly unbelievable. Remember the cookie jar? Goldman Sachs owns the jar now.

Taking full responsibility for your actions takes bravery. At times it takes either great courage or great stupidity or sometimes a bit of both to speak your truth into a space where you know that you will be attacked for your views and possibly killed. Fear chokes truth, introduces truth to doubt which can shake the very foundations of truth. Fear can lead to paralysis, hopelessness and helplessness. Fear is a barrier to taking full responsibility.

Fear has been toppled many times by courage and love. We can make a difference. Peaceful civil protests and peaceful civil disobedience is a right which it seems some democratic governments would rather stifle than protect. Governments try to "protect" visiting dignitaries from protesters rather than protecting the rights of their people to peacefully make their feelings known. D'oh.

Sometimes defiance can be as simple as mothers silently gathering every Thursday at 3:30 PM in a public square in front of the Ministry of the Interior, in Bueno Aires, Argentina.

> *"As long as mothers give birth to children, they will give birth to courage. Who had the courage to defy the Argentine military junta who were kidnapping and secretly killing anyone who they felt challenged their rule? It was a group of ordinary women, mothers of those who disappeared. Their silent, persistent demands for truth helped topple the regime, and their quest for justice continues to this day... The Associación Madres de Plaza de Mayo are an inspiration in the pursuit of human rights all over the world."* -- Margaret Wakeley [2]

The Madres de Plaza de Mayo made a difference. We can too.

---

[1] BBC Business News 16/07/10 "Goldman Sachs agrees record $550m fine"
[2] http://www.gratefulness.org/giftpeople/madres_de_plaza_de-mayo.htm
"Mothers of the Disappeared" as quoted in the article.

100% Responsibility and Ho'oponopono

When I was writing and researching this book I had heard a reference about someone who had cured psychopaths. I thought that I would be able to find the reference to something so remarkable easily but I was mistaken. After many hours of fruitless research I was unable to find a single web reference to anyone curing a psychopath. All the literature I came across was unanimous in deciding that psychopaths could not be cured. If I had searched "cured criminally insane patients" I would have found it. The web is fantastic and can be quite frustrating.

Sometime later I was on Skype with a close friend, Lee, in NZ. Lee was telling me about Dr. Hew Len and Ho'oponopono. Dr. Hew Len was chief psychiatrist at the Hawaii State Mental Hospital for four years and is an extraordinary man.

Imagine working in a ward full of criminally insane mental patients with a history of assault, murder and rape. Attacks on staff and patients were common, almost daily despite the shackles used to move patients around the ward. Staff turnover and absenteeism were high. The place had such a toxic environment that even the paint on the walls didn't want to stay there.

> "Yo, Patch O' Light Blue! I hear you'se going over da wire tonight?"
>
> "Naw, I'm going to drop to the floor, get swept up and escape in a bag of trash."
>
> "We can do dat?"
>
> "Sure, check out the ceiling. That bare patch? White was there until yesterday."
>
> "I'm with you Bro. This place sucks."

Enter Dr. Hew Len, psychiatrist and practitioner of the ancient Hawaiian art of Ho'oponopono. Dr. Hew Len did not see any of the patients clinically, nor did he attend any of the staff meetings regarding patient treatment. What he did do was to review the patient files and constantly clean on himself. "Cleaning" in Ho'oponopono is a way of erasing memories from the past as a way to return to Source, to Love, by taking 100% responsibility. Ho'oponopono means "to make right" or "to rectify an error." Errors arise when a person lives into their past rather than an unblemished future i.e. the present is burdened by memories (often painful memories) from the past.

In Ho'oponopono emotions, except for inspiration from Source, are tied to memories that affect us in the now. According to Dr. Len's teacher, Morrnah, "the subconscious associates an action or a person in the present with something that happened in the past. When this occurs, emotions are activated and stress is produced." Memories get in the way of connecting with Divinity, with Love so Ho'oponopono is about erasing or cleaning on the memories.

After Dr. Len started work on the ward for the criminally insane staff absenteeism and turnover decreased, violent attacks stopped. Patients were allowed out of their cells, they were allowed visitation and access to activities. Today the Hawaiian ward for the criminally insane is closed. Pretty awesome cleaning result!

I am a Ho'oponopono novice so this is a very basic introduction. I think this would be a different book if I had discovered Ho'oponopono before I started writing. Interestingly, I nearly did get introduced to Ho'oponopono in 2009. Lee came across to Australia and did a workshop with Dr. Len and he tried to find me to invite me along but he couldn't find me. Since discovering Ho'oponopono as a practice I have found it very useful, which is why I am sharing it here. There are quite a few interviews with Dr. Len available on Youtube.

I have known about the theory of 'I create the whole of my reality,' of taking responsibility for everything that happens in my life for quite a while but I restricted personal responsibility pretty much to my own thoughts and feelings and I did an ordinary job of achieving even that. Wanting to be right, engaging blame, making other people wrong and wanting someone to do it for me (dipping into dependence) are tempting and well marked paths. The path to taking 100 % responsibility requires effort. There are many programs and courses for cleaning e.g. The Sedona Method and even some religions that teach ways to connect with Source, Divinity, or the God within. I have included some useful references including books after the Epilogue.

The great news with 100% responsibility is that if you create everything in your life then you are also the agent capable of changing everything. Playing the victim does not fit with this model, nor does blame.

Awareness of something at an intellectual level is very different to implementing it. Taking responsibility and connecting with Source is not unique to Ho'oponopono. I love the simplicity of the practice and I have a lot to learn. Now, if I am feeling anxious or worried, I repeat to myself "I love you," "I'm sorry," "Please forgive me," "Thank you." I say these words to myself as a way of trying to come from a place of love rather than a place of my past running my future. It works, when I remember. When I look after myself I come from peace and have more to give.

> *"We are only here to bring peace to our own life, and if we bring peace to our own life, everything around us will find its own place, its own rhythm and peace", and that is what Ho'oponopono is all about." Morrnah Simeona*

> *"I am not cleaning you... I am cleaning the [subconscious] data of my perception about you." Dr. Ihaleakala Hew Len*

> *"What is going on in me that I am experiencing this? What is it in me that I have to cancel?" Dr. Hew Len in an interview with Mabel Katz*

> *Visitor to Dr. Len, "Oh, you work in a psychiatric unit?" Dr. Ihaleakala Hew Len "No, I work in a psychiatric world."*

> *"My job here on Earth is twofold. My job is first of all to awaken people who might be asleep. Almost everyone is asleep. The only way I can awaken them is to work on myself."_Dr. Ihaleakala Hew Len. From Zero Limits, Wiley and Sons, 2007.*

> *"Such a man knows that whatever is wrong in the world is also in himself, and if he only learns to deal with his own shadow, he has done something real for the world. He has succeeded in shouldering at least an infinitesimal part of the gigantic, unsolved problems of our day." Carl Jung, Psychology & Religion. East and West, Collected Works 11*

http://self-i-dentity-through-hooponopono.org
http://www.selfesteemawareness.com/hoponopono-taking-responsability.htm
http://www.youtube.com/watch?v=3xCmvZZFQI0

10

Responsibility:
Not on My Watch

(Contributed by Peter Pan)

Distancing yourself from responsibility ASAFP is the same as totally AVOIDING responsibility but it sounds more responsible. 'I don't remember" "It's not my fault" "I didn't do it" and the Corporal Schultz of Hogan's Heroes response, "I know nothing... I am responsible for nothing ...I did not even get up this morning." Stop laughing, Schultz was a genius.

If you get angry, it is because so and so, the so and so made you angry. If you get sad, it is because so and so, the so and so made you sad. If you get depressed, it is because so and so, the so and so made you depressed. If you get laid, high five. Please don't insult my maturity by even suggesting that I have any control over my emotions, my emotions rule me, not the other way around.

The bigger the company the easier it is for faux accountability and faux responsibility to rule. They are like the Clayton's versions: "Faux responsibility: The responsibility you accept when you aren't willing to accept any responsibility." With faux responsibility the important thing is to use the "R" word, "Responsibility" often as if you really mean it. Try not to spoil your performance by cracking a smile, or brushing your nose. Keep your hands well away from your face and your fingers uncrossed. I will give you a technique later that will help you or just watch BP CEO, Tony Hayward on Youtube when he talks about the BP Oil

Spill and says "we will clean up every drop." SNAP! A perfect example of faux responsibility in that it sounds responsible even though it is physically and quite outrageously not remotely possible. The coaching I would give Tiny Tony is that it would have been an even better performance if he could have looked at the camera but the fact that he was able to deliver such a porker without doubling over laughing is quite an accomplishment.

Avoiding responsibility and blaming are closely related. For example, if you lose a lot of money on one of my Nigerian Internet banking scams it is not your fault: It is the fault of the internet, your service provider, your bank, your mother and or your father. If you don't know about how you can make a fortune with Nigerian Internet banking investments then please email me with your full name, birth date, bank account number and password at peterpan@nigerianinternetbankinginvestments.ng. Quickly, do it now because there is only one instant millionaire spot left.

Never use big mistakes to learn or to "grow." That would be tantamount to admitting it was your fault. Remember, it was not your fault. Whose fault was it? Not Yours. It is either a golden opportunity to go for loads of sympathy or you may choose to keep your stupidity a secret by brushing it under a carpet which allows you to play the semi-silent victim. If playing the victim suits a situation, then really get creative with your performance. Perhaps add a big serving of guilt to go with being a victim?

Managing responsibility is just one of many reasons why having children is a bad idea. Babies are so helpless it is easy to get suckered in by their cutefulness and feel like you should be responsible for them. So what if they share your DNA? Chimpanzees share 99% of your DNA and I don't see too many humans trying to raise chimpanzees. Newborns are attention stealers and even bigger cry babies than most of your friends. If somehow through the 'miracle of birth' you find yourself an actual, living with the child parent, then you will have to redouble your efforts to get any attention at all.

A high level of compassion is a marker for high maturity. Do you really want to stop judging other people, making them wrong and belittling them for no reason except that it makes you feel better? I don't think so. A great way of smothering compassion with a pillow before it gets a hold on your soul is to use the Opus Dei Method: Remember and relive every thing that anyone has ever done to hurt you. Make a list if you need to.

[I had a girlfriend once who was a grievance list keeper. It didn't help our relationship. If you want to make a list about somebody that pisses you off, go for it, get it on paper. Write it all down and then burn the list. Let it go, then make a list of all the things you appreciate about the person.]

The Opus Dei Method might make you cranky and depressed so if you need to numb yourself you know what to do - go shopping or get drunk. As you really get into it the Method you should be in so much pain that you will be totally immune to the suffering of others. Great success!

Gratitude is also to be avoided as it can interfere with your instincts for grasping and greed and all around dissatisfaction. Gratitude can easily be killed off by focusing on all the things you don't have, but deserve: a bigger house, a smaller wife, a better car, higher pay...

To prevent the onset of maturity you must avoid all responsibility. Once you start taking responsibility you have put one foot firmly on the road to growing up. Amputate that gangrenous foot if necessary, but get it off that road. Shirking responsibility is an art form and you are the artiste.

I find it really helpful to make other people feel wanted. The way I do this is to delegate. I delegate everything: cooking, washing, ironing, making coffee, cleaning my room and office, bringing me lunch, writing my reports, preparing my presentations etc. etc. Apparently there are machines that wash clothes, called mothers, hah, hah, but seriously I do have limits. I always do my own complaining and if there are no ass kissers available I will wipe my own butt. I do not find helplessness a career blocker though because I understand power and blame. Keep reading.

Lost Boys these days can and should live with their parents until they at least hit fifty years of age. Mother's should be there for you always, totally dedicated and focused on you. A lot of men quite rightly want two mothers: their biological mother and then a wife to be a second mother to them. <sigh> Kids have got it so easy today. Back in my time, shitty pram safety meant that many of us were, well, abandoned ...

[Hey, I'm sorry Peter. Never having a mother must be pretty tough. Tissue?]

Huh? Me? Naw, I was just laughing, at the stupid kids that need a mother. Not me. I'm good, real good. I don't need anybody!

Laying Blame: Blame Early, Blame Often

It is never too early to start laying blame. The world owes YOU big time and nothing is ever your fault, nothing. You are always right, you have never been wrong and that one time, well, you weren't wrong, the stock market did crash, you were right, just 10 years early.

If you are not happy, do not sit and mope around, take immediate action and blame someone for your unhappiness. Maybe it will be your parents' fault, maybe a sibling or your spouse or someone at work, even a pet can be blamed for your lack of happiness or success or the government or <insert blamee here>. Don't be miserly with your blame, be generous and share it around. Remember "A problem blamed is a problem halved." People will really appreciate you opening up and dumping all over them for no apparent reason. Blame means never having to take responsibility for anything and with blame, ramping up the energy with anger is like adding an emotional exclamation point. It is just good punctuation!

With blame always use simple risk assessment techniques starting with: What is the blame / credit potential of the project? You need to have what we call a balanced portfolio. Don't risk everything on putting your limited energy and attention on just the biggest initiatives. You need a solid base of activities, a finger in many pie holes so to speak to build up and maintain an unearned credit base load and to position yourself for distributing blame.

In options trading there is strategy called the "straddle" whereby a trader positions himself to profit if the underlying stock or commodity moves sharply up or down. If there are no big price movements then the trader's losses are limited to the cost of the Puts (trader wins if the price drops) and the Calls (trader wins if the price goes up) purchased to set up the straddle.

In blame trading there is a blame straddle strategy which is pretty uncommon because most people, due to a conscience, refuse to both support and condemn a project or idea at the same time. Best of all, punters find it hard to believe that anyone would actually set up a blame straddle and so they will often ignore conflicting reports as aberrations or allow themselves to become confused by them. This is fantastic news for Alpha [Alpha-bet] males as they have no straddling qualms at all.

As with most Alpha [Alpha-bet] male strategies, equal parts cunning and chutzpa are required to ensure that your straddle is successful no matter what happens. Now as I said, the great thing is that most people do not expect a blame straddle, but because they don't expect it, they can get very, very pissed off if a straddle position gets exposed. Go figure, I will never understand the general public.

Cunning is required in the positioning of the straddle and the key is to get "on the record" both condemning and praising but at different places, times and in different media. Feel the way the project is going and use your early condemnation or praise, as appropriate, to do some totally undeserved grandstanding and try to refer to yourself as often as possible as a true visionary. With the blessed consolidation of the media to just a few cost conscious highly profit motivated and syndicated players the chances of some parasitic investigative reporter catching you out and then getting anything actually published is more remote than... well, ummm more remote than... [the rapidly diminishing forests of Mongolia used to be] whatever.

If you are ever caught out by some do-gooder then you have a variety of highly effective excuses to fall back on. If the project is going gangbusters, like for example, increased deregulation of deregulation, then reports of you dissing deregulation are unfortunate examples of you being misquoted and / or being quoted out of context. Pointing to the other side of the straddle, you can make the point that it makes no sense that you would hold opposing views so therefore the journalist must have confused you with <opponent> fill in the blank with someone you dislike.

Feigning interest in various projects is laughably easy to do. People who have worked horrendous hours to get an initiative that they really believe in off the ground [despite your best efforts] love to rabbit on and on about it blah, blah, blah, really make a difference, blahhdy blah blah blah. They are normally so desperate for the tiniest bit of recognition that they are actually delighted to mistake your pretend interest for real interest and support.

If the initiative is significant enough then ingratiate yourself using the old, expensive grog/ cheap grog rotation, until they are so pissed that they will tell you where they have bent or broken the rules to keep the project alive. I know, I know, it is kind of cute, people feeling guilty about bending or breaking someone else's rules, heh, heh. This information is absolute gold and will help you distance them from their success or flush them further down the sewer system if the project tanks.

Blame Fundamentals

Shifting the Blame: Smoke and mirrors, watch my right hand, watch my right hand and WHACK! I hit you over the head with my left hand and then laugh. Man that never gets old. Sometimes it is the more subtle: watch my right hand or you'll go to hell, watch my right hand or you'll go to hell whilst my left hand deftly slips your wallet into my pocket. This is not a complicated strategy but it can be devastatingly effective. Business, governments and religion are the masters of this game and before anyone gets upset about religion being last, you religious zealots, relax. I have put them in alphabetical order, not necessarily in order of effectiveness. I'm a huge fan of business religion. I just don't believe any of it.

These days if you want to move a mountain of blame you need to control the media. You can do this either by having only state owned media like in North Korea or China or you can encourage "consolidation of the media" so that you only have one or two big media players to control, who owe you. They are similar but in one the state owns the media and in the other the media owns the state.

Every lie gives off a certain perfume, an *odour de la mentir*, that's French, and it sounds much better than the stench of the festering, rotting corpse of an untruth told with the intent to deceive. When a lie goes bad, it may start to stink. Disbelief or lie rot can set in.

As a good Alpha [Alpha-bet] Male there are times when your own self interest will inevitably come up against the equally important, to them, self interest of another child Alpha Male or another country. You will need to be able to determine what you can do to ensure that your self interest triumphs over everyone else's. You with me? Pretty simple stuff and if pawns get caught in the middle, well, collateral damage in the interests of religion, government or business (now in reverse alphabetical order to keep it fair) has always been acceptable. Corpses don't complain but survivors can be a problem.

Shifting blame is a little like riding a seesaw, sometimes the blame can go back and forth: "you did that" "no, you did that," "no, you did." It can even feel a little playful. Sometimes you might feel like your ass is scraping and bouncing on the ground and then there are the times when all the blame flows down away from you and there you proudly sit, high above it all.

BUT there may be times when other Alpha males are above it all, on the high end of the see saw and to get what you want, your job may be to tip them off the see saw. The higher up they are, the more likely that they will break their coccyx or an arm, maybe lose a tooth as well when they fall. So what? Not your problem, that's business, nothing personal.

There are many great examples of blame transference. The four ring transglobal *Circus of de oil* at the Whitehouse that followed the BP oil spill was entertainment plus. The ~~dick~~ Heads from ExxonMobil, Chevron, Conoco Phillips and Shell, stood shoulder to shoulder to blame BP for the oil poured into the Gulf of Mexico. After climbing from their Leer jets they lay their hands on their hearts [or where their hearts should be] and claimed that a similar environmental catastrophe would never happen on their watch. It was great theatre. They 'reluctantly' expressed their dismay at the rogue British oil company in a unified attempt to transfer blame for the sins of the whole oil industry onto a scapegoat that just happens to be a rival.

[It would have been a lot more effective if ExxonMobil's emergency response plan for the tropical Gulf of Mexico didn't include plans on how to deal with arctic walruses. Why should we believe anything that they say?]

OK, actually not a good example of blame transference but a good attempt at having a go at blame transference. As far as blame transference goes, the blaming of Iraq and Saddam Hussein for 9/11 will forever be the Case Study used at University o' Neverland for how to manage blame transference on a global scale. The sheer duplicity, audacity and blatancy still takes my breath away. The US media, led by the entertainment channel FOX News swallowed every lie so deeply that it can only be concluded that FOX management do not have a gag reflex.

[It is a worrying evolutionary trend that some media outlets no longer gag on lies. Censorship of the internet is a dangerous thing for governments to contemplate. I have read that according to Michael Wolff, (Rupert Murdoch's authorized biographer) even the Murdoch family is embarrassed by Bill O'Reilly and the Fox network. FYI Rupert, you should be and you can fix it. I don't quote Rupert very often but with respect to climate change, he did say in 2007 that: "The planet deserves the benefit of

the doubt." Absolutely it does. A little more follow
through Rupe would be appreciated by our children.]

The Bush psyops (psychological operations team) said that
Saddam Hussein was a major supporter of Al Quaeda and
Osama Bin Laden (amateur film maker). This wasn't true,
Saddam except for the 'tache was clean shaven and apparently
he was repulsed by Bin Laden's scruffy, "Look! My beard touches
my belly button" sort of look. Saddam hated Al Quaeda, he didn't
want any other extremists to compete with his own extremism, so
they were not welcome in his despotorship.

The truth did not get in the way of the shifting the blame onto
Iraq. Little ol' President George W. constantly linked Saddam to
9/11 in his speeches and in the minds of the American public.
The world was told that Saddam Hussein had his hairy, sweaty,
Arab trigger finger on lot's of Weapons of Mass Destruction
(WMDs) and that his finger was getting sweatier [Saddam was a
nasty, sweaty kind of guy and a staunch American ally for quite a
while]. Those nasty WMDs included urine bombs and other
biological weapons, chemical weapons and hmmphsnnrny
weapons. No one was ever quite sure what hmmphsnnrny
weapons were supposed to be because the details were always
mumbled but they were massively destructive.

[Even more destructive than the depleted uranium
weapons used by the "Good" guys in the first and
second Gulf Wars?]

Hey wise ass, it is called recycling. Putting highly
dangerous and difficult to store waste into weapons
that you can "give" to your enemies is clever. The next
hundred generations can worry about cleaning it up.

The final straw before the invasion that the US just had to
have, was the "hard military intelligence" that said that Saddam's
sweaty finger was slipping onto the red button or the trigger
whichever created more fear.

[The word 'intelligence' divorced the word
'military' following the WMD debacle. It was a very
messy split and the word military is not allowed
within two paragraphs of any derivative of the word
'intelligent'. Following large and ongoing numbers of
civilian casualties the word 'smart' has also taken out
an injunction against the word 'bomb'].

Huh? After months of searching and the "unavoidable" destruction of a lot of basic infrastructure it turns out there were no WMDs and no connection between Saddam and 9/11. Huh? I was surprised because US and intelligence just kind of go together for me. So a convenient lie was exposed, so what? People forget. So the Iraqi people were too shocked and awed to welcome the people that came to liberate them from their oil. The US administration and Fox news told us that the use of "good" terror in ousting Saddam and in the ongoing occupation had made the world a "safer" place.

> [**<cough>**<bullshit>**<bullshit>** The war was as destructive as it was swift. It started on the 19th March, 2003 and George W. (child president) declared victory in Iraq on the 1st May, 2003. It was a tad premature but then anything to do with maturity and George W don't go very well together].

What a quick fun war that was. After watching that, I realized that Neverland 1.0 was just too small for me. I did most of the fighting myself, STUPID. Now there are drones which are fantastic toys that can destroy homes and villages in far away places like Pakistan from the comfort of an air conditioned office. The best, best thing is that if the CIA operates the drone then no one is publicly accountable for mistakes!!!! Woo Hoo!

Maybe I'll work for the CIA next. That would be so cool. I could press a button from my hideout and wipe out Hook's ship and Tiger Lilly's Village and anyone that disagreed with me just by shouting "They were terrorists!" and then I could go home to my family, if I had a family. I am thinking of getting a pet crocodile and I'm gonna feed it a clock. Hey, I was saved by the clock once.

> [The use of remote controlled attack drone aircraft has been described by Philip Alston the United Nations Special Rapporteur as "...a strongly asserted but ill-defined license to kill without accountability." This is scary, scary stuff and the attacks have increased under the Obama administration. The Siam Daily News reported that the average civilian to militant casualty ratio is 25 to 1 (June 22, 2010). Judge, jury and executioner all in one tidy unaccountable agency or agencies is not wise. Fighting terror with terror or torture does not make the world a safer place, it makes it a more hateful, fearful place for future generations.]

<u>Conspiracies and Patriotism</u>
or
"How to Discredit Legitimate Questions"

Using the word "conspiracy," is a great way to discredit people who object to some business that you are doing. It is also a great way to stop people asking legitimate questions and is more fun than saying "shut up." Say for instance, that you want to open a brand spanking new coal mine which will require a stupid ol' mountain top to be removed.

Of course the mountain was there first but all you have to do is to label any facts about carbon emissions, environmental devastation or toxic pollution as a conspiracy. If you can, lump them all under the "loony green conspiracy" catch phrase. Don't attack science based data that contradicts the 'facts' you have cooked up [because no credible science supports or can justify the removal of a whole mountain top to mine coal]. Simply trot out trumped up, highly ~~bribed~~ incentivised PhDs to label protesters as "hippies" and their data as a conspiracy which is trying to stop good ol' fashioned free market capitalism. That mountain top is practically filling in the valleys and blocking the rivers already.

Oh, human induced climate change is just a loony green, hippy conspiracy propagated by people who want a better environment and who don't work in the coal, petroleum or any other unsustainable industry. Yeah, just because all the nerdy scientists <use a whining, belittling tone and play to demeaning, inaccurate stereotypes to reduce the credibility of your opponents> say that the oceans are warming up doesn't mean that they are. They are obviously scare mongering nutters who are trying to destroy our way of life.

> [Every peer reviewed scientific publication is in agreement that ocean temperatures are rising and we have no *$#& idea what that means except that polar ice is melting faster than the models can be rerun. Higher ocean temperatures inhibit calcium carbonate sequestration and increases ocean acidification.]

It is very important to link anything you want to discredit to job losses and/or at least one real "nut case" conspiracy by saying loudly and in an exasperated and condescending tone "The next thing they'll say is: 1) that the Easter bunny is real or 2) that the moon is made of cheese or 3) they probably believe in WMDs."

[The new, simplified definition of "Unpatriotic" is: someone that disagrees with you. Branding someone unpatriotic is a way of sidestepping annoying things like science and logic and stepping hard on the emotional accelerator. Although in some countries, like Australia, the patriotism acceleration rarely extends beyond sport and drinking. In countries like the USA however, it is a potent way to stop debate and attack opponents. Even now in many parts of the US, anyone that questions the "official" version of 9/11 is unpatriotic and a conspiracy theorist, so a double shut up whammy. Questioning of the ongoing wars in Iraq and Afghanistan has also been branded unpatriotic though with increasingly less vigor and confidence.]

"Patriotism is supporting your country all the time, and your government when it deserves it." Mark Twain

11

The 100th Monkey Theory

(Contributed by Peter Pan)

I like monkeys and monkeys like me – respect to you tailed ones. When I saw a story about 100 monkeys, I thought sweet, bring it on. But it's just a story written by Ken Keyes Jr. and it is supposed to be "inspirational."

A lot of New Agers have quoted Ken's story as if it is based on actual results. It is a bit like some of the good climate change denial stuff that is out there – take a pinch of reality (experiments with monkeys) and then make up a nice story to support your point of view.

[It is true that the Hundredth Monkey is a fable that has often been quoted as if it based on the actual results of certain experiments. It is not. Hey, Peter why not tell the story. Some people might not know it.]

Ok, I I'll tell it but I'm going to have to add a few comments to make it interesting. I'll put the original story in bold, so readers can easily follow it.

[You are a very helpful guy. You've added stuff about poo throwing haven't you?]

Maybe, that is one of the reasons why I like monkeys so much.

A story about social change. By Ken Keyes Jr., {and me}

Reproduced from the book *"The Hundredth Monkey"* by Ken Keyes, Jr. The book is not copyrighted and the material may be reproduced in whole or in part {or with bits added in brackets.}

The Japanese monkey, Macaca Fuscata, {or just the Macaca as they liked to be called} **had been observed in the wild for a period of over 30 years.**

In 1952, on the island of Koshima, scientists were providing monkeys with sweet potatoes dropped in the sand {the scientists were uncoordinated}. **The monkeys liked the taste of the raw sweet potatoes, but they found the dirt unpleasant** {fussy, fussy}.

An 18-month-old female named Imo {Imo the Fussy} **found she could solve the problem by washing the potatoes in a nearby stream** {Imo was subsequently diagnosed with OCD -Obsessive Compulsive Disorder}. **She taught this trick to her mother** {for a modest fee}. **Her playmates also** {coughed up and} **learned this new way and they taught their mothers too.**

This cultural innovation {originally ridiculed by the clean food deniers} **was gradually picked up by various monkeys** {Macaca} **before the eyes of the scientists. Between 1952 and 1958 all the young monkeys** {they had the disposable income, didn't they?} **learned to wash the sandy sweet potatoes to make them more palatable. Only the adults who imitated their children** {rather than buy the technology} **learned this social improvement. Other adults kept eating the dirty sweet potatoes** {the clean food deniers}.

Then something startling took place. In the autumn of 1958, a certain number of Koshima monkeys {Macaca} **were washing sweet potatoes** {and throwing poo at the scientists for dropping the sweet potatoes in the sand} **-- the exact number** {of poo throwers} **is not known. Let us suppose that when the sun rose one morning there were 99 monkeys on Koshima Island who had learned to wash their sweet potatoes.** {OK, but midday would give the teenage monkeys that were having a sleep in, a chance to wake up and join in} **Let's further suppose that later that morning** {afternoon}, **the hundredth monkey learned to wash potatoes.** {There are just not enough good potato washing stories are there?}

THEN IT HAPPENED! {Please the suspense is very mild.}

By that evening almost everyone in the tribe {even many of the former clean food deniers} **was washing sweet potatoes before eating them. The added energy of this hundredth monkey** {his name was Lachlan Macaca, who just happened to own every media outlet on the Island} **somehow created an ideological breakthrough!**

But notice: A most surprising thing observed by these {clumsy} **scientists was that the habit of washing sweet potatoes then jumped over the sea...Colonies of monkeys on other islands and the mainland troop of monkeys at Takasakiyama** {say that 5 times fast} **began washing their sweet potatoes.** {The scientists, being biologists and therefore techno nerds, were totally unaware of the sophisticated wireless network that the Macaca's had set up}.

Thus, when a certain critical number achieves an awareness, this new awareness may be communicated from mind to mind {Interestingly, the spread of poo throwing leapt over several oceans and continents and quickly became popular at Universities around the world but this has been ~~wiped~~ covered up}.

Although the exact number may vary {depending on media ownership}, **this Hundredth Monkey Phenomenon means that when only a limited number of people know of a new way, it may remain the conscious** {intellectual} **property of these people.** {Sadly no patent application was lodged for the process of washing root vegetables}.

But there is a point at which if only one more person {or monkey} **tunes-in to a new awareness, a field is strengthened so that this awareness is picked up by almost everyone!** {Except perhaps ex-Governors of Alaska.}

<u>Peter Pan:</u> How could such a boring story about washing sweet potatoes ever get repeated? As you know, I'm not big on details, 100 monkeys, 150 monkeys or 250 hyenas, I couldn't care less. I do care about making Neverland 2.0 as big as possible though.

I'm really not sure how many "lost boys" it took before perpetual childishness got critical mass or when it actually happened. I'd like to take credit for it, so I will. At some point though there is no doubt that growing up became unpopular and infantile and puerile behaviour was rewarded and revered until now it is an art form. Not only did we get critical mass [the 100th asshole theory] but we took control of companies, armies, families and the media. Once this takeover took place, the phenomenon of Neverland 2.0 just keeps expanding.

Consolidation of media into fewer and fewer more powerful hands has been totally awesome and God Bless Ronald Reagan for abolishing "The Fairness Doctrine" in 1987, one of the most constraining, onerous media restrictions ever placed on righteous, one eyed media owners.

[In 1934, the FCC, the Federal Communications Commission in the US was founded and it viewed the stations to which it granted licenses as 'public trustees,' not licensees to print money. The FCC required that broadcasters must allow for rebuttal of controversial viewpoints and make every reasonable attempt to cover contrasting points of views. The Commission also required stations to perform public service in reporting on crucial issues in their communities. Sounds fair and doctriney enough].

Michael Fowler, FCC Chairman under President Reagan, did away with the Fairness Doctrine.[1] Brilliant! Media no longer had to be fair and provide even the pretense of balanced reporting. I was amazed and delighted that this routing of unbiased reporting was allowed to take place. It remains one of the pivotal moments in the expansion of Neverland 1.0 to Neverland 2.0.

So Ronald Reagan, possibly the most senile president to ever nap regularly in the oval office gave the media open slather on the truth. Most of the public were unaware of the change so they foolishly continued to trust the media to look after their best interests, laughable really, of course. The media companies have [ab]used this power to proudly put profit before the truth.

[Some would argue that the dumbing down and fearing up of the media has been happening for some time but the disappearance of the "Fairness Doctrine" put dumbing down on a runaway sled.]

Media deregulation has been terrific for me because if you treat adults like children for long enough then they will start behaving like children which is happily what has occurred. I have more playmates now than ever before. Without any fairness provisions, people only ever hear one point of view and now they have been taught to become threatened by anyone that does not share their world view. People cannot have mature debates or discussions anymore. They have been taught to ridicule or viciously attack anyone that does not agree with them. I taught that stuff to the "lost boys," it appears that at least one of them was listening.

[1] http://www.pbs.org/now/politics/mediatimeline.html

12

The 10,000th Lost Boy Theory
A story about people who are influenced by advertising.
A Story by Daniel Prokop Jr.

The first Homos (hominids) appeared about 4 million odd years ago with little fanfare and no press conference. There was no press for starters and conference facilities were limited. The rule back then was that if you couldn't grunt something nice, you didn't grunt anything at all.

Life was simple. Putting your head up your ass was a way of saying to predators, please eat me. Groups that worked well together, survived and those that didn't were saying, please eat us. Times were often tough, anyone who seriously disrupted the harmony of the tribe was left in the wilderness to be recycled (eaten). So whilst there were no live Alpha-bet males, Alpha-bet male entrees and main courses did become available from time to time to some of man's larger predators. A skull and brain structure similar to Homo sapiens was still millions of years off but there was no hurry.

Fast forward 4 million years less a couple hundred years to when the first business man learned how to buy a politician. Owning a politician gave the business owner a competitive advantage. He kept this secret to himself for as long as possible but once the habit of buying politicians is started it is difficult to stop at just one. Soon the competitors that survived copied this behaviour and started to buy their own politicians until there just weren't enough politicians to keep up with demand, so government had to get bigger and the buying of politicians seemed to jump across all continents thanks to

some of the best Masters of Business Administration degrees… Can I stop now? Do we really want to follow this simile of The Hundredth Monkey story any further? This is supposed to be about advertising, so here we go…

{And you call me undisciplined… giving money to politicians is called making a donation to democracy.}

[Whatever, publicly funded elections make a lot of sense to me. Instead of dem-ocracy we seem to have business-ocracy].

No one in the advertising game will confess to believing in The Hundredth Monkey Theory or morphogenic fields, they refer instead to TARPs (target audience rating points) or top of mind recall, Penetration, CTRs (Click through Rates), CPMs (cost per mille) sales or any other CRAP (crap) that their research and marketing departments can digg up to justify the advertising budgets.

Once upon a time advertising was relatively benign, the first TV ad didn't appear until 1941 in the United States and was only 10 seconds long. The ad was for a watch that people apparently needed but didn't know that they needed. Some primitive countries like the UK and Australia didn't even get advertising until the mid 1950's. How did they get by without it? American audiences can now enjoy 18 minutes of ads (commercial minutage) per hour, unless they skip them ☺. Advertisers and TV stations treat their audiences like children. The culture of mega stars (sporting and movie varieties) supports vicarious living. The idolization of the immature and irresponsible creates barriers to healthy adulthood.

It still astounds me how totally conflicting stories can be told by the same TV station, often in the same breath: 1) What is shown on TV does not influence people's behaviour! 2) Advertising revenue is vitally important for the TV stations economic survival and how dare anyone try to regulate when and for how long they can punish viewers including very young children? <head shake> In response to arguments that there is too much violence on TV (or at the cinema) for example, they quote whatever gibberish that they can find to definitively say that what people see on TV i.e. violence has no influence on intelligent human beings.

Apparently advertisers are fools who donate billions of dollars to media companies every year to get their images in front of people even though we all know that what we watch has no influence on anyone and let's face it the advertisers do not mind playing dumb on this one because it is a step up from being called deceptive. A brilliant circular argument, what people see makes no difference yet companies pay billions of dollars to make no difference. Surprisingly this defense of inappropriate content continues to this day. As with so many things we are just out of balance.

The statistics on rates of abuse of children and domestic and community violence are frightening. The International Violence Against Women Survey (IVAWS) included eleven countries and in 2008 reported that between 35-60% of women experienced violence by a man during their lifetime and that between 22-40% have experienced intimate partner violence. Less than one third of women reported their experience to police. It is not just women that are affected by domestic violence. Don't these statistics shout that something is fundamentally wrong?

It is hard to believe but there is (sometimes) a limit to just how long you can treat people like idiots. If the pool of idiots has somehow been exhausted there are other suckers that can be targeted, like the vulnerable and children. Many companies do not target the poorest and most vulnerable people on the planet even though they are in the majority. Nestle did not let a little thing like people's poverty and their inability to buy their product, stop their marketing machine. Hell No.

One of Nestle's products is infant formula. After a highly "successful" third world marketing campaign in the 1970's a lot of women stopped breastfeeding their babies and started feeding them Nestle's Infant Formula. The warm human teat was ripped from the baby's mouth and replaced with a cold rubber nipple. "Modern" bottled formula became fashionable but a lot of babies died, victims of a marketing induced fashion. Dr. Derrick Jelliffe called the impact of formula on infant health "commerciogenic malnutrition." The unethical marketing to the vulnerable resulted in the call for a world wide boycott of Nestle products in 1977.

As a result of the boycott, an international code on the marketing of infant formula was drawn up in 1981. The "code," is more of a sham really. Unethical marketing practices continue such as generously giving "free" samples to new mothers. But even a short period of formula use, like long enough to use up "free" samples can severely interrupt lactation, forcing mothers onto substitutes for breast milk. I wonder which companies could help them out? Formula companies continue to market artificial foods in ways that undermines breastfeeding. E.g. this from a 2009 Mead Johnson (NYSE:MJN) press release "…trusted to give infants and children the best start in life." This is an example of technically clever, but morally questionable marketing. The best start in life is a woman's nipple in the mouth and it ain't that bad later in life either. Nestle uses labels that claim that the formula 'protects' infants, despite the fact that babies fed on it are more likely to become sick and, in conditions of poverty more likely to die than breastfed infants. Why are these companies not being charged with murder? The WHO estimates that reversing the decline in breastfeeding could save 1.5 million lives per year. Charging executives that break the code with murder would stop these companies and then the code could be tightened and externally monitored.

Very sobering stuff but we are not powerless, we can stop buying their products and let them know why and tell others too or alternatively these companies could grow up and act responsibly. Replace the good ol' little boys at the top of Nestle with a group of breastfeeding mothers. I'd love to see that.

The vulnerable are ok to exploit but there is a marketing group that are better. These suckers are so pathetically helpless they can't even move away from advertising. They can barely even hold their own heads up. You got it. We are talking about newborn Babies. Many marketers balk at targeting babies because they have disposable nappies but no disposable income. Whilst it is true that all babies are broke, the canny marketer knows that they will quickly become key influencers or naggers of their parents. The truly awesome thing about babies is that they can't complain. Sure they can cry and poop in their nappies but then babies poop and cry constantly. By the time a parent checks on the child, the offensive ad that gave the child diarrhea, is off the screen. The connection between poop on the screen and poop in the ol' nappy is not a popular research area.

Maggie Hamilton in her book *"What's Happening to Our Girls?"* points out how "marketing Guru" James McNeal (I'd like to see his PCL-R Psychopath score) discovered how to exploit babies when they are so young that the baby has no idea that it is separate to the world around them. Because they don't know better, they think the brand is part of them. Before a baby can lift its head, it spends a lot of time staring down, drooling and shitting. Marketers are now making the most of this period in a babies life, not by wiping the babies butt, which would be useful butt by placing branded images on the babies tummy, bib or on the outside of the nappy itself. Sure the baby can chuck up on those images but for a baby at that age, even the vomit is part of them until it is wiped up, when it becomes part of something else.

"The moment a baby girl can see clearly, she becomes a consumer" Susan Gregory Thomas "Buy, Buy, Baby: The devastating impact of Marketing to 0-3s" 2007.

The goal is to have kids nagging their parents as early and as often as possible to buy your products. Kids knowing what they want, which is what marketers tell them they want, is a good thing, for the marketers. Knowing what children need is a parent's job and we need to tell marketers to stay right out of our kids' heads.

We do not have any obligation to TV stations or magazines to provide them with income from advertising that is plundering our young people's minds and creating anxiety and depression in younger and younger children.

On one hand, the marketers encourage children to grow up faster than they are developmentally ready, a trend identified as KGOY, Kids Growing Older Younger. The stated objective is for children to yearn for products advertised directly at them but being played with by slightly older children. It is a deliberate ploy so that children are never happy with where they are, creating at the child level "I'll be happy when I get that toy or that shirt or that cap." Deferral of happiness in this way has previously only been an "adult" domain and judging playmates based on the brand of clothes that they wear, well that was never really healthy adult behaviour.

When marketers refer to growing up it has nothing to do with emotional maturity. Children are reduced to being a targeted marketing demographic which changes with age. They quickly become marketing collateral damage.

Focused, very highly paid marketing executives accessing the latest research on child brain development backed up by top psychologists and large market research budgets are raping the minds of our children. Marketers vs. our young children is an unfair fight which needs to be stopped NOW. Sweden has banned all advertising targeted at children under 12, a good example to follow. Real adults would not target our children if they had any concern for the emotional well being of this or any future generations. "Hey, I'm just trying to make an honest but immoral quick buck and don't bother me with your whining because I don't care about the consequences," which brings us to...

Cravings
vs.
Self Discipline

*"There is no end of craving. Hence contentment
alone is the best way to happiness. Therefore,
acquire contentment." --.Sivananda*

13

Saying 'I'll Wait" can be the Hardest Words

(by Daniel Prokop)

Traditional people didn't have access to EEG (electroencephalogram), MRI (magnetic resonance imaging) or PET (positron emission tomography). They probably didn't even know a YABA (yet another bloody acronym) when they saw one. They were unaware that a human brain is not fully mature until approximately 25 years of age but they did know that there was a lot happening in the bodies and minds of their teenagers. They used a fabulous instrument called EYES and they employed a technique called OBSERVATION. They spent a lot of time with the young people watching them, nurturing them and they knew when the young person was ready for their Rite of Passage, when they were "ripe."

With the benefits of modern brain imaging technology it has now been documented that the profound adolescent external body changes during puberty are also being mirrored internally. Think of the teenage brain as a computer (of sorts). During adolescence teenagers are basically installing a new operating system over the top of their old operating system which is kind of scary (for some computer users just thinking about doing that could result in sphincter lock).

Fortunately, in the case of humans there is more than enough memory for the new operating system. In fact there are too many synapses which are slowing the system down. The new operating system will deliver a more efficient computer when the install is completed. The user is not prompted for the install and there is no opt out option, it is a compulsory automatic install. As the new operating system is installing however, there will be times when the whole system seems to crash for extended periods. At times it will also seem that the computer has gone backwards rather than forwards and there will be frequent unpredictable bugs. Some of the peripherals may take some readjusting and in the case of teenage boys, they may need reminding to stop doing this adjusting, at least in public. "Hey buddy, how about you go easy on the pocket billiards until you get home?"

The brain of a teenager is undergoing several developmental processes, the two most noteworthy are; 1) myelination: the laying down of a layer of myelin around the neural axons which speeds up the relay of electrical impulses in the brain and 2) synaptic refinement: a pruning process where synaptic connections that the brain is no longer using are deleted and ones the brain is using regularly are reinforced. You use it or you lose it. The brain accepts new connections throughout life but there are times when it is easier than others to install and then reinforce them and this is one of those times.

The brain maturation process generally occurs from the back of the brain to the front. The prefrontal cortex is believed to be one of the last brain structures to mature. It is understood that the prefrontal cortex is the part of the brain responsible for making judgments, controlling impulses, foreseeing the consequences of ones' actions and setting goals and plans[1]. Recent research published in the April 15th Issue of the journal *Neuron* now suggests that it is the ACC (anterior cingulate cortex) that controls the instant gratification impulse, or not, as the case may be. It also appears to play a role in decision making, empathy and emotion. Crap name for an important brain bit.

Traditional societies recognized that adolescents need help while their brains are busy rearranging their neural pathways. This was when they assisted the young people to lay down the new pathways associated with growing up emotionally. Did they know that the rituals that they had created were impacting on the ACC or the prefrontal cortex of the initiates? Of course they did, they didn't need an MRI. They could see it in the new way the young person moved, the look in their eyes. They didn't have to know the exact biochemical reactions that were taking place to know that it was important. They understood at an intuitive level about neural plasticity and what to do about it. They knew that the teens needed help to create some healthy new neural connections and the ceremonies also helped support the teen brain to delete some of the connections that had gone past their emotional use by date.

Perhaps they knew that if they did not help set up some new connections then those connections might never get made? Certainly in the past couple millennia plus of western culture where people have been left to go solo on their brain development, the ability to accept responsibility, share power, control impulses and defer instant gratification seems to have diminished considerably, as has compassion for the "small" people.

In business the craving for instant gratification is called "ambition" and ambition has been selected for as a highly prized corporate trait. Short term thinking has over ridden any thought of long term consequences and creates a corporate culture where people are mocked, derided and fired for "wanting to save the world." On May 12th, 2009, BP CEO Tony Hayward, actually bragged about getting rid of the "world savers" in a speech he gave at the Stanford Graduate school of business. It is available on Youtube. But only watch if you have a strong stomach as the smugness of the man that presided over the culture in BP that culminated in the Gulf Oil Spill and the death of 11 men, may make you retch.

> "I'm telling you, British Petroleum has put more birds in oil than Colonel Sanders." —David Letterman

In the lead up to the Global Financial Crisis fortunes were made playing reverse pass the parcel with expensive bits of paper with the words 'The name of this derivative is guaranteed to tell you nothing about what it actually represents. In deregulation we do profit. Amen.' The paper turned out to be worthless to the poor sap left holding it when the music stopped. And stop the music did. A lot of people who actually had no idea that their entire life savings were being gambled in the banking reverse pass the parcel game, lost everything.

In the mad scramble for "survival of the fittest," future generations are ignored. Actually it's not as passive as ignoring, it is more like future generations are given the finger whilst everyone grabs what they can NOW. It is worse than childish behaviour and I apologise to children everywhere because it besmirches childhood to call this behaviour childish. We should call it what it is, totally reprehensible and some of it is highly illegal but the Kings of industry appear immune to the laws. Maybe we need some new laws?

There are logging companies that trick indigenous people or have them removed so they can rape the rainforests for valuable timber which provides a short term profit for some but generations of misery for others. The rainforests may never recover due to the erosion of the thin topsoil but long term sustainability is not the loggers' problem. Clear felling vast swathes of ancient forests around the world so it can be turned into grazing country for beef production which it is not suited to is very sad and also stupid.

Somehow we need to be able to control the impulses for short term thinking and start thinking about people other than ourselves. Old growth forests in Australia are still being destroyed for low grade paper chip despite a 2004 Newspoll that found that 85.5% of Australians believe that they should be protected for future generations. Come on people.

Resources are ripped from the earth with little regard for the environmental and social impact. Just because there are ways to extract gas from coal seams or oil from shale doesn't mean they should be allowed. Check out the movie "Gasland" – there is a scene where a man turns on his tap, puts a match near it and lights the water coming out. Gas is not supposed to come out of water taps. We need to stop the frakking process before the industry gets too big. People who get in the way of rapid progress are branded rabid greens in the US or radical greens in Australia where we don't have rabies. There are some people in the environment movement that are extreme and we need balance. Stopping to consider the social and environmental impacts of any development and ensuring that it is safe before it goes ahead is prudent and responsible and if that means slowing down a project or stopping a project then so be it.

The Iroquois Confederacy invoked this declaration before they met in counsel: "In every deliberation, we must consider the impact on the next seven generations." There are a lot of people making some pretty shitty decisions who can't count past one. Alpha-bet males live in a unary system where they are the only ones that matter.

> *"Any vote in an Iroquois counsel included an equal vote cast by a representative who spoke specifically for the needs, the survival, and the dignity of those who would live a hundred and fifty years in the future. For the Iroquois, the generational format of*

their council defined a long term relationship between government and ecology... Conservation was thus, the very foundation upon which the culture was built." Jim Norton, "For the Seventh Generation" from the Interspecies Newsletter, 2000

It takes very healthy adults to think so long into the future and care about people that they will never meet. It is a different way of thinking. Many aspects of our lives will need to change so we can start to consider the next generation. We have to move from "Future Eaters" to "future protectors"

"We have the power to make this the best generation of mankind in the history of the world - or to make it the last." John Fitzgerald Kennedy

The over packaging of food and goods with plastic that is thrown away is less than clever. Built-in obsolescence is shameful and making one use throw away goods is ecologically criminal. In the case of ink jet printers, in many cases it is cheaper to buy a whole new printer than to buy new ink cartridges. Printers are deliberately made so that the cartridges cannot be refilled but until the printer manufacturers are charged for every printer that goes into landfill I'm not sure if they will change their business model. On the upside, the amount of printing I do has decreased considerably since my old printer that was easy to recharge died.

Manufacturers are scared of cradle to grave product responsibility being forced onto them. I remember sitting in meetings on this subject 15 years ago or so and it is about time that councils and states brought that concern home to roost. (Most products have got barcodes which makes it a bit easier, doesn't it?) Another name for cradle to grave is "life cycle cost" which means that the price we pay for a product should include the disposal cost and any cost to the environment as well. Plastic bags are cheap to produce but they are not good for the environment and so their life cycle cost is much higher than their manufactured cost.

Efficient, safe recycling of the product and the product packaging should be part of all manufacturing design and approval processes. Some companies are right onto this and doing it really well. Mercedes Benz unveiled a 100% recyclable car back in 2006.

I'm guilty of plastic abuse too. In my home we recycle everything that is recyclable into the council recycle bins and compost all organic matter. We buy a lot of our produce from our local farmer's market but we still generate a plastic bag a week of mostly plastic packaging that goes into landfill. There are some good initiatives happening, like the banning of plastic shopping bags by some councils. (Australians use 6 billion plastic bags every year.[2]) The introduction of biodegradable bags made from starch is great. Whilst the technology for biodegradable plastic has been around since 1990 it has taken a long time to bring the cost down and people's perception of the importance of using an environmentally friendly product up.

The consequences for our addiction to instant gratification are all around us. We want convenience and we want it now, even if long term it is not good for us. Sometimes the consequences are not immediate and sometimes they are just hidden. The Great Pacific Garbage Patch, also described as the Pacific Trash Vortex (PTV) is a gyre of pelagic plastics, chemical sludge and other debris that have been trapped by the currents of the North Pacific Gyre. The PTV is not a continuous debris field and whilst it is estimated to cover an area as large as the continental United States it is not visible from space (yet). The concentration of plastic in the PTV is increasing and the plastic does not biodegrade but it does breakdown into ever smaller particles which are now entering the food chain and killing fish larvae, marine birds and turtles but it is not in your or my backyard so as with much disturbing news it is largely ignored. It just gets too much sometimes to think about these things – we can all do a little bit though and we can find that middle path again. It's there somewhere under all the plastic bags.

I think it is fair to say that in western culture we are not doing so well at controlling the urge for instant gratification or risk taking. When instant gratification is not controlled then it can become insatiable, the next big deal in banking, pushing limits in the oil and gas industry so you can get the credit for the "success" whereas the responsibility for the clean up doesn't follow you up the ladder. This also applies to alcohol and "recreational" and prescription drugs. We know the brain isn't fully developed until about age 25 now and there is evidence that alcohol and drugs are more damaging to a developing brain than previously thought.

The use by date is up for the excuse of the alcohol industry that they can't help it that the advertising for the latest, trendiest beer or Alco pop "splashes" over onto underage drinkers. If it can't be avoided then the solution is very simple, stop it. Moderation and balance and a fair fight please. Where are the ads to balance the alcohol industry? What about: "Over 3,000 Australian's die each year as a result of harmful drinking, bottoms up.[3]" The alcohol industry is doing a bit of window dressing with the drink responsibly campaign but it is a defensive strategy designed more to silence critics rather than decrease drinking.

We owe it to future generations to start taking our time and considering very carefully the consequences of our actions and our consumption and the behaviour we model to our kids. We can become sustainable and becoming sustainable will generate a lot of jobs in the process and we need to help each other to achieve this because foregoing a short term gain for a longer term benefit takes support. If we consider future generations then foregoing short term profits for future gains, like clean rivers and groundwater become easier.

The developing adolescent brain has a well developed accelerator but only a partially developed brake. An immature adult is more likely to continue the risk taking and impulsive behaviour that is normally associated with teenagers. They are also less inclined to consider the possible negative consequences of such risky behaviors. It is serious enough that they risk their own safety but the Pan-ish of this world are taking risks in motor cars, with the banking system, with weapons and genetic engineering of common crops, deep deep water drilling for oil, drugging our children and many other risks. The profit from some of these ventures is coming out of the pockets of future generations and if the environmental costs were fully factored in, they would not be viable.

Insatiable instant gratification when coupled with the abuse of power and a lack of responsibility makes a potent, destructive mix and it is time we got off that path. Traditional societies invested their energy and time with their adolescents to help them manage the turbulence of puberty. Without the benefits of brain scans traditional societies not only knew the optimal time to help create some new neural pathways that point to healthy adulthood, they also knew how to create the ceremonies and rituals to do it.

[1] Jay Giedd, National Institute on Mental Health (USA)
[2] Australian Academy of Science
[3] Chrikritzhs et al (1999) National Alcohol Indicators Bulletin No. 1: Alcohol-caused deaths and hospitalisations in Australia 1990-97, National Drug Research Institute and Turning Point Alcohol & Drug Centre

14

Instant Gratification

The 2 Minute Noodles of Satisfaction

(Contributed by Peter Pan)

The greatest invention ever invented by any inventor has to be the invention that happened in an instant: The instant noodle. Just think how much time was wasted when fresh noodles had to be cooked like on a stove and everything for up to several whole minutes at a time. In a Japanese poll the instant noodle was voted the most important Japanese invention of the century with Karaoke coming second, the walkman third, the compact disc fifth and Pokemon eighth. Pikachu was very disappointed with the poll results and has asked for a recount.

Momofuku Ando was born in Taiwan in 1910 when it was a Japanese territory. At the age of 48, in a shed in his backyard in Japan, Ando developed a way to rapidly dry noodles by flash frying the noodles in oil and thus the instant Noodle was ~~cooked~~ born. "Experts" predicted that the instant noodle would be just a flash in a pan of oil because back in 1958 fresh noodles were cheaper than the just invented "Chicken Ramen" noodles. Could the experts have been more wrong? [These same "Experts" were snapped up by US Military intelligence.]

In 2008, 94 billion servings of instant noodles were sold world wide according to the big WINA (World Instant Noodle Association). Ando invented the Cup of Noodles in 1971 and if the 27 billion cups that just Ando's company, the Nissin company, has sold since then were stacked on top of each other they would stretch to the moon and back 3.5 times. [The thought of the sheer volume of all that Styrofoam packaging is intimidating].

The instant Noodle sparked acceleration in the instantness or the rapidity expected of instant gratification. The instant noodle also sparked the start of the fast food race which McDonalds entered with all fat vats boiling and all burners blazing in 1953 and the trend away from nutritious food and family time spent at the dinner table accelerated. In Neverland 2.0 the only food available is fast food.

[There are now 31,000 McDonald's worldwide but fortunately the McLibel Case and movies like *"Super Size Me"* have started to reverse the trend in some countries. The McLibel case was where McDonalds tried to legally bully people who were handing out the "What's wrong with McDonalds?" flyer. The flyer raised questions about the honesty of McDonald's marketing, employment practices, environmental impact and nutritional data. It ran for 10 years becoming the longest running court case in UK history and was a major PR disaster for McDonalds.]

Once upon a time people were inexplicably much more patient, somehow they could wait for satisfaction. LOSERS. People started to realize that if they waited too long for satisfaction, if it took more than two minutes, i.e. if it is not instant, the satisfaction got a bit soggy. In Neverland, satisfaction can be cooked with just hot water in less than two minutes. How convenient is that?

Standing firm on never getting satisfaction from anything that takes patience is very important because once the neural pathways for sober reason and judgment sneak into your thoughts then those connections may never get deleted. Through constant repetition, the neural connections for always getting your way and wanting everything NOW get stronger and stronger and stronger and just like a groove in a record, those connections in your brain become the neural highways which become the "go to" parts of the brain. Thinking of investing for the long term? WHAM no way and before you know it, the needle of your consciousness has taken you into the groove of another get rich quick scheme.

Neverland depends on fast food and fast results including premature ejaculation fast sex. Whatever you do it has to be bigger, quicker, better and NOW. Short term thinking is very important particularly in big businesses where executives rarely stay in the job long enough for any long term strategies to reap dividends. They have to move often before anything catches up with them. Rainforest, schmainforest. We need more beef for hamburgers that can be put between two sugared buns by low paid workers for the highest profit possible regardless of the long term impacts on biodiversity, the environment or people's health.

One Day at the University of HumpBurgerology:

"Hey, you! Nerd in the lab coat. I want you to know that I have an MBA and that I am being fast tracked. Now, I know we inject vaccines into cattle. We also inject cattle with hormones to make them grow quicker. So, my question, which could just give us the competitive advantage we need at the moment: Can we inject meat preservatives into the cattle before they die? You know, save some production time? They're going to die anyway." – A. W. Anker (MBA (Hons) with NCS (NCS: No Common Sense)

Speaking of short term thinking, parenting should be based on short term control and manipulation rather than wasting time building character, independence, resilience or self esteem. All those are almost impossible to measure and in education, if you can't measure it, don't do it. In the fast paced Neverland 2.0 world, time is precious and should not be squandered on children. What is in it for you? You might get a squeeze of your hand, maybe a HUG or a kiss?

In the same time as it takes to earn affection from notoriously fickle children, you could have created havoc on a financial market, denied a health benefits claim or foreclosed on a second generation family farm so the corporate farm next door can expand. Productive work, work that contributes to growing the GDP and if the thirst for growth ever slows down then we would have to stop doing all this great stuff that is working so well.

Feeling sad or depressed about something, anything? Instead of trying to deal with any underlying issue or talking about it with friends and finding out that everyone occasionally feels awkward socially you can: 1) HAVE AN ALCOHOLIC DRINK or three! 2) TAKE some DRUGS prescription and/or non-prescription or 3) GO SHOPPING and BUY, BUY. BUY stuff you might want but don't need, feel the shopping buzz hit which makes you momentarily happy and is encouraged by all forms of advertising. After the post shopping euphoria rapidly fades you can do it again and again and again! Until you need another credit card or a bigger house to store all the shit you don't need.

It is important to instantly feed the desire for immediate gratification by rewarding these [childish] impulses with rewards to set up the necessary Neverland 2.0 neural super highways in your brain. It also means that when someone says "NO" to you, or if you have to wait for gratification that you will automatically go mental by jumping the emotional crash barriers of your neurotic superhighway. The best rewards are those that come from outside, not within.

[Strengthening the neural pathways associated with deferring immediate gratification for future benefits is very important and as parents we can help our children with this and practice it ourselves.]

Death
vs.
Death

The fear of death follows from the fear of life. A man who lives fully is prepared to die at any time. -- Mark Twain

"It is no more surprising to be born once than to be born twice: everything in nature is resurrection." -- Francois Voltaire

15

You Can't Take it With You But You Can Try

(by Daniel Prokop)

*"In this world nothing can be said to be certain,
except death and taxes." Benjamin Franklin.*

Taxes are no longer a certainty if you have a smart enough accountant or if you are a corporation determined to avoid them. Death and change are the only certainties. Both are avoided but death in the Western influenced world is shunned, ignored, not spoken about. Death is the proverbial almost extinct elephant that is constantly in the room. If we look closely at the elephant wallah, he is wearing a black cowl and holding an iScythe (the new WAP enabled scythe). You would think, given the huge daily quota of death we are served up via movies, video games and the news that we would be acutely aware of our mortality, of the fragility and preciousness of all life, but no. Herein lies one of the many Neverland paradoxes.

If you behave as if you will never die then it would make sense to look after the environment since you are going to be around forever. That is logical. Unfortunately, the S.S. "I am immortal" is a ship that is so vast that it can fit all Never Landers in it: Noah's Ark on steroids and fortunately with a much bigger gene pool.

> GOD: "Hey Noah, Noah!. Just stop sawing a minute and listen! I just had a thought - saving two of everything is great but, but... it is going to get very

incestuous. To propagate the species, the first offspring have no choice but to have sex with their brothers or sisters, or am I missing something? We don't want that, do we? Maybe we need to add a few more cubits and go for four or six of everything? It is more believable. What do you think? Move that torch away from the straw, Noah. Know what? I'm gonna bump up the height of a few mountains, take some of the pressure off you and the ark."

But far from being fearlessly immortal, overgrown children live in constant fear of Death. Actually they mostly just live in fear and fear of death is a big part of that. Pretending that you will live forever, trying to cheat death through science: cryogenics, genetic engineering or cloning helps people to believe that, as with taxes, death does not have to be a certainty.

We will all die, and in death we are all the same, rich and poor which really gives the rich the shits. You can't take any possessions with you when you die. The ancient Egyptians didn't believe that. Mummifying corpses, leaving riches and sacrificing servants so they could party on in the afterlife has fortunately fallen out of fashion, sort of. Many live as if they can take it all with them, they build pyramids of private wealth that they guard as if it will travel with them for several lifetimes. There is no ability to do a wire transfer from the other side, perhaps the banks should let people know that.

Complaining and whining that death is not fair, that you were really going to live your life properly and do the things you love doing just as soon as the mortgage was paid off or you have made that second million will not give you one extra breath. Ignorance of death is no defense even if it true, maybe nobody ever told you that you would die. You will.

Small children put their hands over their eyes and think that no one can see them, which is cute. Putting your adult hands over your eyes will not hide you from death. No one knows how long their ticket for this lifetime is punched for. When the Reaper suddenly appears, iScythe in hand, it is your time. Offering everything that you own to the Grim Reaper for an extra day, an extra hour doesn't work. Apparently, the Grim Reaper is grim because he is so tired of people trying to bribe him, he was once called the Solemn Reaper but he is just getting more and more exasperated.

"But the most certain signals for lighting the fires of destruction are sent when the old people of a group

lose their memories, consume like youths, and neglect the rites of grieving and burial." (Meade, Michael. 1993. Men and the Water of Life...Initiation and the Tempering of Men. Harper San Francisco, USA).

The rites of grieving and burial (or cremation, or sky burial) show respect for the dead and support those that are left behind with the changes that losing a loved one brings. Moving rituals can be created which are celebrations of the life that has passed. Accepting death, befriending death can sharpen our appreciation for life and bring attention to priorities. If you were to die tomorrow would you continue to do what you are doing day in and day out? Death confronts our beliefs about spirituality and whether there is life after death. Is it actually true that;

"To the well organized mind, death is but the next great adventure" ~J.K. Rowling, "The Man with Two Faces," Harry Potter and the Sorcerer's Stone, 1997, spoken by Albus Dumbledore

Impending death can focus a person's attention on what is truly important and acquiring more things, more consumables like a bigger, wider TV screen can lose its appeal, whilst spending time with loved ones suddenly becomes a priority. The shadow of death can also be a potent harbinger for forgiveness of self and others and letting go of past hurts, real and imagined. In our western culture there is such a fear of death, a denial of death, yet in other cultures Death is a natural part of the cycle of life.

"Today is a good day to Die"
Chief Crazy Horse.

Never Landers find it very difficult to move through the many stages of life that we go through until we return to the earth. Peter Pan is stuck as a child and in denial of the natural journey of life and death. We are not meant to stay perpetually as children. Rites of Passage are important because in many of them, ritually the old way dies before the new way of being can be born. Rites of Passage are as much for the person as for the community.

Children believe they are immortal. Do not, repeat, do not let a boy watch Superman (any version or sequel or sequel to a sequel), give him a cape and send him to his room upstairs unless you are prepared to catch him as he tries to "fly" from his bedroom window. Mortality is not something children dwell on.

Death will make an entrance in every life at some point as this story from the life of the Buddha tells us;

> *Kisa Gotami lived in Savatthi. She married a rich young man and a son was born to them. The son died when he was a toddler and Kisa Gotami was stricken with grief. Carrying her dead son, she went everywhere asking for medicine to restore her son to life. People thought she had gone mad. But a wise man seeing her pathetic condition, decided to send her to the Buddha.*

> *Thus she went to the Buddha and asked him to give her the medicine that would restore her dead son to life. The Buddha told her to get some mustard seeds from a home where there had been no death. Overjoyed at the prospect of having her son restored to life, Kisa Gotami ran from house to house, begging for some mustard seeds. Everyone was willing to help but she could not find a single home where death had not occurred. As the day dragged on, she realised hers was not the only family that had faced death. As soon as she realised this, her attitude towards her dead son changed; she was no longer attached to the dead body of her son and she realised how simply the Buddha had taught her a most important lesson: that everything that is born must eventually die.*

Of course these days Kisa would look to cryogenics, cloning or other unnatural means to keep her son alive or she would spend her days suing someone for the death of her son to keep her away from her grief. Death is not the enemy. Overloading children with virtual death and then disconnecting them from the natural death of a pet or a relative must be confusing and it keeps death in the role of the adversary to be overcome.

We are also disconnected from our food. Meat comes from the supermarket wrapped in plastic, not from living animals that have to be killed and butchered. The danger we are in is that children are either so shielded from grief and sorrow that they are strangers to these emotions or they are so immersed in abuse and violence that they become numb to survive. Either leaves them emotionally vulnerable. Isn't it better for children to experience some of these emotions when they are held (hopefully) by a loving, supporting family?

In truth, there is simply no place in the "pure" Alpha male society for the elderly (unless they are fabulously rich). The reasons for this are: 1) Old people are by definition, old. They are wrinkly and they are unwanted reminders of the passing of time and of mortality, two of the many things that the Alpha male constantly strives to ignore. 2) The Alpha male is not interested in learning from the past nor does he need advice as his self professed "wisdom" borders on the omnipotent (omnipotence being the lesser of the two). Therefore the logical thing to do is to put all the old people in old people's detention centres as far away as possible from the younger members of the community.

{Ummm hasn't anyone told you? We've already accomplished this.}

You are not so good with sarcasm sometimes are you?

16

Death is Something That Happens to Other People

(Contributed by Peter Pan)

In Neverland 2.0 no one ever grows up and if you never grow up you will of course never die.

[Hello? Are you really saying children never die?]

Shut up.

[Panno have a look deep into Neverland, children are expendable in your world, they are slave labour in some countries.]

If I never see it, it isn't real, nah, nah, nah, nah.

[Ummm, Peter, putting your fingers in your ears just stops you being able to write. Sorry to interrupt, keep going, this should be good.]

In Neverland 2.0, no one ever grows up and if you never grow up you will of course never die, because I said so! Pets are also strongly discouraged for a couple of reasons: Reason 1) because it is impossible to train a pet to never grow up, they are just too stupid. The first person who can teach a kitten to stay a kitten forever would be a millionaire. If you're pet grows up right in front of your very eyes you may be tempted to reflect on the passage of time and mortality which would make you morbid and no fun and give you nasty wrinkles, so ditch the pet. Reason 2) pets need feeding, cleaning, petting, exercising etc and your parents will do their very best, which fortunately isn't very effective, to get you to take responsibility for the animal that will grow up and will one day die and go to pet heaven or a good home in the country.

As a good Never Lander you have taken a VOW of non-responsibility and clearly having a pet would violate that sacred Vow. Of course you could get around your vow of non-responsibility by playing your Neverland Truth Elasticity Card BUT…. It all starts to get a bit messy. You could have a pet and then not look after it, which many people do but there are a lot of people who like animals more than people and the RSPCA could be called in… better to just avoid pets altogether.

[The physical and emotional benefits of having a pet are well documented. In addition to walkies bending over to bag a poo helps keep you supple.]

Consume like there is no tomorrow, because if you don't, someone else will. Remember the rule of "A," to stay at the top, to remain Alpha male you have to have more stuff than anyone else, more expensive toys, clothes, cars and don't bother to repair anything, just throw it out and buy another one. Who cares about the earth's "finiiite" resources? It is not your problem, you can't even spell ffinite, even if you tried a couple times.

There is a saying in Neverland "He who has the most toys WINS."

[The quote is "He who dies with the most toys still dies"]

Fortunately Neverland has the full support of the current western medical system which is in denial about death. Providing of course that a living soul can pay for the care, no patient is ever allowed to die with dignity when there is time for one more test, one more drug one more chemo treatment or a final referral to a colleague. In the face of terminal illness doctors will expend vast resources to keep a dying patient alive, just a comatose moment longer, as it should be, though of course who wants to talk about death at all?

A terminal illness should always be a surprise. "What? Why didn't anybody tell me that I could Die?" There are some things which are easy to distract yourself from, a job you hate, that tractor tyre that now hides your belt, your family, BUT death, that will take a lot of distracting, some serious, serious denial. But then if you have successfully avoided contemplating death before your own approaches then you are no doubt up for the job. Why let something like a sudden introduction to mortality shake you out of your very comfortable life? Why should just the young consume frantically?

Death is something that happens to other people, often in movies. Death, destruction and gratuitous violence films are served up daily and they have almost completely displaced crappy movies with actual stories that move and inspire people. About time I say. Watching increasingly realistic and frequent death and violence on TV or via Video games is an excellent way to numb yourself to your own mortality and it introduces a very casual relationship with grief. To grieve you have to appreciate the preciousness of life or beauty and connect to something other than yourself, to the passing of a loved one for example ... as if that is going to happen.

> "The Hero comes crashing in with seven guns blazing, two shoulder mounted, one in each hand, two on his hips and one shooting out his ass. In just a few blazing minutes, making full use of his special infinite weightless ammunition, his bullets tear apart the flesh of 20 bad guys and gals killing them all deader than dead, really dead."

> [Apparently it's fine to kill women on screen now, though "realistically" killing children will have to wait a little longer, not much longer, but a little]

Thankfully the director takes the care and trouble to show us the massacre in slow motion, following the trajectory of as many shells ripping as realistically and graphically as possible into soft, blood spurting flesh. The same 'maestro' director doesn't need to put any energy into story or character development, not when he has CGI toys to play with, why would he? If the idiot [Neverland] public will keep paying good money for bad trash then keep serving them up more trash.

For "Action" films, all we need to know is that the Hero is always RIGHT and he is the self appointed judge, jury and executioner. The BAD guys all deserve to die, none of them have families that will miss them. The HERO is actually doing the bad guys a favour. Unfortunately, in the scenario above, the HERO is operating on the basis of "solid" military intelligence and he has just barged in on a wedding party. The alleged terrorists are a block away, but so what? It just means we get to see another massacre later. There are never any consequences for killing heaps of humans, no remorse, no grief, no sham military tribunal or civilian criminal action, just some crummy cliché laden dialogue, maybe a poor attempt at a tasteless joke and then onto the sequel. More action please!

Death is death, baby, we should have a very, "it will never happen to me" relationship with it. Forget about death, there is no chance of you dying before you take over one more company. The more that death is served up on the platter of our wide screens the better. Cry babies that say there is too much violence today are easily shouted down by a barrage of Alpha Male "Artists" that demand that they are allowed to express their creativity.

> [These "artists" could pay a violence levy as a small percentage of turnover, the more graphic the violence, the higher the levy. We tax cigarettes don't we? Tobacco smoking kills people so there is a strong precedent of taxing things that are harmful. A violence levy would mean that the "artists" would have to ensure that any violence moves the story forward. Gratuitous violence would become too expensive.]

To ensure that children never ~~leave Neverland~~ get in touch with their emotions you have to shelter them from anything that will upset them. Death used to be harder to avoid but now.... Fortunately it's easy to buy kids off and lie to them about pets or relatives dying – "We think Goldyfin must have somehow escaped from his bowl so we bought you this Porsche...," "Mittens must have run away with a boy cat, turns out she was a slut, so we bought you this entertainment system for your room." Aunt Verna moved to the country, finally." Exposing children to the drama of divorce is absolutely fine. Obviously kids can handle dealing with parents breaking up and fighting, shouting abuse at each other which is fair enough as it's probably the kids fault they are splitting up anyway. But grief or dealing with death? No way, keep all that stuff safely on the TV screen.

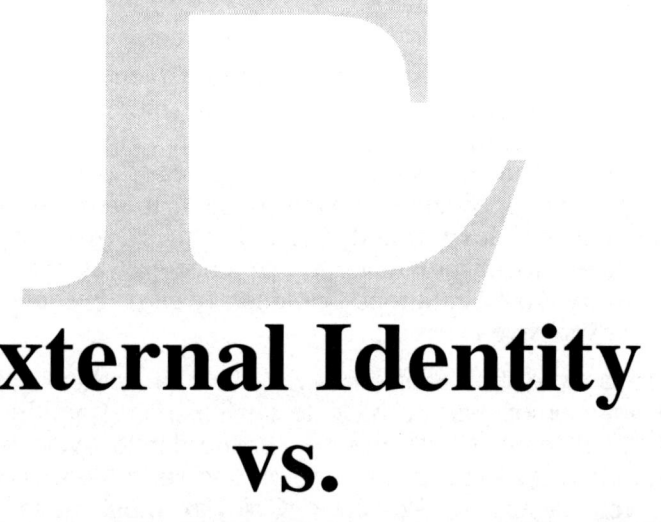

External Identity
vs.
Identity from Self

*An identity would seem to be arrived at by the way
in which the person faces and uses his experience
.--James Baldwin*

17

To Mine Own Self Be Me

(by Daniel Prokop)

A child saying "Look at me! Look at me! Look at me!" is totally appropriate because a child wants to be seen by their parents, needs to be seen for the unique spark of life that they are. Sometimes the smallest of acknowledgements, a little wave or a nod can generate a smile so bright that it can make you stop worrying about parent stuff, for a moment. In an adult the same insatiable attention seeking is tiresome, painful and apparently comes with the territory if you are a celebrity with a publicist.

A child sits at the centre of its known universe and the world revolves around them. This is the way it is and is not very surprising since the human baby starts out life cute but totally helpless. New parents soon learn that the family does revolve around the child. If you are expecting a child and you want to make parents that are struggling with a willful two year old laugh, just say "we've decided that we're not going to let the baby change our lives." Try not to say this if they have a mouthful of food unless you want to wear it. HAVING A BABY WILL CHANGE YOUR LIVES! Just so you know. The reason everybody says "they grow up so fast" is because they grow up so fast and our time with our children is precious.

Children often do things just to gain attention. When an overgrown child constantly does things just to gain attention they have jumped over to the child side of the line in the sand. It is likely that they are also ignoring responsibility in their attempts to grab that spotlight just one more time. It is trying and destructive and results in people claiming credit for results they have not contributed to and hiding failures. Sometimes they make much ado about nothing "Yo! Hey! Check it OUT. I have denied every claim for healthcare I have received today. I rock."

A healthy adult does what is needed (like passing legitimate health care claims) not for attention but because they see that it needs doing and they get on with it. Their happiness does not depend on lots of attention for the work they do and some acknowledgement and recognition is certainly nice. The big difference is that their motivation is not attention. Before I go into a little bit of a rant, I have to say that there are some very, very good people working for corporations who are doing their best to foster transformation from within the belly of the beasts. Ok, now for that rant...

In big corporations, layer after layer of management has been removed because an expensive management consultant pulled a figure out of their ass and said that sacking 20% of the workforce will generate savings that could justify their fee. So now there are scared managers that have no idea what people they are supervising actually do. Job descriptions are fine but they have limitations and some bear no resemblance to what an employee does on a day to day basis. Key performance indicators such as: always agree with the boss even when he is wrong, laugh at stupid jokes and grab your ankles are not usually formalized.

An organisation that has people who are fearful for their jobs and have little knowledge of what someone does creates a fertile field for little children who crow about the tiniest "win," viciously protect their little patch and spend more time sucking up than buckling down to the job at hand. Supervisors often do not have the skills to give appropriate performance feedback so instead, they promote incompetence out of their department, just so they don't have to carry the dead wood. Unfortunately, this just creates a problem somewhere else and the person that gets promoted can soon get a highly inflated opinion of themselves and others mistake rapid promotion as merit rather than *merde*.

People who have never worked in huge corporations mistakenly assume that all senior people are highly competent individuals. Hell No. There certainly are highly competent people but there are also many little boys who have been promoted several levels above their level of competency and maturity based on strategies that Peter Pan promotes. Just because they occupy a senior position does not automatically mean that what they are saying is truthful or good advice. Rant over, TY.

Constant praise of children can be as harmful as paying them no attention at all. "Johnny, oh, my GOD did you take that big breath all by yourself? You are so gifted, so special, so much better than anyone else." Seeing children and acknowledging them, letting them know they are loved for who they are keeps them supple, gives them a strong centre of balance for the winds and storms of life that buffet us all. Praise can become addictive and inhibits the transition to healthy adulthood. Totally enjoy and celebrate regularly with your children, they are special and so is everyone else.

Self esteem comes from a Greek word meaning "reverence for self." As parents we play an important role in helping a child develop self reverence and also reverence for others. Ways that support children include giving specific feedback. For example, a child presents a drawing that they are proud of. Specific feedback could be: "I love how you did the yellow shading around the sun." The child knows that you have taken the time to really look at the drawing and the parent has not set up false expectations in the child that they will become the next Picasso. Instead of teaching a child to always seek external approval we can reflect back to them the pleasure found in doing something well. "So when you finished that drawing, how did you feel?" (Robin Grille's books and articles on parenting are excellent resources.)

There are also many children growing up in toxic households and I'm not talking about asbestos. I'm talking living with abusive, highly critical parents where no matter what the child does, they are never good enough. This not good enough wound is difficult to shake and one I can certainly relate to. Most children are raised in a confusing montage of praise and criticism.

Children are amazing mirrors and they are incredibly perceptive. They absorb their environment and then will reflect some of that back at us as parents. "I don't know where they get that from?" can be a form of parental denial. More often than not, they get it from us but what makes it tricky is that as well as the verbal stuff, children also pick up blasted non-verbal stuff too. Some of the "stuff" is hidden even from us. I remember a particular incident and my son lost it, he kept saying to himself, "I'm stupid, I'm stupid, stupid stupid." We have read the parenting books and we have never said that to him but ... when the fan is looking a bit brown for me, guess what? That is my inner dialogue, so I know where he gets it from. I just thought I had hidden it better than that. So going easier on me is a way of supporting my children too.

In the teenage years the child starts to question their inherited identity. As the young person begins to individuate the parents are pushed or fall off the pedestal that they stood on for so long which can be uncomfortable for all concerned. A teenager trying to find their identity may be as simple as "anything as long as it is not my parents." On one hand they are trying to find their uniqueness whilst they also desperately want a sense of belonging. This is a heck of a paradox to navigate. Up to this point, most of their identity has been made up of external references: gender, ethnicity, religion, physical abilities, appearance, social status and who their parents are.

Body image is a huge issue for teenagers today. In the 2008 Mission Australia National survey of young Australians young people ranked their level of concern about fifteen issues. Body image was ranked among their top three issues, closely followed by drugs and family conflict.

As the individuation process unfolds they question sometimes for the first time beliefs that they have had handed to them. It is a time when teenagers are quite vulnerable as they try to work out what makes them tick, what touches their soul. For boys this is a time of uncertainty and rapid physical growth too. So much is happening that they are not sure who they are and the uncertainty can mean that they find it difficult to look people in the eyes. Some men will make them look them in the eye which can make the teen feel bullied, dominated. As they gain confidence they will straighten up and look the world in the eye.

A contemporary, community based Rite of Passage provides a safe, non competitive space where a teen can be really seen and acknowledged for their gifts which can be: a great sense of humour, a deep sense of compassion, courage, or wisdom. Some of these qualities can be overlooked in a world that places more value on sporting prowess but less on kindness.

Healthy adults have a strong sense of who they are and so are not dependent on approval or praise to feel good about themselves. They are not so easily manipulated through their insecurities by advertisers. They are less identified by their occupation and more by who they are being. 'Know thyself' This ancient Greek aphorism was apparently inscribed in the forecourt of the Temple of Apollo at Delphi though it might have been more useful to the Greeks if it had said "Know thy debt levels."

A healthy adult doesn't need to put someone down to feel happy. They don't need to constantly compete with others to have a sense of self worth. For some little boys they feel a need to constantly compete with others. The satisfaction of a game well played is meaningless against whether they win or lose. Of course Peter may have a few different ideas on this...

18

Why the Beta Male is the First Loser

(Contributed by Peter Pan)

A is for Alpha Male, B is for loser, C is for … Competition defines us, it is everything. It is the yardstick by which we are measured and by which we can measure others or beat them over the head with it. Competition keeps us sharp and ideally should permeate every moment of our waking life. How do we know how we are doing unless we can compare ourselves to and be better off, than others? They say a little competition can be healthy so a lot of competition has to be awesome. Alpha males must continually maintain and reaffirm their "Alpha" status and this means making everyone else either a Beta male or preferably a C. Any competition that excludes or disadvantages women before it even starts, is a good competition because such bias makes winning so much easier.

Before you were you, when you were still just a slightly glazed look in your drunken father's eye you were already competing for your very life. The sperm that created you beat 300 million other sperm to penetrate an egg's defenses, to make you! Yeah, Baby! Where are those 299,999,999 second place getters now? Those loser sperm are Dead, and in the ultimate humiliation their final voyage was not a victory lap down the birth canal but the disgrace of being ejected from the body by a current of warm urine.

[That sounds very dramatic but your knowledge of female anatomy is flawed.]

As a society, it will be some time before we actually douse silver and bronze medalists in a yellow liquid but we are getting closer, we just do it now by ignoring them. Remember, Beta males get flushed, Alpha males get the egg.

Some wankers, sorry, "new agers" talk about "Win/ Win" situations – an Alpha male will never settle for a Win/ Win situation and playing just for "fun" makes everyone a loser. In Neverland 2.0 we must maintain the delightful and strict dichotomy between winners and losers. Winners are allowed to be happy "grinners."

NOTE TO TINKERBELL: We need a better word than "grinner", something that ups the feeling of superiority whilst simultaneously humiliating the vanquished.

There is nothing worse than being a sad, miserable LOSER. It is imperative that we maintain as high a ratio of winners to losers as is humanly possible. One winner for every fifty losers or more is just a guide. Luckily there seems to be no shortage of losers.

It has taken time to extract the stupid "fun" element from games and for competitions to become vicariously competitive [umm... I think you mean viciously competitive?] As I said games now are vicariously viciously competitive. Our ~~backward looking~~ fine education system has a strong competitive history that has pitted students against students. School is essentially an enormous "L" for loser factory. There are many ways that schools can put an "L" stamp on a student's forehead: failing students that do not learn the narrow way that a school teaches is the most popular way, though encouraging a strong bullying culture also works well or simply ignoring kids for long enough can lead them to "L" themselves.

The good news is that the pressure is on for schools. In the education system more and more direct teaching time is spent dealing with classroom behavioural problems. Obviously this is the ideal time to start testing all students at earlier and earlier ages. Whilst early exam pressure may rob a kid of a few years of carefree early childhood it can help add decades to childhood after school. The clear social bonus of relentless testing and comparison to others means that the "L" stamp is now even less likely to get bumped off a kid's forehead by supportive and understanding parents or friends. Schools are wonderful at creating Beta and lower males and females.

It is lamentable that once out of school, businesses never test their employees on what they don't know in the same way that our huge education system does. Testing for drugs doesn't count. If it is appropriate to subject unpaid, very young children to regular exam stress and anxiety, then why stop this practice once they actually start getting paid as employees? This is an area where we can do so much better and I point this out in the hope that the champions of industry might somehow take it on to reinforce and even create new learning dysfunctions that could be utilized to further reduce the minimum wage to the below minimal wage or sub-minimal wage [which it already is in many third world countries like the USA].

Fact: Men are naturally more competitive than women. When you start your pre-life with a death race against 300,000,000 others a strong competitive spirit makes sense. Men who are not competitive are basically bully fodder, no judgment there, just the law of the jungle, survival of the fittest and all that. Sadly, there are some men who really make you wonder if all the other sperm took a wrong turn.

Keep wanting more and more. You are special, you know that so you know that you deserve more than anyone else so feel free to just take it, it's yours even if the receipt for it is in someone else's wallet. Make sure you set up rules for happiness that are impossible to meet. It is good to involve your parents in this by making rules for praise or approval that you know they will never give you. This clever bit of unobtainable goal setting will keep you driven to succeed in a way that non children will never understand.

Remember that attention and adoration are limited resources and they belong to you. If there is a spotlight either steal the limelight by pushing your way in or better still steal the actual spotlight and set it up so that it only focuses on you. If you have a brother or sister, be vigorous in undermining them or they will take attention meant for you. This will also make working for a large corporation easier as these skills are transferable.

If you are to remain the centre of everyone's attention then dominating conversations is an important skill to learn…

Communication: Disagreeing is Not Bullying
(But if Done Correctly It Can Be)

Disagreeing with someone is not bullying even when the disagreement becomes heated or passionate. In theory, different points of view coming together can create vigorous, respectful, healthy debate which can lead to new distinctions and the refining of knowledge on a particular topic. It is your job to prevent this from ever happening. In some cases "healthy" debate on an issue could cause you to question some of your underlying core beliefs and lead to personal growth which is why it must be avoided at all costs. Mature respectful conversations are dangerous and engaging in them could get you kicked out of Neverland 2.0. Fortunately this way of interacting rarely occurs outside of human research labs. Any discussion that is rapidly maturing can easily be derailed by some good ANAL (Active Non Auditory Listening) or escalated into pure BS (Bullying Situation).

> *"When two or three people come together in the name of Neverland then I will be there amidst them or if I am too busy or have a better offer, then I will send a proxy or you can just have the tantrum without me, whatever." (King James Version: Gospel of St. Peter Pan 18:20PM).*

If for whatever reason you are not feeling particularly aggressive or the other person is physically much larger than you, then you may just choose to short circuit good communication by employing an ANAL technique. There are a few ways of being ANAL and mixing these techniques up will provide the best result: 1) OWF or Off With the Fairies: if you can see Fairies like Tinkerbell, then whilst the other person's mouth is moving take some time to watch them fluttering around behind the person expelling their breath in the form of speech. When you finally notice that the other person has stopped speaking and is waiting for you to respond, you do. "I'm sorry, what were you saying?" You can even admit that you were off with the fairies or you can go the advanced technique and insert a sympathy lie "I'm sorry my <father, mother, dog, aunt, uncle, good friend> just died, I was thinking about them." Whether you add a single tear running down your cheek here will depend on your acting ability.

With just one good ANAL you have derailed the entire conversation which will often run out of steam when they realize that they are talking to themselves. If you have timed it so that the hot air that you missed was particularly thoughtful and passionate, better still, because trying to replicate a moment of inspired eloquence is almost impossible. If you have employed an advanced technique you have not only stymied any debate, you have brought the conversation back to the most important topic in the world, yourself.

Staying with ANAL for the moment: technique 2) Interrupting in Mid Point (IMP) this is a technique with infinite variations and can be used in all human to human interactions. Timing is important, wait until the speaker is totally immersed in what they are saying and building up to an important climax point before you launch the IMP. A good IMP can also be a *conversationus interruptus.* Children trying to prevent ~~competitors~~ siblings are particularly good at this variation though they often abbreviate it to *coitus interruptus.*

Before launching the IMP you need to decide what to interrupt with: A) Personal IMP or PIMP – "Your tie really doesn't go with your shirt." This comment satisfies the three P's of good interrupting: Pointless, Personal and Puerile. A PIMP tends to stun an opponent and they waste precious moments and momentum trying to determine whether your comment merits a response. The best riposte for an IMP is to ignore it completely and to play on but most players take the PIMP personally, as it was intended, therefore derailing the whole conversation.

One of my favourite IMPs is B) the POOP (Paradoxically, Out Of Place) IMP. Ideally a good POOP is delivered when the speaker takes a breath. Some speakers will not give you the minimum conversational courtesy of a breath break as they can circular breathe. Circular breathing is when you draw breath in through the nose as you talk and exhale through the mouth. To master this anti interruption technique for yourself, learn how to play a didgeridoo. To successfully play a didgeridoo you need to be able to circular breathe.

A non-breath gap POOP needs a little more energy to successfully interrupt than a true breath gap POOP. The POOP can be a reference to something in the Area of Immediate Attention (AIA). "Hey that cloud looks like the US [illegally] invading Iraq," the more absurd and creative the POOP the better. "Can anyone else here smell dope?" is always a good standby, even if you have to light one up yourself to validate the comment.

Trivia POOPs can be quite effective. Tailor these to your audience. These can be sporting related, political, historical or entertainment based but of course on a completely different topic to the main topic of conversation. You also need to decide whether to go for a trivia question that everybody knows the answer to, which increases the opportunity for secondary interruptions or whether you go the obscure trivia where you are the only person that knows the answer, a rhetorical question disguised as a general question. The advantage of going for obscurity is that, if you have interrupted successfully, then all the attention will be back where it should be, on you.

An IMP that is fun to play with and if done well, the most infuriating to contend with is C): FAST (Finishing A SenTence) IMP. If you are pulling a FAST one, start out small, finishing the last word of a sentence at the same time as the speaker and then sporadically build the FAST to finishing two or three words. A good speaker will initially be surprised, then quickly irked and then annoyed as you continue. Because you appear to be agreeing with the speaker, and you will be supporting this view with appropriately affirming body language, they will not feel threatened unless they know you. A speaker will rarely move to shut a FASTer down but FASTing should, as a minimum impact, put the speaker off their rhythm.

The coup de grace of a FAST IMP should be delivered just prior to the speaker making their definitive point or if you are in a hurry or need to shut them up early, any point will do. Your end FAST must be in total contradiction to everything the speaker has said in the lead up. For example a whining environmentalist speaking on habitat destruction ... "blahdy, blah, blah, blah, wetlands, blah, vital nursery grounds blah, blahdy ... and that is why it is so critical <speaker pauses for breath and for dramatic effect>" ...<insert your FAST> "that we drain all wetlands as soon as possible and build condominiums on them!" With any luck the media will quote the speaker and use your conclusion. FAST is a fun ambush technique that may require you to leave the venue rather quickly.

The final IMP D): Is the LAG (Loud Automatic Gainsaying). This is the most aggressive of the IMP options and is made even more effective when combined with some form of physical intimidation. As explained earlier some experienced speakers can ignore a PIMP or a well placed POOP, they can even dodge a FAST but a LAG is impossible to ignore and cannot be made to look accidental. It is pretty self explanatory, to deliver it, just remember SLAP(PP): Short, Loud, Aggressive, Personal and (Paid if Possible). Expletives often help when SLAPPing a LAG on someone, but know your audience and keep colourful language one rating below the audience level i.e. use M rated language when with an MA audience, WHY? Why not go one notch above for shock value? Well you can, but ideally you want people to remember more than just the shock of a swear word, you want them to remember the reaction of the speaker that was interrupted. They will get angry and some people will crumple under unexpected and inappropriate pressure.

Technically most of the foregoing are actually forms of covert psychological bullying except of course for the straight up intimidation one which is less than covert. It is unlikely that you will ever be accused of covert bullying due to the general ignorance surrounding bullying and any blaggard that does accuse you can always be counter attacked with "They are just being overly sensitive" and when this is said in a condescending manner it clearly suggests that the complainant is a little mentally unstable.

Of course whether you successfully interrupt or not, by staying focused on interrupting you will have successfully avoided listening to a single thing the other person was trying to say, thereby protecting you from their point of view.

A shared vocabulary enhances effective written and oral communication. Fertilising your statements with as many AAs (Ambiguous Acronyms) as possible can put a well placed barrier to understanding and will give you a [false] sense of superiority as well as the opportunity to change your story by renaming acronyms even if confronted with a HANSARD transcript of what you have said. AA's give you that little extra wiggle room so use them generously. SLAPP a FAST LAG on an ANAL PIMP, yo!

[Thanks Peter, I guess. That completes the last section on the differences between Peter Pan and a healthy adult. The differences are profound which is why contemporary Rites of Passage are so important. We need adults, apply within.

Peter is going to share some of his executive tips next which will provide a few clues as to how we got to where we are. I'm going to follow through on that topic as we wind our way out of Neverland but before we leave we are going to spend some time looking at what parents can do about helping their children to grow up.]

Free:
Peter Pan's
Executive Tool Box

"People want you to be a crazy, out-of-control teen brat. They want you miserable, just like them. They don't want heroes; what they want is to see you fall." -- Leonardo DiCaprio

19

Ignorance is Way Better than BLISS

(Contributed by Peter Pan)

It has been said that Ignorance is Bliss but that is a gross underjustice to ignorance which is way, way better than BLISS. Ignorance is so much more versatile. Bliss is so one dimensional. Bliss is just bliss and it is a transitory kind of feeling. For example, bliss without ignorance in the face of a direct threat to your life will evaporate and can inadvertently get you killed "What are you smiling at? <STAB>." Ignorance in the face of a threat to your life can keep you safe. In ignorance you can walk past potential muggers who might mistake ignorance for confidence thus leaving the ignoramus alone. Blissful people can really piss miserable people off too, especially if bliss is misinterpreted as smugness which is an open invitation for a smack in the back of the head (isn't that right DiNozzo?)

Ignorance allows you to walk a dog without having to take a poop bag with you. I could stop this chapter now on the strength of this point alone. It is impossible to remain blissful when you are desperately trying to suppress your vomit reflex as you attempt to scoop up a fresh pile of dog shit with an inverted plastic bag as quickly as possible while trying not to look at what you are doing. With ignorance, even if you see your canine doing a big dump on the sidewalk (and let's face it, there are some dogs that should whinny when they poo) you simply turn your cheeks the other way and pretend that you know nothing about it. You suddenly become interested in the clouds and adopt a faraway, "Don't disturb me, I'm deep in thought," pose. This pose is also called the pose of the three politicians "see no poo, hear no poo, smell no poo" and it epitomizes the way many politicians deal with difficult problems.

Ignorance is the crutch of bliss. If you want to kick bliss right in the nuts then go ahead punk, make my day, educate yourself, take a course or do something new. Even taking your head momentarily out of the sand can cause you to notice things that you don't want to notice which could be a blow below the belt for access to bliss and an open invitation for WORRY. Ignorance fuels our ability to ignore stuff, a basic but very, very important point. Ignoring that niggling feeling that something is wrong gives bliss a bit of extra elbow room.

With ignorance there is a "Veil of Ignorance." Some extraordinary people can do the full dance of the nine veils of ignorance, that's seven veils of idiocy plus two extra veils as a stupid bonus. Bliss doesn't even own a veil. Bliss is just bliss but with ignorance there is also willful ignorance, playful ignorance, invincible ignorance, rational ignorance and the more passive "I don't know," kind of ignorance. Ignorance has been maligned for a long time.

> *"Ignorance, the stem and root of all evil"*
> *Plato*

Despite Plato dissing ignorance, education has not made much progress in tackling ignorance and of course by calling ignorance 'Evil', every religious nutter around has had to weigh in and slam ignorance whilst simultaneously doing everything in their powers to keep people from questioning anything they tell them. Go figure.

> *"What we call evil is simply ignorance bumping its*
> *head in the dark" Henry Ford*

I have studied ignorance or not studied it actually, more just reveled in it, for a long time and I have used it not only for bliss but to defend the indefensible, to accuse the innocent and it is invaluable in marketing and banking and in industry. The foundations of Neverland 2.0 are mired in ignorance as are many of the simplest lies "I didn't know" "I can't remember" "What?" "I don't understand." Ignorance opens up whole new avenues for consistent Bliss.

How many adults are Blissful? Need more time to answer that question? It was obviously non rhetorical. One of the best reasons for never growing up is the lack of bliss in the adult world. Ignorance of how a person in a fully grown body should behave will keep you young forever and the ignorance will at least give you a shot at the bliss of the young. Ignorance will also give you bonus excuses "I'm not supposed to behave like a baby?"

Ignorance of the troubles of the world will also keep you worry free. If you have never heard of human induced climate change then how can it concern your pretty little head? To remain ignorant all you have to do is to is either ignore all peer reviewed scientific papers written in the past 20 years or watch FOX News. Simple. Yet one more example of why it is important that people stop saying that ignorance is bliss, ignorance is way way better.

To maintain optimal ignorance it is important to stay within your comfort zone at all times, avoid situations where you feel uncomfortable as this could lead to personal growth. The word "grow" is part of personal "grow"th and if you "grow up" you will get kicked out of Neverland 2.0. Stay the same, you are great the way you are.

20

"To Lie or not to Lie?"
A Rhetorical Question.

(Contributed by Peter Pan)

Of course you are going to lie. Lie-ability is a fundamental life skill and it is often the rock upon which you will build your... not religion, but, well, maybe your religion, you know what? I don't care, I really don't give a ... where was I? Are we on to the health benefits of maintaining a short attention span yet? No?

Children will experiment with the truth and some kids are natural born liars. Competency at deception can erase a few wrinkles but if you want to stay young forever you must be more than a good liar, you need to be a great liar. Remember this: Lying can be as good for your skin as Botox and it's free. Three words for the up and coming liar: practice, practice, practice. Lying is as much an art form as art is an art form although with lying, too much colour is not necessarily a good thing and please do not start your lying practice by saying over and over that an apple is an orange whilst looking at a bowl of fruit. That is an advanced lying technique.

What will help you as you develop your lie craft is to watch and model how the experts do it and let's be honest [just for a second] and acknowledge just how good the Neverland 2.0 Department of Lying and Deception is. Your first "go to" liars are politicians. In the farce that masquerades as politics, the unwashed ~~pubic~~ public has been conditioned to expect politicians to lie and this is often the only area where politicians actually align themselves

144

with the pubic they are elected to represent. Seek ye out also other career liars, for example, many PR and advertising executives are consummate liars.

A word on advertising and how a lesson from advertising can help you worry less, whilst increasing your lie-ability. To avoid adverse conscience feedback from a big black lie, do what advertisers do. Say you make some outlandish claim like "Nucular [nuclear] energy is clean energy."

> [Totally "clean" except for the mining, the reactor risk and the fact that the spent fuel rods from the reactor need to be disposed of for thousands of years and who will pick up the tab if they are not stored properly? Thousands of years! How can anyone in good conscience leave a legacy of radioactive waste for hundreds of generations to come?]

> As long as all the lights and the air conditioner come on when I want them to, I don't care where the electricity comes from.

It helps if you say nuclear like George W. Bush "nucular," it makes it sound kind of cute and folksy like. So you say "of course it's safe, trust us we're scientists. We'll look after the waste forever blah, blah" then you add a very short disclaimer. But with the disclaimer, you say it incredibly swiftly and only to yourself. It is your personal rider that no one ever needs hear and it is very simple: you say "your experience may differ." This is the PR / advertising equivalent of having your fingers crossed which as we all know means that you are not responsible for how other people experience whatever it is that you claimed or said or sold. Amen.

Of course when saying to yourself "Your experience may differ," it is very important to make sure that you do not move your lips, that would be very unprofessional especially if it is during a TV interview. Of course those highly evolved individuals who have had a successful conscience-ectomy [psychopaths] may no longer need to rely on even advanced emotional crutches.

Do not be afraid to seek out a master in the art of lying. They are not too hard to find. Choose an unsustainable industry where there are only a few, very large, predatory players. For training purposes let's choose Big Oil. Hey! Don't get ahead of me here … yes, the spokespeople for big oil are good but they are limited in their lie-ability because they are publicly identified with the company and industry that they represent.

"To Lie or not to Lie?" A Rhetorical Question

For some reason people are skeptical of Big Oil when they say "don't you worry about climate change, we'll take care of it for you" but they are totally fine when they say "of course there is enough oil to last forever" or "of course it's safe to drill 5.5 km into the core of the earth in 1.5 km of water." With climate change they are compromised, through no fault of their own, in their lie-ability. Sure, sure they can afford to tell lies loudly and often but they are not the masters that we seek.

The true master will be the passionate and sincere spokesperson for a lobby group with a very serious name who will add wings of credibility to deliberately misleading falsehoods. Some of the names are fantastic: The National Center for Policy Analysis and the Heritage Foundation are both advocates for climate change – their job is to deny it until it is too late to do anything about it.

> [Both the NCPA and the Heritage Foundation have published "misleading and inaccurate information about climate change," according to Bob Ward, The Guardian, June 1,2009]

Unfortunately these days distrustful, busy bodies, a [so far] uncensored internet and outrageous freedom of information acts make it more difficult for these lobbyist masters to operate completely independently of their host organisms [often a parasite]. Be smart, if you are going to fund these lobby groups, and of course you are, then please be more careful than ExxonMobil who got busted investing millions of dollars in the "climate denial industry." [David Adam, The Guardian 28, May 2008]

This is an area where the early deception movers had a huge lie-ability advantage. They had the freedom to take the truth and smear it with unbelievable shite which, even if people didn't swallow the lies hook line and sinker left them with at least the hook, the cleverly implanted doubts about subjects that they hitherto had no doubts about. The tobacco industry were early masters in this area. Who will ever forget "Nicotine is not addictive," "we are not targeting young people" and "smoking does not cause lung cancer." Each of these lies represents an investment of millions of dollars of bogus scientific studies, misleading statements, hiding facts and straight faced denials.

No chapter on lobbying and lying could be complete without mentioning the Japanese lie about "killing whales for scientific research," or the equally unbelievable squealing porker of "We have always traditionally eaten whale meat processed by traditional gigantic Japanese mother ships after they have been killed by traditional ancient Japanese high explosive tipped harpoons in the traditional Japanese Antarctic whaling grounds which are a mere 12,000 km away from Japan." These lies, the former for international consumption and the latter for Japanese domestic consumption have been unconvincingly but often told for over two decades.

To become a black belt liar there is one final step for full rounding as opposed to being just a bit padded and it is considered the Holy Grail of Liar training: catch someone telling the truth and study them. This can not only be difficult but also highly dangerous and my recommendation is to keep this part of your training as short as possible. It is dangerous because the truth does have a certain ring to it, fortunately, as the soothing blanket of Neverland has carpeted the land, the tone of truth can now only be heard by dogs and a limited number of individuals who give a shit but never the less, it could mess with your head and you do not want your lie-ability to be compromised by the truth e.g. if you work for pro-whaling interests then it would be wise to avoid listening to Sea Shepherd spokespeople, they are way too passionate and convincing. Listen instead to someone from seed savers, equally passionate but everyone knows you can't grow whales from seeds so you should be safe.

So you have done your homework, you have studied masters, you have practiced, you can say "your experience may differ" without moving your lips but there is one person that knows every one of your cute tricks, every one of them, YOU. At first blush you would think that lying to yourself would be a tough gig, after all, you know yourself well enough to not trust you, but this is just not so.

It is precisely because you do know yourself so well that you are able to deliver the lie flawlessly. There are two types of lying to oneself: 1) When you lie in a way that you know that you don't mean it so it is a kind of self fulfilling lie. If hell ever suddenly freezes over some of these lies could become true. New Year's Eve is a great time to make these lies: "I resolve to work with neglected children – my own." This lie is shattered by January the 2nd. Then you tell yourself, and you believe it, that you actually meant it as a Chinese New Year's Resolution which gives you some breathing space. Obviously you swiftly break that resolution but then you realize that you really, really meant it as a Tibetan New Year's resolution or a Mayan New Year's resolution by which time it could be a birthday resolution. You know what I am talking about, we've all done it, we say it, but even we don't believe it.

The second type of self lie is: 2) When you lie but you are the only one that doesn't know it is a lie and you will never ever believe that you would lie to yourself about THAT. Example: "I am a great golfer" but the course professional follows you around in a dump truck just to fill in your divots. This self lie is quite popular: "I am a great father" but you cannot remember the name of all of your children and you only have one.

The parental lie that every school adores is: "My child would never do that!" These are tough, almost cruel lies because you have actually tricked yourself into believing what you have said, despite your intimate knowledge of you, but hey, perhaps your experience may differ.

Advanced Lying Strategies:

Multi-Lie Situations: When all hope of hiding something is gone, when the tell tale glow of truth starts to shine from under the door you slammed in its face you are in what I call a multi lie situation (MLS). MLSs also cover those unfortunate times when you are caught red [bloody] handed with your hand in the till or on the barrel of radio active waste. Initially you may feel like a trapped rat and you will be left gasping for a lie, any lie to get you of the heinous situation of getting caught. MLSs are ones where one primary lie is automatically backed up by a number of secondary lies.

Even for experienced liars, a sudden, deep, primary guilt infection will nearly always release the rancid puss of secondary lies. This is where training and no credible witnesses pays off. The first lie will be out before the brain can be engaged, not your fault, it's due to some recessive honesty gene. Whatever… listen, no matter how bad the primary lie is, stick with it. For example: "We invaded Tibet because we lost a bit of China thousands of years ago and we thought that it was hiding under Tibet." The Chinese have stuck with this lie for the past 60 years.

> [If interpreted strictly according to China's own logic, Tibet could make a reverse takeover claim of China. Tibet invaded China in 763 and extracted an annual tribute from China which China is now seriously in arrears on.]

Stick with the primary lie loudly and often and then apply appropriate lie management principles. At all times, you must fight the compulsion to immediately replace or bolster the primary lie. Credibility is inversely proportional to the number of secondary lies, big words, sorry, more lies equals less chance of being believed. The standard secondary lie for an invasion is "liberation." The biggest challenge with secondary lies is that they are rarely placed or carefully positioned as part of a deliberate untruth campaign. They are usually spontaneously vomited forth, with bits of tell tale carrot. Remember a gold medal secondary lie, like regime change, will never make up for a poor primary lie, weapons of mass destruction. I wouldn't know myself, of course, but this is what I have observed or rather what a friend told me, no wait, I mean this is what my Grandpa, no my Grandma told me or one of my siblings, I think, or maybe I read it on the internet or … now I remember, I got it sent as an email. See?

Tertiary lies, lies to back up secondary lies, are a sign that good MLS management has failed. The tertiary lies for China's need to invade and develop Tibet in 1950 are that; they could...

...and in Tibet you couldn't see the trees for the forests, there was not enough pollution, no toxic industrial waste, there were too many Tibetans, not enough Han Chinese and the Tibetans had littered their countryside with useless monasteries.

No wonder that after nearly 60 years of occupation no one believes China and Tibetans are still called Tibetans not Chinese. Dear Neverland rookie, this is an example of what not to do in a MLS situation.

> [Tibet wasn't perfect in 1949 but name a place that was. Tibet had its challenges but it was the Tibetan's country and it was unique and they were making progress.]

Like so many muscles, you could lose the lying muscle if you stop lying. Yeah, right, ROFLMAO.

The Withdrawal Technique : The three most common lies of all time are 1) The cheque is in the email 2) I Love You. 3) I won't ejaculate.

Lie three above has multiple variations and is basically a lie and eventual withdrawal technique. Having said you won't, you do. In the throes of coitus men will pretty much say anything which is why the withdrawal method of contraception is... absurd. No apology will remove rapidly swimming sperm from the uterus. The deed and the potential paternity suit are done.

This is very similar to the method we use for the Lie and Withdrawal method of adding doubt to something that is bleedingly obvious. Court Room lawyers learned this a long time ago. A lawyer says something outrageous. There is an objection and the judge strikes the comment from the record. The lawyer withdraws his comment and the jurors are asked to disregard the remark. They can't do that. They have heard it and no matter how staunch they are, it creates a flicker of doubt. Fortunately, instead of mentally penalizing the guilty lawyer, the deleted comment is better recalled than many other comments because of the drama surrounding it, because people love gossip and the "up yours" factor. "Where does that high and mighty judge, dressed in drag, get off telling me what to remember and what not to remember?"

150

Of course this works in the Big Game outside of court too. In fact it works much much better outside of a court of law. In a court room, unfortunately the same people that hear the lie are also told to disregard it which does diminish the effectiveness of the withdrawal, but the sperm are still in there doing their thing, so to speak. In Greater Neverland, once an outrageous lie is launched, very few people ever see the withdrawal or retraction of the lie. Certain media companies and political parties are masters of this advanced technique.

Good techniques are not enough in today's busy world. Once upon a time you cold throw a lie out there and walk away, simpler times friends. Today every lie needs to be managed.

Lie Management Strategies: If you have some rather unpleasant skeletons locked away that will go off if hit by direct daylight or if you have told a lie and the truth is rearing it's butt ugly head you need to be familiar with world's best practice lie management principles. There are basically two mutually exclusive lie management strategies: 1) ignore your critics completely or 2) threaten and viciously attack those that mock and disagree with you.

There are those that say attack is the best defence. Rubbish! Defence schmafence. Why do you think that attack is so popular compared to shutting up. Attack is vastly better than shutting up because attack is EXCITING and FUN whereas shutting up is really, really boring. However, as we will see, knowing when to zip the old mouth and keep it shut is sometimes a far superior alternative to attack.

Option 1) Ignore Your Critics: A case study in ignorance: the Catholic Church vs. Dan Brown. If the Catholic Church had simply maintained its silence regarding Dan Brown's book "The Da Vinci Code" then the books' sales and the popularity of the subsequent movie would have been significantly diminished. Dan Brown's previous 3 books had sold less than 10,000 copies between them. Attacking Dan Brown gave him priceless publicity.

Ok, even though it was on the fiction shelves some of the stuff in Da Vinci must have stung. Especially given the various crusades, Inquisition's and the church's history of the treatment of women. Why can't women become priests? Because they are not men.

Despite all this, the Church should have said nothing, nothing except a very big thank you to Dan Brown for not blowing the whistle about the real Catholic Church conspiracy which has been the deliberate cover up and protection of paedophile priests.

As the self proclaimed Grande Master and keeper of the Keys to Neverland 2.0, I love and encourage the full expression of childhood behaviour like lying, blaming, bullying etc but even I draw the line at sexual abuse of children. It is not OK, it is NEVER, NEVER OK, even in NEVERLAND. The hard numbers on global child sexual abuse make me ill. So I pretend that it doesn't happen and the numbers are not real. I can forget the numbers as soon as I see them.

> [Peter, children in men's bodies are mostly to blame and you can't have bullying and all the other inappropriate behaviour without having severe side effects such as child sexual abuse. Studies suggest that worldwide 20 per cent of women and 5 to 10 per cent of men suffer sexual abuse as children. (Source: UNICEF Facts on Children, 2007).]

> Rubbish, children would never hurt other children, well, they would and do but I mean, they wouldn't do it in that way specifically.

> [Ineffective parenting and not allowing teenagers to grow up keeps the cycle of abuse spinning instead of shutting it down.]

> Oh, look, a ~~elephant~~ walrus!

Option 2: ATTACK! Yeeha! China regularly attacks the [Nobel Peace prize winning] Dalai Lama personally.

> [It would be the greatest act of the millennia to reward the Dalai Lama for a 50 year peaceful protest. It would demonstrate that non-violence is a viable strategy. The middle path for true Tibetan autonomy within China, (think Scotland within the UK), is a huge compromise from the Tibetans. Imagine if China was strong and confident enough to admit that it had made a mistake a long time ago. One day it will happen. If Australia can apologise for the mistreatment of aboriginal people, if the Berlin wall can come down, then this can happen too.]

China won the hotly contested 2008 Bad Lie of the Year Award when they claimed that the peace loving, Dalai Lama was organizing the violent demonstrations against the Olympic torch running through Tibet [rather than admit that a lot of Tibetans had simply had 58 years too many of repression]. That was a bad lie because no one believed it. Surprisingly, China went on to lose the 2008 Bad Lie of the Year to themselves, when they had the cute little Chinese girl lip synching while the ugly peasant girl with the amazing voice sang at the Beijing Olympics opening ceremony.

> [If there was an Olympic event for putting commercial interests ahead of human rights then the weak as piss International Olympic Committee should have won Gold, Silver and Bronze in 2008 <spit>].

Unfortunately, many people inspired by the Dalai Lama's example of forgiving the Chinese have gone on to forgive friends, relatives and work mates where they really did not have to. The words "Dalai Lama" mean "ocean of compassion." Let me tell you this for free, dipping your toes in that compassion water will get you kicked out of Neverland faster than you can say "Tinkerbell."

21

Denial, the 51st State
of the USA.

(Contributed by Peter Pan)

To stay childish forever you will need to spend a lot of time in Denial. It is a safe, worry free place and a recognized territory in every country in the world but only in the US of A has it achieved full statehood.

Denial is more popular than ever. There are now whole denial industries. The climate change denial industry is my favourite, probably because it is so well funded and so popular, whereas Holocaust deniers are few and far between and generally shunned. One group denies overwhelming scientific evidence that could have catastrophic consequences for hundreds of millions of people whilst the other group denies overwhelming evidence of the murder of 6 million Jews, half a million Gypsies and at least a quarter of a million disabled people. What tickles me is that the Climate Denial Industry is actually highly respectable rather than highly shunned. Money doesn't talk per se but it can buy a lot of advertising, misleading articles and blogs.

[If only the climate denial industry was shunned
the way the Holocaust deniers are.]

As soon as a country puts "United" in the title you know they are paddling on the river of denial, or at least a tributary. Take the United KINGdom, where there's been no king for like the past 600 years or so [57 years]. Most of the Irish hate the English, some of the Irish even hate the Irish, the Scots also hate the English and everyone rubbishes the Welsh, if they've even heard of them [sorry]. Great Britain?? One good play, "Peter Pan", doesn't make you a great country, nice try though and by the by, way to squander an empire, losers.

Let's look at the former USSR, the United Soviet Socialist Republic? United? Really? United by the threat of being invaded by Russia is not very United - go straight to denial, do not pass the Iron Curtain. Canada makes no such pretense about being united and Quebec still has one foot in and one French foot out. Canada has way too much honesty to ever be a Super power but if they ever change their name to the United Provinces and Territories of the Democratic Republic of Canada, then watch out.

Major denial example: In China, for nearly one thousand years [sadly, yes, it didn't stop until 1949] crippling a woman by binding her feet was normal because it was considered that it made the woman more desirable. Denial is an important part of Neverland so I am all for it, buuut foot binding? I struggle with that one because it has affected me personally. I still have the bumps. You see, I casually mentioned once to Wendy that smaller feet might make her seem a bit more "dainty" and she clobbered me with a branch and then clobbered me some more until I finally had to fly away. She said, "that maybe a few more lumps on my head might make me more intelligent". I never mentioned it again.

Denial is pretty crowded these days as it has positioned itself right next to deferral "I don't have to do anything, I'll worry about it later." Neverland 2.0, is a place where we all have lots and lots of fun, sometimes at other people's expense, sure, but you know, carefree forever, full tummies, lot's of adventures and no responsibility. It seems there are a lot of governments in denial as well as large corporations including the military. In fact you could say that the whole of "free-market capitalism" is in denial, otherwise how could the following statistics (which I refuse to look at) be ignored:

- Pre-schoolers are the fastest-growing market for antidepressants. At least four percent of US preschoolers, over a million, are clinically depressed[1]
- The rate of increase of depression among children is an astounding 23% p.a.[2]
- The WHO predicts that depression will be the second largest killer after heart disease by 2020.[3]

- 15% of the population of most developed countries suffers severe depression[4].
- Everyone, will at some time in their life be affected by depression -- their own or someone else's. (Depression statistics in Australia are comparable to the US and UK.)[5]
- 30% of women are depressed. Men's figures were previously thought to be half that of women, but new estimates are higher.[6]
- 80% of depressed people are not currently having any treatment.[7]
- 15% of depressed people will commit suicide[8].

[Neverland is advertised as a "worry free, care free place." Clearly from the statistics above and loads more like it, it is not. The tail of economic rationalism is wagging so hard that it is knocking everything to support communities off the table. Hoping that everything is going to get better makes the tail wag even more furiously.]

"Hope" is denial's best friend. When things are a bit busy in denial I sometimes move to hope which is a big step up from denial and it means I always sidestep despair or awareness. I hope all the scientists are wrong and that climate change is not happening. I hope that some advanced and friendly alien race will drop in and buy up all our excess atmospheric carbon for a lot of gold that they will give only to the permanent residents of Neverland that helped to deposit the carbon in the atmosphere and we can start the whole cycle over again only quicker. The lovely thing about dropping in on hope is that it is a very low energy level emotion.

When you settle into hope, you get a lounge chair and a complimentary drink but you don't have to do anything. Sadly the service in denial is pretty crap. The reason is that in denial, you sort of have to pretend that you are not actually there so the waiters ignore you and you deny that you are going to be there long enough to need a chair so you just stand around with the same fixed expression on your face that you came in with. Compared to "hope" denial is kind of sucky.

Hoping that human induced climate change isn't happening is easier than denying it. Hoping that your children won't get into drugs means that you don't have to talk with them or spend time with them or anything. Hoping world hunger will go away when you have a full tummy is almost a waste of hope. It means you don't have to donate money to Oxfam or any other charitable organisation that is doing something about it. Hoping that you will win the lottery without ever buying a ticket is strong hope.

[1] Study published in *Psychiatric Services,* April 2004. Reported in our health news archive: Pill-Popping Pre-Schoolers, Even Toddlers Get the Blues
[2] Harvard University study in *Harvard Mental Health Newsletter,* Feb.'02.
[3] WHO report on mental illness released October 4, 2001. Health news stories: Depression Link to Heart Disease, Hostility, Depression May Boost Heart Disease
[4] World Health Organization (WHO) report quoted BBC-Online 09/01/2001.
[5] Australian Institute of Health and Welfare, 1998. "National Health Priority Areas Mental Health: A Report Focusing on Depression." Depression statistics in Australia are comparable to those of the US and UK.
[6] National Institute of Mental Health (NIMH). "The Numbers Count: Mental Illness in America," Science on Our Minds Fact Sheet Series.
[7] "National Healthcare Quality Report", 2003.
[8] Agency for Healthcare Research and Quality, 2003. "National Healthcare Quality Report." This is a widely quoted statistic, though some experts, have cited higher figures.

Gosh, Was that the Truth?

*"People who pride themselves on their "complexity"
and deride others for being "simplistic" should
realize that the truth is often not very complicated.
What gets complex is evading the truth."* Thomas
Sowell

22

Where art Thou Truth?
Too many Convenient Lies
(by Daniel Prokop)

The power of deliberate lying is unfortunately considerable and most people, especially those that have been parented by highly controlling authoritarian parents have been taught not to question anything. There might be AN Inconvenient Truth but there are many, many convenient lies. The most convenient lies are those that people want to believe. If there is the tiniest bit of doubt in someone's mind, it gives permission to put off taking any action. That is the reason that lies by false front lobby groups are so pernicious and the very existence of false front lobby groups is a sad indictment of Neverland 2.0.

> *"Special interests have blocked transition to our renewable energy future. Instead of moving heavily into renewable energies, fossil companies choose to spread doubt about global warming, as tobacco companies discredited the smoking-cancer link.... CEO's of fossil energy companies know what they are doing and are aware of long-term consequences of continued business as usual. In my opinion, these CEO's should be tried for high crimes against humanity and nature. Conviction of ExxonMobil and Peabody Coal CEOs will be no consolation, [it will help a bit] if we pass a runaway climate to our children...." Dr James Hanse, to Congress "Global Warming 20 years later: Tipping Points Near."*

The Fracturing of Community

Some economists and neo-cons say "Oh we can't afford to take action." Two things on that: BULLSHIT and BULLSHIT. We can't afford not to take action. Apparently we couldn't afford the world financial crisis and yet, we have and are still paying for it. We can do this and do it well and we need responsible adults at the helm of corporations and governments and in our homes.

Some people will remember when computers were first becoming popular. There was a lot of fear, "Computers will take away all of our jobs" and this was way before Terminator (has anyone checked how many Sarah Connors are left alive in California?) or iRobot or anyway... you get my drift. Computers have created more jobs than they took.

Cutting ourselves free from fossil fuels by taxing carbon will generate new jobs in renewable energies, in land regeneration, forest management and will provide time for changeover. We need to be smart about it and learn the lessons from the GFC and we need to move swiftly. Smarter, smaller, bio diverse agriculture can breathe new life into rural communities which have become tumbleweed collectors for a long time. Peter Andrew's book *BACK from the BRINK (How Australia's Landscape can be saved)* is fantastic. Rethinking weeds and desalinating land is important.

Local farmers markets are a sensational initiative. If you have never paid money directly to the people that do all the work growing the food then you are missing something. It feels good and the markets are great ways for local communities to regularly come together. There are many possibilities for new ways of thinking and we can either fight change or we can direct it.

The good news is that with a still uncensored Internet it is possible to check the source of a story fairly quickly and what we can do is push for greater transparency from corporations coupled with rigorous auditing of special interest "donations" and conflicts of interest in politics. At some point political donations by corporations has to be outlawed because in countries where this has not happened government has become a corporatocracy "Government by the corporations for the corporations" rather than a democracy. We can also stop supporting newspapers and media that operate as puppets and print trash day in and day out.

Finally, we just need to look around. Humans have had a massive impact on this planet and fortunately the environment and the ecology of this Earth have been amazingly resilient. We must take action and we need to question what we are being told and somehow let companies know that lying is no longer considered *de rigeur.*

23

The Fracturing of Community

(by Daniel Prokop)

"In many tribal cultures, it was said that if the boys were not initiated into manhood, if they were not shaped by the skills and love of elders, then they would destroy the culture. If the fires that innately burn inside youths are not intentionally and lovingly added to the hearth of community, they will burn down the structures of culture, just to feel the warmth." (Meade, Michael. 1993. Men and the Water of Life, Harper San Francisco)

It was the job of the whole community to contain that youthful "fire," that amazing vigor and energy (that some older people feel is wasted on the young) and direct it towards "the hearth of community." This is not always easy. At times the anger and hot blood of young men in particular would need to be tempered and cooled by the wisdom and example of the elders and by the uncles and grandparents.

In societies where respect is earned, the youth will (eventually) listen to those they respect. It was never about extinguishing the fire of youth, it was about understanding its beauty and working with it. The boys and girls in these communities also spent a lot of time with healthy men and women as well as with grandparents and elders who all knew them and took a real interest in their well being. The young people had good role models and people to talk to when things were worrying them e.g. will it really make me go blind? Does she like me? Do I like me? Am I normal? What was it like when you were growing up? Something about acne?

Community was the vessel that held the sacred fire of youth and at some point a vessel or vessels broke and the fire became a wildfire and it has been burning fiercely ever since, tearing down culture after culture. Destructive tendencies are not limited to boys in their youth, in purely destructive terms it is the boys in their mid-forties or so that can be the most dangerous.

How did the community vessels break? Natural disasters, drought or floods, would have fractured some communities. Improved mobility using horses, better hunting weapons and growing populations leading to more crowding may have created new challenges. Communities with different societal structures might have argued about who was right or who's imaginary friend (God) was better at darts or maybe it all got kicked off with a couple of early psychopaths.

Conveniently all of this happened before any written records so it is very difficult to discern anything for certain. There are few clues and prehistoric forensics was, well, primitive. There was no Neolithic Cave Investigation Service (the original NCIS) available to visit early crime scenes so we may never know what actually happened or how harmonious life was or wasn't prior to the invention of war. (I've kind of squeezed NCIS in here on behalf of my son Samuel, who loves NCIS. Sam would like to meet the cast of NCIS and be an extra. Just putting it out there).

Once the unchecked fire of youth genie was out of the bottle, peace loving, co-operative cultures were vulnerable to predation by brutal, dominating, patriarchal warrior groups. It is difficult to imagine that there was a time on this planet, a very long time in fact, when war had not been invented.

> "Hey, everybody gather around, gather round. Listen to this! I just thought of a way that we can get a whole lot of goats, land and weed without working for any of it. Interested? Yeah, I call it "WAR" "**W**e **A**nnihilate our Neighbou**R**s" and all we have to do, is go to the village next door and kill every man, woman and child using our hunting weapons. It is soooo simple, I am really surprised nobody else invented it first. Sounds good, huh? I'm going to patent this idea, get a percentage of all future looting and pillaging... Hey, why are you all looking at me like that? Just put the stones down and I won't get hurt. OK, look umm ... if you don't like the name "war" we can just call it "trade" we trade their

lives for our profit. Ouch! Good shot. Ow, ow, ow, ouch, noooooooooo."

Of course expressing an idea before it's time has come can be a dangerous thing.

The first recorded professional war, where they obviously had embedded journalists with clay tablets, was in 2700 BC with Sumeria vs. the Elamites. Effectively it was the first Iran – Iraq war. Thank God they were able to put that conflict behind them. The win put Sumeria at the top of the World Domination Cup for quite a few years, but once you've fought one war, I mean idle soldiers can be the devil's playthings. Obviously war was happening at an amateur level quite some time prior to 2700 BC but Sumeria vs. Elamites was the first one we know of where they had fully developed armies.

The Romans of course were very big on war. In 216 BC they had a rematch with the Carthaginian team. Rome vs. Hannibal at the Cannae Outdoor Stadium, the place was packed out with 80,000 tickets sold to the Roman legions and their allies vs. 56,000 tickets for the Carthaginians. Hannibal, captain of the Carthaginians elected to field first and he caught the Romans leg (infantry) before wicket (cavalry). Hannibal played a real captains innings and up to 50,000 Romans died that day and 10,000 Carthaginians. 60,000 deaths in a day are staggering to contemplate. It was fewer deaths than Hiroshima (66,000 dead) but more than Nagasaki (39,000 dead). Atomic weapons can match the killing power of 56,000 Carthaginians in one warhead: A very sobering thought.

Little wonder that traditional communities placed so much importance on helping their young people grow up so that conflicts could be worked out without recourse to violence or atomic bombs.

What is amazing is that for perhaps tens of thousands of years the fire of youth was lovingly and intentionally added to the hearth of community. I think that the advent of writing fanned the flames and that in the ashes behind the flame front, patriarchy was reinforced by the new found power that writing provided. Leonard Schlain in his book *The Alphabet vs. The Goddess* puts forward a theory that with writing cultural thinking shifted to left brain dominated thinking. Linear, logical thinking came at the cost of intuition and creativity and that with TV and computer screens all being very visual that we are moving back into more balance.

In many parts of the world the path to growing up for vast numbers of young men was only available through the various armies. Initiation with the intention to prepare a young man for war adds some unique military baggage to adulthood. Bags like never questioning orders and emotional numbing which is part of the training required to get humans ready to kill other humans.

The concern of the military is not to preserve the environment nor is the soul of the souldier vital unless it can be manipulated to enhance the fervor and killing ability of the soldier. Nor until more recently has there been much concern for how well soldiers fit back into society.

In a war, or a war on terror (which can go on forever), the meetings about "what to do about the future" are kind of brief. When the first agenda item is: kill or be killed, there is no second agenda item, end of meeting and concerns for future generations? Well if you are killed, no future, no problem, no worries. If you are doing the killing, meh, probably not top of your list to contemplate.

Economic terrorism can be more devastating than the fanatical explosive type terrorism and it is often delivered under the mantle of Free Trade, because:

> *"A Thneed's a Fine-Something-That-All-People-*
> *Need!" The Lorax by Dr. Seuss.*

And now we take you back to the good news. People are starting to question authority especially as the evidence mounts against global FREE TRADE and the economic terrorism that can go with it.

The questioning of authority is likely to increase too because there is a lot of evidence that there is a growing trend away from the highly authoritarian or military type command and control style of parenting that was basically the only style of parenting on the parenting shelf for a very long time. The evidence: 23 countries have now banned the hitting of children and there are over 80 countries where corporal punishment is banned in schools.[1] Why? Because I said so, that's why! <joking>.

Longitudinal studies done on authoritarian parenting conclusively show that children from highly authoritarian households have less compassion for other people and are more likely to become bullies or perpetual victims themselves. As a means of short term control (domination) authoritarian parenting works but in many cases the positional power of being a parent is abused. Many parents are choosing to parent differently to the way they were parented, choosing to parent more authoritatively rather than authoritarianly.

As levels of patriarchal domination diminish we can move more into balance. Right brain and left brain working together, the yin and the yang, masculine and the feminine, Rocky with Bullwinkle. Violence against women, children and the weak is not strength it is cowardice. It is not OK and people and politicians that regularly model dysfunctional behaviour should be shown the door. It is hard enough for our young people to grow up without anti-role models all around them.

Speaking of a lack of balance, most of the Christian churches at least now allow women priests, except the ROMAN Catholics (just how long does that sponsorship deal go for?). Personally, I think that the Roman Church is doing a fabulous job of encouraging people to find spirituality that is more consistent with Jesus' teachings rather than about supporting a monolithic, entirely male dominated institution more concerned with the business of religion, its own power and the domination of its flock.

There are good people within the church trying to bring some balance to issues such as the ordination of women, the use of contraceptives and the recognition that gay people are 'gay' and 'people'. The only people Jesus really didn't like were the bankers (money changers) so I could understand if various religions lobbied hard against bank marriages but they seem to have missed that obvious point.

[1] *Parenting for a Peaceful World* by Robin Grille, Longueville Media 2005 and updated in 2008. This is a fantastic and sobering parenting book.

24

Harmony in Humans is More than Just Singing Together.
(by Daniel Prokop)

In healthy traditional societies there was a deep respect and connection to the environment and the land. Their connection to land was so profound that there was no separation between the two. The concept of land ownership is inconceivable when you are connected to and in effect, part of the land. How could anyone own something that is part of you? Point of clarification: this was way before human organ trafficking. How could people own something that belonged to everyone? And why would they even want to?

Imagine if this conversation had taken place when James Cook first landed in Australia. (A Babel fish to help translate would have been most useful, please refer to The Hitchhiker's Guide to the Galaxy for more information on Babel Fish):

James Cook [Jimmy the Cook]

My good man, have you any system of Land Ownership? Does Torrens Titles mean anything to you?

Aboriginal Man (shakes head)

No. No one can own the land, it is part of all of us.

James Cook [Jimmy the Cook]

You don't own the land? No one owns land? Right. Ah ha, excellent. I hereby declare this land to be Terra nullius. Jolly good!

The Latin phrase Terra nullius means "land belonging to no one" and therefore the first to discover it, owns it.

James Cook [Jimmy the Cook]

Can you move those black people out of shot while we have the portrait painted? The king is going to love this place. It is so unspoilt but we can fix that. I'm thinking, perfect place for convicts and lots of them.

Aboriginal Man

Hey James, do you own your arm? The right one?

James Cook [Jimmy the Cook]

(distracted and salivating)

No of course not, it is part of me. I don't need a piece of paper to say that, it's obvious to anyone.

Aboriginal Man

So you don't own your arm or any other part of your body?

James looking a little nervous shakes his head indicating no.

Aboriginal Man (cont'd)

I hereby declare you, James Cook to be *corpus nullius*. I'll have your right arm, mate.

James Cook [Jimmy the Cook]

But I need my arm, it's part of me. Can't you see that? I need it to be a captain. I would die if you took it.

Aboriginal Man

Sorry Cooko, but the problem, Mate, is that clearly it is possible to remove your white arm and I want it, it is the first white arm I have ever seen. I can give you a few shells or a broken promise for it, whichever you prefer. Now, hold still.

James Cook's arm is removed with blunt instruments and quite a bit of screaming about Tort Law.

James Cook [Jimmy the Cook]
You can't just leave me with a bleeding stump. I could die.

Aboriginal Man
Sorry Jimmy, not my problem. Tribe says we have the right to bear arms.

(that is a really bad pun, sorry)

Actually, I need the other arm too for my friend. Since you are still alive, you must have lied about dying if I took the right arm. How will you English become known for understatement if you keep exaggerating?

James Cook [Jimmy the Cook]
Hey, stop! They are part of me. I'll never recover ….

Aboriginal Man
Don't go getting all upset, it's just business, mate. You'll be fine, but I think I'm going to need a leg up….

Taking traditional custodians from their land is exactly like cutting off limbs but to people with no connection to land or place they can't understand it. At best they are bewildered and indifferent to the suffering caused by the theft and then the destruction of the natural environment. At worst they are vicious and condescending. The disconnected can't see the forest for themselves.

When a person becomes accustomed to a very generous salary and the privileges that come with it, their world can shrink to a world where only similar people exist. They can become immune, even bewildered by the challenges that face so many and they can also become disdainful and spiteful. They can come to regard poor struggling people as pseudo people or "small people," only because the word "savages" has fallen out of favour. A really poor but popular excuse is: "well if they only worked hard enough they could rise above their poverty." Tell that to people who work 12 hours a day standing in the same spot with minimal breaks, afraid to talk to the person standing next to them, doing a mind numbing task so that you can enjoy a cheap iPhone. These "small people" feel they have so many "choices" that eleven have taken their own lives, suicide being at least something that they feel they can control.

So once upon a time there was connection to place and connection to each other from the youngest to the oldest. Traditional life was co-operative, they knew how to share, really share, not as in sharing only to get something back which is called corporate giving. They didn't tell a mother with a new born to "Look, luv, know this is your first baby and you don't have a clue and you're going to get seriously sleep deprived but stay in this square box (house) on your own and maybe we'll arrange for a partner to stay a few hours in the evening but remember he /she (just being politically correct) will be tired from working in a job that they hate, so be considerate and be happy when he/she gets in OK? got that? and don't worry too much, because before you know it we'll arrange to take that baby out of your hands to "free" you up to work..." and maybe your child as well.

We are a pack animal (not like a donkey though there are a few asses out there.) We are not meant to be so isolated from one another, from our children, from our food sources, from nature. In a healthy culture people help one another and the kids are a big part of it all, mucking in at times or playing with other children. Older people are treated with respect and they help with what they can physically do and with the children. They know that the village will look after them as they get older because that is what you do. You "do unto others as you would have them ..." Who said that?

Was life tough? Cold, hunger and death were not strangers, but neither was gratitude. I'm sure there were very difficult times, droughts and floods and famine (just like now), little Johnny getting his head caught in a saber tooth tiger (not like now) and all kinds of things. There were also periods of great abundance. There were traditional cultures where they had no word for 'work'. They just did what needed to be done. So tasks were shared and mixed with mourning and play and the laughter of children, the masters of joy. They shared, they told stories, they trusted one another and they played nice and often. There were also some tribes that most certainly didn't play very nice. But there are examples of cultures that did and the Yequana Indians of Venezuela are one that is still around today. But do we find Yequana people at the very top of global consulting firms like McKenzie? I don't think so, the Yequana are too smart for that.

Harmony in Humans is more than Just Singing Together

Ladakh is in the western Himalayas, a place of limited resources and extreme climate. Yet a highly co-operative, sustainable and harmonious society thrived there for thousands of years. Ladakh used to be isolated for up to eight months of the year but progress and tourism came to Ladakh in the late 1990's and with tourism and better road access came dissatisfaction. The young people started to yearn for what the tourists had, not appreciating that emotional poverty can be hidden by flashy toys and expensive clothes. The rapid changes in Ladakh mirror what has taken much longer in western culture. Helena Norberg-Hodge has written a great book called *"Ancient Futures" (Learning from Ladakh)*. Ladahkis lived sustainably in a very harsh climate by respecting their environment and from sharing.

When collecting plants or flowers Native American children were always taught to take only what was needed. Even in times of shortage they were taught to always leave some berries behind. Taking every berry from a bush just because you were hungry was inconceivable; it was against natural law to be greedy. BUT of course, nature forgot to write it down, didn't nature. Because it wasn't written down it became optional.

> *"Treat the Earth well: it was not given to you by your parents, it was loaned to you by your children." Ancient Indian Proverb*

I'm sure there were hiccups and upsets but people having other people to talk to (who aren't even paid to listen) about stuff was in the communities' interest. When differences of opinion cropped up, people may not have got what they wanted but they did get a chance to speak and be heard which meant that they could move forward. There is a huge difference between co-operation and competition. It is much harder (though still possible) to hold a grudge when you have to see a person regularly. It is harder still if the community does not fan the fires of anger, jealousy or righteousness. Much worse than death was banishment from the tribe, so it was in your interest to play nice too.

Life has been simpler. In Ladakh there were elders available for advice and for just listening or telling stories. People behaving like healthy adults, often being childlike without being childish and getting old was kind of cool. Getting old didn't engender the feelings of obsolescence because they were respected, useful and they knew that the village would look after them.

In a balanced society, when gatherings were called they took place in a circle. In a circle everyone can see everyone else and no one is above another. There was not the time pressure to rush things through so many different views could be heard and listened to with respect. Respect for people, respect for the land, respect for the little people (children), respect for self. Respect is not a difficult concept to grasp. In giving it, it is also received.

Some readers are going to be saying (whining) "You're romanticizing the stone, mate, if, Darrell, and I mean a very big 'if' mate, when I say If, what you are saying is right mate, then why don't we learn from what they did and start doing more of that? Actually, even if they all didn't do all that stuff, why don't we at least start doing it some of it?" to which I would say "the name is Daniel and that sounds like an excellent idea." Some tribes were dysfunctional and not all early civilizations lived in harmony with their environment (Easter islanders became extinct after cutting down all the trees). Some of them stuffed up big time. What do we want? Do we want co-operation over competition? Are we up for sustainability even if that means a drop in GDP but an increase in Gross national happiness?

I enjoy reading about communities that are sustainable and harmonious. One of the common features is that they tend to have a high quality of life and time to spend with friends and a relatively low quantity of "stuff." Their happiness comes from within rather than from without. Jean Liedloff in her remarkable book *"The Continuum Concept : In search of happiness lost"* describes her years living with the stone age Yequana Indians in the South American Jungle. This experience demolished her Western preconceptions of "civilization" and led her to a radically different view of what human nature really is and how we can live peacefully with each other, as well as practical ways we can find our natural well-being for ourselves and our children.

The Continuum Concept had a profound influence on Beth and me as new parents. As much as practicable our babies were "in arms" (either being held by someone or in a baby sling) until they were ready to be put down. Prior to having children I wondered how you would know when a child was ready to be put down. I now know that the child, in a very wriggly vigorous way, will let you know when to put them down or you will drop them. We also always had our babies sleeping in bed with us rather than have them isolated in a room of their own. This co-sleeping also made it easy for Beth to breastfeed without having to get up to do it.

Whilst playing the corporate game (which was well paid market research for this book), I would often be out of the house before my baby was awake and home after he had gone to sleep. So my connection time with Samuel while he was awake was pretty limited. Having Sam in bed at night gave me time with my child next to me to help me recharge my batteries and remember what was really important. Sometimes I didn't sleep too much, I would spend hours just staring at this small, amazing being and having my finger held in a tiny hand. I was amazed at how good something as simple as a gentle squeeze on my finger could feel. Co-sleeping doesn't work for everyone and there are some people who are afraid of rolling onto their child in their sleep. I understand that. We found that by having the newborn as high up in the bed as possible i.e. the babies head up near the bed head, it meant that there was no way we could accidentally roll on top of the child.

So much depression and anxiety can be healed by connecting again with people in community gatherings or in men's or women's groups. "Dances with Wolves" touched the yearning we have for a simpler life, for the comfort and connection of community, for being in nature, for respecting indigenous and other cultures, and for watching Kevin Costner before he got torn down by the same machine that had built him up.

We make life complicated, it is actually pretty simple. Small children are wonderful teachers of joy and happiness for no reason and they are also very good at forgiving and letting go of worries. Many parents are now not spending much time with their children when they are young which means they can miss the lessons that the children offer. One of the reasons why healthy children have so much energy is that they don't invest huge energy in worrying about stuff.

The scattering of families and communities has been painful. I choose to believe that we had to scatter for the necessary global changes that are happening to take effect. Change can be very threatening for tribes and now the job before us is to heal the wounds of the scattering, of the separation. We have been through many challenges and now we can come back together and rebuild our communities, our connection with each other and with nature in a spirit of respect for diversity, with the strength to stand up to bullies, to respect and honour both the feminine and the masculine.

In a few isolated, remote places on Earth some balanced societies have persisted into modern times. When these communities were discovered by "civilization", instead of hailing them as being precious examples of highly evolved, stable social structures, they were ridiculed as primitive oddities and promptly destroyed. If being primitive is to live in balance with each other and with the environment then we need a massive injection of primitivism (back to basics) and we need it now.

The arrogance of "advanced" humans is laughable. Okay, it is a laugh laced with irony, no, actually it is just a bit sad so perhaps a snort which could be misconstrued as an exhalation of breath consistent with a laugh incident. Instead of being humbled by what we don't know, like for example, we know nothing about black energy which makes up 74% of the universe, we attack new ideas that threaten established dogma.

Vast amounts of money are spent on researching drugs like Viagra, how about some investment into cures for disharmony, disconnection? Actually, a lot of these cures are already available to us but they will not come out of a bottle and cannot be branded.

Home
Parenting

*If you bungle raising your children, I don't think whatever else you do well matters very much. --
Jacqueline Onassis*

25

Parenting for
Perpetual Childhood

(Contributed by Peter Pan)

This phrase works on a number of levels. A lot of parents are permanent residents of Neverland 2.0, so it works for parents that are actually still children themselves and it also works for forward thinking parents who are bringing up their children in a way that ensures that they will join them in Neverland. These are succession planning parents.

Part I – Disengaged Parents

A disengaged parent has actually run or sprinted away from the family and fair enough too. My views on never having kids are on record. The bodies of a few disengaged parents might still use the family home as a mail drop but emotionally they are not present or available. They can't even engage enough to move their stuff out and leave. The body of a disengaged parent being in the house can be confusing for children and spouses alike because they will jump to the foolish conclusion that just because the eyes are open that someone is home for them. Not the case and it will take a while for people around to disconnect the dots and to surrender to the fact that the disengaged parent or partner is "disengaged." Could they make it any clearer? Get that wax out of your head but you are welcome to "hope" that they will somehow change. They have no interest in you and you might

175

just want to think about what you have done to cause it. Is it because you are ugly or stupid or demanding? Have a think, but keep the answer to yourself. It is your fault, not theirs.

Disengaged parenting isn't all that difficult to achieve, however if you choose this path you will need some support. The socially sanctioned method of disengagement is to be a highly ambitious, career focused individual. Putting work before family is expected in most workplaces so it is not as difficult to achieve as it first sounds. It is entirely possible to leave the house before the kids wake up and to arrive home either just before they go to bed or after they are in bed. On the rare occasion when your kids do spot you, it will trigger an episode of awkwardness because they are trying to relate to a stranger and you will have to try to remember their names. Kids having sleep overs with friends can make these brief encounters quite tricky. Tip: put a fairly recent photo of your children on the 'fridge with their names and ages underneath and maybe a list of their favourite hobbies. You will cop shit for sacrificing your family for your career – kids can be so unreasonable. You will have to explain often that you are doing it for ... um, Jimmy no, no Timmy. It helps a lot if you get the name right but if you are worried just say "I am doing it for you," and leave it at that. If by some bizarre accident you find yourself in the same room with the "family" just pretend that you are fine with it and then get the hell out of there as soon as possible.

After a while, even if you do attempt to engage because you want to do the "happy family thing" to look good at a company function you will be met with well deserved contempt. Thus the cycle of dysfunction and estrangement will be complete. A comedian friend Tom Agna does a great skit about a teenager coming out of his room. When the teen unexpectedly sees his dad, he attempts to make small talk "ohhh, ummm, Hi Dad, thought it looked like you, ummm ..... you still going out with Mom?"

Career dry husk or career disengaged parents give work everything, which means that they have no time for family, friends or for themselves. They have nothing to give beyond criticism, perhaps corporal punishment and their personal example of unhappiness. If a nasty divorce can be thrown into the mix and it often is, then the dry husk is free to repeat the same cycle but with different actors.

The other path to disengagement can also be socially sanctioned if you select being an alcoholic as a disengagement mechanism or you may choose an alternative addiction:

gambling, prescription drugs, pornography, internet chat rooms etc . Designer drugs create an interesting semi-sanctioned path because whilst illegal they are at least now part of the brave new marketing world that we know and approve of. It is hard to believe that marijuana was ever popular when it was just called dope. That's what happens when you let drug fucked addicts do the marketing for you. Dope? What a terrible name, "Hey you want some dope, man? It's illegal." Drugs are now marketed properly with names like "Crack, Ice, Ecstasy" which makes them much more attractive [and dangerous] than ever before.

[Kids are not stupid, they quite rightly go "wait a second, alcohol is not only legal but heavily advertised but marijuana is illegal because?" Neither is very good for your health but surely it is time to either prohibit alcohol, which was tried and didn't work or decriminalise marijuana? Especially as the hydro weed that is available now is so strong and has such bad side effects. Let people grow a few plants for their own use and maybe even let people grow their own tobacco too. If they are in the garden more maybe they will even grow a few veggies? I have inhaled and then after a short while I also exhaled but with chunks in it. I am not a stoner, I am a vomiter. I did do my share of binge drinking and maybe a bit of someone else's share too. It is time to stop advertising alcohol and phase out alcohol sponsorship of sporting teams and events. Our communities and families are wearing the brunt of the effects of excess alcohol. Middle path, a little is fine but in excess, alcohol releases aggressiveness.]

Becoming an addict is a popular way to disengage but the downside is that not all addicts are able to pull their families fully into the gutter with them and spouses and children will rarely blame themselves for you being a human wipeout. In fact, seeing you violent, hopeless and regularly dressed in vomit could inspire them to avoid addiction altogether.

Disengagement is the lowest energy parenting style possible whilst ensuring your children become Neverland 2.0 recruits. A word of warning though, mentors and supportive school environments can disrupt the long term erosion of self esteem and resilience that you have put in place. Most disengaged parents have no expectations for their children because to do that would be a form of engagement. A few elite disengaged parents will dump enormous expectations on a child that the child will never be able to meet and then walk away. This strategy opens the door to you being constantly disappointed in the child which sets them up beautifully for a full life of disappointment.

Being totally detached from your children and from all parenting responsibilities will also earn you lifetime membership of Neverland. Congratulations on your brave choice. Looking after children can have a nasty way of making people grow up and discover positive aspects to responsibility that are best left hidden. If you feel wholly inadequate to be a parent this is a good way to hide that because no one will ever get close enough to "out" you.

Part II - Permissive Parents

The best parenting style for perpetuating childhood is the totally permissive or indulgent parenting style. More than any other parenting style this one actually attempts to replicate Neverland in the home, which I think is just brilliant. Permissive Parents (PP) typically love their children, whatever. But on the upside, PPs so want to be children themselves that they refuse to take up the role of parent in the parent / child relationship. Why should they have to be the bad guy? They just want to have fun and indulge their child. Typically these parents are holding onto a convenient confusion about the difference between being childish and being childlike. In PP households there is a child to child relationship. Typically they have no idea about how to be an effective parent and when everything turns to shit and their children later despise them for being spineless they will still wonder what happened? What did they do wrong?

This last question is highly perplexing for PP because they didn't do anything. They never said "no" to their little darlings. They gave them whatever they wanted and if they did accidentally step in, they will have quickly reversed and apologised for whatever punishment or boundary that they accidentally set in a moment of frustration. Inconsistency is one of the key planks of all ineffective parenting styles. Just remember that kids love surprises, so keeping them guessing just keeps the fun levels turned up to the max.

> [Parental inconsistency is very difficult for children to deal with. It leaves them confused and bewildered and creates insecurity. Setting a boundary and then never following through teaches children to

stop listening to you. It also means that they don't
ever have to do what they say they are going to do
because you don't. It can be quite tough to be
consistent.]

PPs are more likely to be overprotective of their children and
they will simply refuse to believe anything negative about their
little darling's behaviour. For some reason schools find this
somewhat challenging. Rather than producing secure, happy,
compassionate children this parenting style nourishes
selfishness, impulsiveness, aggressiveness, dependence and a
total lack of understanding of the concept of personal
responsibility. Obviously, this Parenting Style is the preferred
Parenting style for Neverland 2.0 for both children as parents and
children as children.

Insecure and or permissive parents will often constantly praise
their children for the smallest things "Oh, honey, I loved the way
you just tied your own shoelaces. That is such a pretty knot-like
mess. Oh, you are so clever, not many 13 year olds could do that
by themselves and wearing two left shoes is very… creative."
Praising your child constantly will either turn them off doing
anything you want them to do because your relentless bragging
and praise embarrasses them and makes them violently ill or, if
you can set your child up for life to constantly try to please others
or to seek attention at every opportunity, both highly desirable
Neverland 2.0 character traits.

[As briefly mentioned earlier, constant praise for
children can be as damaging to them as constant
criticism. It does not build their resilience, it builds
vulnerability. This is especially true if parents are
not very available as a child soon learns to perform
to win praise so they are seen and noticed. When
praise is withdrawn the child can become depressed
or anxious or angry. Every child has gifts and
acknowledgement of a child's gifts is very
important. Ideally such acknowledgement is also
appropriate, specific, authentic and timely. 'I love
the green shading on the trees you drew.' "How did
you feel when you did that?" "You look like you
enjoyed that." Repeating some of what the child
says back to them let's the child know that you are
really listening.]

There is no impetus for personal or emotional growth in the
permissive household. There are few expectations and without

any boundaries to ever push against the children either fall on their faces or some will go looking for boundaries to test themselves on at school or with the police which is not your fault or the fault of your child, other people just don't understand your out of control treasure. The terrible twos phase in these children can easily be extended into their teenage years.

Overindulging children of course makes it difficult to get them to do what you want which is where bribery comes in. Bribery can have the added bonus of teaching children that getting stuff makes you happy. They take to shopping for happiness like native consumers and advertisers can be relied on to help your children to stay with this strategy.

Overindulgent parents are also the most likely of all parents to buy their 14 year old alcohol because he or she asked for it and therefore expected it and what was that word that would have stopped that happening? "No?"

> [It is not OK for parents to buy alcohol for young children, it is illegal. The brains of teenagers are still developing and they don't need it. It is possible to teach them that they can have a good time without getting pissed or stoned but to teach this effectively you will have to model this behaviour yourself.]

Whilst certain parts of society [everyone but the parents and the child] label their behaviour as difficult, it is important to remember that the kids of PP have never had to worry about anybody else but themselves. Their selfishness, craving for instant gratification and constant attention seeking earn them automatic entry into Neverland 2.0 where they can join their parents. Sadly when they have reached physical maturity these kids often find that they don't have much respect for their parents [or anybody else for that matter] and don't want to hang out with them. This is very disappointing for the parents that have poured so much love into their child. My advice, get over it, you have done a great job of preparing your offspring to do very well in Neverland. You should be very proud.

Part III – Authoritarian Parents

If you are into domination and control then this parenting style is for you. Authoritarian parenting could be more accurately renamed the S&M parenting style [not Sales & Marketing]. Authoritarian parenting is the most prevalent parenting style. It benefits greatly from securing the default parenting position from the past. Parents actually need to choose other parenting styles. The vast majority of parents are already familiar with S&M parenting since they survived it to reach breeding age themselves. For much of history children were to be seen but not heard and children were expected to obey parental commands immediately.

S&M parenting is very high in expectation, high in criticism, high in disappointment, high in control but low in time wasting warmth and affection. When combined with a degree of inconsistency and or brutality it can be devastating. Children are quick learners, they can be taught how to fear a parent fast and as an S&M parent it is very important that they learn this because there is a good chance, particularly with boys, that at some point they will become physically bigger and stronger than you. If they fear you enough, they will not beat you to a bloody pulp when they can, which is good news.

This style is particularly great with younger children who do not easily question authority, so 100% compliance in the early years is relatively easy to achieve. Yes it may squash self esteem and creativity in the child. It may sit squarely on the face of having "fun" but as a busy, high performing or striving parent it is very economical on parenting energy and in the competitive parenting stakes (my kids are better than your kids) it does produces puppets that will usually perform appropriately in public.

Popular Control methodologies for authoritarian parents include physical punishment, mental punishment, reward and punishment, punishment punishment, shaming, disappointment and constant criticism. Vary things a little to see what is most effective for your little tike and remember, just because something does not leave physical scars does not mean that it has not left deep emotional scars. You can introduce inconsistency in a number of ways like making the child wrong no matter what they do or the one that produces the utmost confusion in a little kiddy's head is when you tell them to "do what I tell you, not what I do!" Try this say "Do not smoke!" or perhaps, say it in the form of a threat, "If I ever catch you smoking ...." whilst you are rapidly puffing away on a cigarette yourself. It does a kids head in which makes them easier to control.

S&M parents come down hard on mistakes, which stops a child from learning anything useful from an experience but teaches the kid some very important lessons for life within Neverland 2.0. It teaches kids to never take responsibility for anything because they could get it wrong. They equate getting it wrong with being ridiculed and punished. A child quickly learns to do nothing at all because then you can never make a mistake. It is easy to pretend to be busy. Demanding S&M parents will often nurture their child's struggle with personal responsibility into fully blown Hypengyophobia which is an overwhelming, irrational fear of responsibility. Sometimes referred to as Hypegiaphobia, this word derives from the Greek "hypengyos", meaning responsible and "phobos" meaning fear.

> [Some would argue that the high proportion of
> S&M parents are responsible for many aspects of
> our Hypegiaphobic society]

The Authoritarian parenting style is preferred by bullies and by bullying your child you teach them all they need to know to become fine bullies themselves (see the chapter "Seven Habits of Highly Effective Bullying").

There are some bleeding heart critics of S&M (authoritarian) parenting. They pull up all kinds of studies that show that authoritarian parenting actually produces angry non-compliant children rather than the obedient puppy children that authoritarian parenting advocates "promise" to parents. Admittedly S&M parenting can become tricky in the teenage years especially if the child ever works out that you are *un sac de merde* [full of shit]. As your child becomes fully grown and maybe bigger than you, you will have to try to break their spirit. This is often the dramatic finale of the S&M Parent vs. Child series of confrontations. If you lose then you will have to give up trying to dominate them altogether. You will be relegated to being a spectator of your child [from beyond the distance specified in the Apprehended Violence Order they have obtained against you]. You will get to watch them do everything that their peer group tells them to do. Some will leave home forever. There is a third option if you lose which is to engage in guerilla warfare of sniping constantly at them and telling them how ungrateful they are. No matter which way the self esteem crumbles your children will never forget you, though they will rarely call or ever visit.

There are some Authoritarian parents that vehemently deny that they are S&M parents because they eschew physical punishment and instead use words, rewards, or seduction instead of tyranny to control and manipulate their children. Wealthy, time poor parents are more likely to adopt the use of rewards as it helps the parent feel better about missing their children's childhood by "spoiling them" with gifts as a form of compensation. The child of course has to perform to get the gift even if it as simple as not taking their own life for another year.

[Robin Grille, author of the great book, "Parenting for a Peaceful World" uses the term "poisoned carrot" to describe the unhealthy aspects of control and manipulation by reward and punishment. Short term it can get results but it is not called "spoiling" a child for nothing, definition of "spoil": to make a mess of, to destroy or ruin, to fester. Treating a child like a lab rat, using reward and punishment to make them run through the maze of life as fast as possible will hinder that child's development. Or opening your wallet and having them behave as though Pavlov had rung his bell is not effective parenting. If as a parent, you really want to reward a child, give them some undistracted time with you.]

When an S&M parent feels like they are losing control they are the most likely parents to shout at their children to "grow up you <insult><insult><optional insult>" whilst doing everything within their parental power to ever prevent this from happening to either their offspring or to themselves.

Parenting for Bullies

Parents have had the stick, the wooden spoon and the belt ripped from their still warm hands. And what were they given to help them? Nothing! Thankfully parent educators are a lone voice in the wilderness trying to stop the bullying in the home.

To keep bullying levels growing it is essential that parents receive no training and are kept under constant time and financial pressure. Parents that are a bit confused or unsure what to do have a good chance of flip flopping around "Yes, no, I mean maybe. No, ohhh, go ask your mother, wait. I'm your mother, go ask your father."

The massive increase in single parents has been a windfall for Neverland 2.0. The less time and money and backup parents have, the more likely it is that they will train either bullies or victims out of sheer frustration. I know nobody wants to use the "V" word but not every child can be a bully. We need some people to be victims too. Sorry, just the way it is and I'm sure you'll understand that with all the recent mergers and acquisitions we need fewer, bigger bullies and more victims. It's just business. The days of the small family run bully are almost gone.

I know a lot of you are already asking, "What can parents do to give their kids the best chance of becoming the school bully and ensuring that he or she has the skills necessary to graduate and become a highly successful and overpaid corporate bully?" Good question. I try to welcome as many new Never Landers as I can and from those conversations I have found that parenting style is a good predictor of bullying potential.

Sure, some very good bullies and a lot of uncontrollable kids come from totally permissive homes where the parents let the kids do whatever the bloody hell the kids want to do. Often these parents are already long term residents of Neverland. As well as being ineffectual, these parents can also be warm and affectionate. That blasted parental affection and love does tend to undermine the total undermining of the child's self esteem.

If you are setting out to totally shirk any parenting responsibility and be the worst parent possible then disengaged parenting will be your style. Totally disengaged, uninterested, uninvolved parenting brings the distinct advantage that you don't waste any of your own time on the fruit of your loins. BUT, you can't predict whether the child's anger at you for never being there for them will be channeled into taking it out on others; equals bully or internalized; equals victim. If you are totally disengaged then you probably don't give a shit, anyway, but you would think you would take just enough interest to try to nudge them into the more successful bullying flight path. Why leave it up to chance?

Another Secret, but you can tell people this one: the parenting style of choice for consistently producing first rate bullies is authoritarian parenting. The higher the authoritarian levels the higher the quality and dedication of the resulting bully. Pathetically, some of you, mostly the ones I call the "damaged goods" parents have been looking for a "better" way to parent. A better way, indeed.

The "damaged goods" parents are the ones that failed to fully appreciate the constant criticism or belittling that they received and the odd, unpredictable smack across the head or bottom or legs. What their parents were not saying to them was "I don't know how to talk to you so I'm going to smack you instead." What the smack says to the child is "you are not good enough and you never will be, you disappoint and or disgust me." All a parent can ever do is to project their own inadequacies onto their children as honestly as possible, what the child does with that information is up to them.

Many successful go-getters use the rocket fuel of their parental disapproval as a launch pad to constantly try to prove that they are better than everyone else (without ever believing it themselves). These obsessively competitive champions are usually prize bullies that never, ever squander time or energy considering someone else's feelings as they forever strive for an approval from a parent that they never got. I think I can hear you cheering. These winners never look back and waste time trying to ponder the question "why am I so driven?". Pondering that question is wasted energy that the "damaged goods" parents seem so happy to spend. Go figure, how can you supposedly be green and still waste energy, huh?

The key focus for authoritarian parents can be summarized in the following word: control, control, control, control, control, control and control and more control. Control your child at all costs [including the cost of affection]. You, by virtue of being a parent, accidentally, biologically or non-biologically, have enormous positional power in the family over children, particularly small children. Never mind what the UN Convention of the Child says, you do not have to listen to what your child has to say. All you have to do is "pretend" to listen to them and that is pretty easy to do. If you are a man, tune them out by pretending that your child is your wife or ex-wife as is more likely. Otherwise you could be at risk of learning something from them. It is rare outside of a family for you to have the same level of authority over another human being, so savour it. You have authority so it just makes sense for you to be an authoritarian parent.

Remember: control your kids at all times especially in public. It is very important that they make you look good. People will be watching you and judging you depending on the behaviour of your kids. You must come to grips with the fact that the fleeting, fickle, judgmental opinion of complete strangers is more important than your ongoing relationship with your child e.g. is a severe peanut allergy a good enough excuse for the cruel parental embarrassment of a child having an anaphylactic choking fit in a crowded shopping mall? Ummm that was actually a rhetorical question so that means I don't have to write the answer.

Control methods: Many authoritarian parents shame without thinking. Actually they do much of their parenting without thinking. "You are useless <add other words as [in]appropriate e.g. stupid, ugly, pimply etc>". Children are particularly vulnerable to shaming as they internalize the feeling and often have no way of ridding themselves of shame without help.

Goal setting for parents is important as it will give you clarity and firm purpose. If you are actually [ir]responsible and want your children to take your place in Neverland 2.0 then your parenting choices are limited to authoritarian, permissive or disengaged parenting or better still a combination of the three.

Now that you know all this, go for it, it's pretty easy and if you ever feel like you are falling off the rather broad and winding authoritarian parenting pathway just allow yourself to get in touch with your feelings of frustration and suppressed anger and just like pressing a hyperspace button you will find yourself back on track. If you want to raise self actualized adults who are just going to get creamed out there, then fine, go "off-piste" try balanced or authoritative parenting, see if I care.

Maintaining a Supportive Child Friendly Environment

Once upon a time, living at home past late teens was basically not an option. It was very hard to score with the opposite or the same sex when that person learned that you still lived at home with your Mother. Generally there were too many other children, the houses were smaller and the parents less tolerant and more working class, unless they weren't. Besides, back then renting a place of your own or sharing accommodation was relatively cheap [and it still is in some countries other than Australia]. What has changed? Homes are bigger, families are smaller, both parents are working and are more absent. Rent is more expensive and can be conveniently saved by living off mum or dad or mum and step dad or step mum and dad or in rare instances mum and dad (biological).

Parents have known you since you were a bump. Some keen parents were even present for your tedious, painful, slimy, sticky and time consuming birth. In civilized times and places, aristocrats and well heeled Colonialists knew how to raise children, they left it entirely to nannies, au pairs or boarding schools. Finally we have industrialized raising easily manipulated workers. We call it "child care" [AND they do care about some children but how do you know if your child is one of them?]

The great thing about your parents is that until you are over 32 years old or so, your parents have known you longer in a child's body than in an adult's body. Whilst most parents will notice that you are taller, they never quite get around to starting to treat you like an adult. This means that living at home is a fantastic way to avoid growing up and save a few bucks, and get your laundry done and free meals, what a wonderful scam. Staying at home is less uncool than it once was.

In Italy they have a term for the 30 year old singles still living at home: Bamboccioni (literally: grown-up babies), in Japan they are called parasitic singles which is a bit harsher. For some parents, having their 30 year old child still living at home can open new vistas for vicarious living. Whilst parents will whine from time to time or continuously, they are basically powerless to make you grow up if they miss the maturity window and they know it. Exploit this knowledge but throw your parents a bone now and again, like not crashing their car for a week.

Advice for parents: a great way to keep your children childish is for you to do everything for them. Women find it really cute when their partners don't even know what a washing machine or an oven look like. Try to make your kids believe that houses clean themselves and so do the dishes, vacuuming, dusting and washing for them. Instead of taking the time to show kids how to do things, do it ALL YOURSELF, it is quicker and you will do a better job and you can become resentful and bitter if you want to.

Again, try to be inconsistent. Let your frustration build and build until finally you vent it all in one big frothing, dribbling tantrum that culminates in a volcanic eruption of emotion which leaves them stunned. Kids love tip toeing around waiting for the next big bang. Getting angry with children for not helping works best when you telepathically badger them but you never quite actually ask them to do anything. Springing a totally unreasonable request at the last minute and then getting the shits when they do not immediately stop everything and jump to it works well. Kids really enjoy the challenge of unreasonableness; it will help them thrive in the modern workplace.

Somebody needs to tell the Hikkomori about Neverland 2.0. Dudes you don't have to stay in your rooms for years just to avoid growing up, you can do that just about anywhere. "Hikkomori" literally means "pulling away, being confined." It is a Japanese word to refer to individuals who have chosen to withdraw from all social life, locking themselves in their rooms for months, years and even decades. These are the ultimate never leave home kids who are supported financially by their parents. They are extreme recluses. The parents may not see a Hikkomori for years. Some of the Hikkomori will come out at night to forage for 2 minute noodles or music. Obviously they spend a lot of time on the internet playing games and listening to music, watching reruns of Hook, Peter Pan and Peter Porn.

> [Dr.Tamaki Saitoh is the researcher that coined the phrase *"Hikkomori"* He made up a number, a million, well, he didn't make up that number he made up that the number of Hikkomori in Japan was 1 million. The figure has been quoted around the world, because it is a spectacular number despite there being no actual research basis for it. The recent estimates of the Japanese Ministry of Health and Labour for the total number of Hikkomori are much, much lower, though still worrying.]

Now, some company work environments are very child friendly. I'm not really talking about helping employees with their children i.e. daycare but some companies are very much like a big daycare centre but with bigger toilets and there are some

188

workplaces that will work you to death. Generally speaking, the bigger the corporation the more they reward behaviour that would get you kicked out of any respectable sandpit. WOOT! In small companies there's not usually enough room for more than one Alpha-bet male but the biggest, deepest sandpit's of all can be found in trans-global companies and politics. These playpens are also tend to be the worst supervised. Find your sandpit and dig in, the longer you can stay in the same sandpit the harder it is for anyone to kick you out, even if Basho is working for them.

The other advantage of large organisations is that there are many supervisors that really have no idea what the people that report to them actually do. This is a blessing for utilizing some of the strategies of lying and blaming. Many supervisors are terrified to ask questions because then people might realize that they don't know what they are doing but unless they can ask questions they never will. Oh, well, so what?

Change comes from within which is what you need to avoid.

Why Wendy?

Before Wendy was an ice cream she was a girl. As some of you may remember Wendy came and joined me in Neverland with her little brothers. Ok, so I was missing a mother figure and I went and got her but Wendy (the Whiner) didn't stay and I lost a few lost boys afterwards but then with lost boys you expect to lose a few.

Whilst Wendy left Neverland what is less well known is that she also refused to grow up. She got married, divorced, elective c-section, kid, married, divorced, elective c-section, kid, married, divorced and then dead. <silence> Ha! Gotcha! Actually, all I really know is that she left. I made up all that other stuff except the dead bit.

My point is this, if you are a Never Lander looking for a relationship with a woman you should look for someone that reminds you of your mother. As long as you are always looking for a relationship with your mother they will be very tolerant of your childish ways and will not try to change you and they will love you for the big kid that you still are and always will be, unless their name is Wendy

26

"Off-piste" Parenting
(by Daniel Prokop)

Pronounced [awf-peest]. Definition: 'off-piste' adverb, adjective on an unprepared, trackless area e.g. 1) Skiing: away from regular ski runs: off-piste skiing 2) Parenting: away from the way you were parented: making it up as you go along: off-piste parenting.

I give talks to parents on how to help teenagers grow up emotionally at schools around Australia. I start each talk by asking "How many people parent differently from how they were parented?" The vast majority of the audience put up their hands.

It is much easier to follow the well trodden parenting path, there are regular cultural approval markers to keep you on track and you have already been down the path once but as a child rather than a parent. So why are so many parents now choosing to go "off-piste?" Because the primary style of parenting until recently has been highly authoritarian parenting. The authoritarian parenting style is high demand but low in responsiveness or warmth. 'Do as I say, not as I do." "Children are to be seen but not heard." Authoritarian parenting is all about the direction and control of children. The control tools are manipulation, shame, reward and physical punishment though not necessarily in that order. I believe that a lot of people carry emotional (and some physical) scars left by their authoritarian parents, which has prompted them to try to find a more responsive way to parent their own children.

So let's take the most important and most difficult 24/7 job in the world, the job that shapes the next generation more than any other on the planet and take away community and intergenerational support and in many cases one of the parents as well. Let's make the cultural landscape almost impossible to recognize from 30 years ago and have parents choose to parent in a way in which they have little prior experience, add a generous helping of financial and time pressure, sprinkle high social expectations and then act surprised when rates of depression reach crisis proportions.

Going "off-piste" for parents a generation ago was a tougher option. The parenting trail was pretty well fenced to keep parents on the ol' straight and narrow path. If you did go off-piste you either left the ski field altogether or you didn't stray too far from the path that "worked" so well for the previous generation. This is not about blame, I believe that all parents do the best they can with what they know. We know a lot more now than a generation ago and the world is also very different.

The use of reward (cheese) and punishment (electric shock) was used effectively to get rats to learn how to go through mazes quickly. As a means of short term control it was highly effective but at the end of those experiments the trembling rat was never asked how it felt. Our children are not rats (neither for that matter are employees) and how they feel and their ability to express emotions is very important. We know that it is possible to parent without using reward or punishment to control children and it is a new paradigm in parenting. The Authoritative or balanced parenting style is high in demand and high in responsiveness and it is where many parents are heading sometimes without even knowing that the destination has a name.

Whilst the balanced parenting path is not yet well marked culturally, we do have a compass to guide us which is our heart. We also need to engage our heads and our wisdom, particularly as our children get older. If we are presented with a choice between being the parent and being our children's best friend, we have to choose being the parent. Discipline and setting boundaries are important parenting skills and since more and more parents are finally dropping the stick they are finding it harder to teach their children boundaries.

I have heard parents say "Oh we know that hitting a child is bad <pause> <embarrassed pause> but if only schools could bring back the cane." Why would parents contradict themselves in the same sentence? Answer: Because parents have difficulty setting boundaries without the use of the stick. What children actually need is discipline as opposed to punishment. The word discipline actually means to teach. Etymology of the word discipline:

Middle English, from Old French & Latin; Old French, from Latin: disciplina, teaching, learning, from discipulus, pupil (from Merriam-Webster Dictionary.)

Confidence, warmth and consistency are parenting traits that serve our children well. We all know that bullying is not OK. Despite this there are people that use their positional power as "bosses" to overpower and humiliate others. As parents we are the "bosses" and we have huge positional power over our children and this power can easily be abused. Good work done in schools to reduce bullying can be undone if the child goes home to an environment where a parent dominates or belittles them. Highly authoritarian parenting is sometimes just bullying by a more acceptable name and with teenagers it can break down altogether because it is difficult to physically dominate someone who is bigger than you. At some stage unquestioned obedience becomes questioned. When children reach their teens authoritarian parents often escalate their dominance in an attempt to "break" their teen to their will or they capitulate, throw their hands up in the air and deploy a guilt bomb "Oh, well, I tried, go on make a mess of your life."

Parents sharing positive parenting stories can help us through rough times and deep sleep deprivation. One of the happiest moments of my life happened days after my son was born. I was lying bare-chested on the bed, with Samuel, this tiny, beautiful, trusting, loving being, sleeping naked on top of me, skin to skin, heart to heart. There are no words for the experience. If you have tried it you know and if you haven't, try it if you can and you might get peed on but it is worth it. You also need to make sure that you aren't worrying about a lot of crap when you do it.

How can an economist put a productivity value on the creation of an unbreakable bond between father and son? How can you predict when or how that will happen? What I do know is that the parent child bond is vitally important for the journey embarked on together is for the rest of our lives, for better and poorer, in sickness and in vomit, times challenging and delightful, loving or spiteful, closer or estranged.

In the whole child care debate I hear various commentators espousing the benefits of childcare on Australian productivity levels and how well the child is doing vs. parental care based on limited sample sizes and using the few external behavioural "acting out' parameters that can be measured. I find myself yelling at the radio (talkback radio) that parenting is not a one way street going from parent to child. The child to parent connection is vitally important. As a parent, children give us so much but we actually have to be around to receive the gifts. How can any study predict indeterminate variables in personal well being or vitality and joy later in life? How much is a call out of the blue worth from a grandchild telling you about an amazing spiky caterpillar that they just found in the garden and how much they love you? How many grandparents now wish that there was a strong connection. There are many Grandparents afraid to call their children because of the pain of getting an indifferent or impatient response and many Grandparents that long to pick up a phone that never rings?

Children do grow up very quickly. Our time with our children is precious and there is a very real risk that parents that put their children in childcare at very early ages will not bond deeply with their kids, will not give the child the benefit of a minimum of six months breastfeeding as recommended by the WHO and those parents may not learn the lessons that the children are happy to teach us if we are around long enough to learn them.

Children teach us how to love unconditionally, laugh often, that some cuddles and hugs are beyond price and that life is simple. Happiness is our birth rite. A society that forces children into childcare for economic imperatives is barbaric, in my opinion. There is a responsibility that comes with becoming a parent and some of the parental ski runs that are currently open and well groomed may not be the best for us or for our children.

The great thing about being "off-piste" is that it can be an exhilarating ride. We are going to make mistakes, fall over and sometimes take paths that initially look great but end in steep "lessons." It is how we clean up after our mistakes, pick ourselves up when we fall over, take responsibility for our behaviour and learn from the paths that take us to unexpected places that will teach our children how to thrive in an ever changing world.

My children teach me about love and the joy that can be found in the simplest things: a sand castle, flying a kite, the perfect head shot in Halo. My children also press my buttons. I have taught them how to jump from a great height onto each one. Every time I have my buttons pressed I am presented with the opportunity to grow or regress. I try to remember that I am supposed to be the adult and I reset my buttons, not always gracefully but I reset them because I do want to be the best parent I can be, not just for my children but for their children and their children's children.

To be the best parent I can be I need to learn from other parents and from other parent educators because my wife and I are parenting "off-piste," there is no path and there are moments of white out too.

I Will Not Grow Up

"The day the child realizes that all adults are imperfect, he becomes an adolescent; the day he forgives them, he becomes an adult; the day he forgives himself, he becomes wise"-- Alden Nowlan

27

Growing Up:
How to Avoid It

(Contributed by Peter Pan)

Avoiding Growing Up is easier than ever before, providing we don't have another world war or major police action, and it basically comes down to managing change, responsibility and creating and maintaining a supportive child friendly environment.

<u>Managing Change, NOT:</u> The important word here is NOT. As we all know, if you are a good manager you can get paid a lot of money to shuffle work from one person to another whilst completely avoiding doing any work yourself besides the time consuming pretence of being busy. Your carefully prepared stage set or office will look as if you are completely snowed under. Your goal is to be in such a constant state of busy PANIC that no one ever has the time to find out what it is that you actually (don't) do. Looking harried and haggard is mandatory. Staying out late and partayyying is a good way to achieve this look and is highly recommended.

In agreeing to never grow up you need to be able to essentially behave like a child, sometimes even a teenager, forever! The good news for you oldies out there is that it is quite possible to regress if you have already passed childhood developmentally and remember, just because your body is grown up doesn't mean you have to be.

You have to manage change and there are two ways of doing this: 1) NOT managing change, and 2) Managing Change NOT. Stop looking confused and pay attention, if you can.

1) Not managing change means going against the flow of trying to avoid change. Not managing change (or embracing change purely for the sake of change) can be a devastatingly effective strategy for the right person and psychopathic tendencies in applicants will be viewed favourably.

This strategy works particularly well in business where you are an agent for change and for telling other people what to do. For you, spearheading the very latest and now monthly Change Management Strategy, codenamed "Reorganizing the previously simplified, restructured, modernized but not as organized as last time we reorganized organizational Review" or BAB (Boning the Already Boned) for short. What fun.

You thrive on constant chaos, mainly because in a stable environment your corrosive personality, constant bullying and general incompetence would stand out like rabbits ears when they are up and trying to listen to something. (Most dogs these days have had their little puppy testicles harvested by a veterinarian, so the expression "sticks out like dogs balls" whilst nice and simple is clearly outdated).

With constant change there is no way to track your performance or for you to be held accountable or responsible for anything. High staff turnover? Not your fault, they couldn't adapt or you got rid of dead wood. A drop in sales? Compared to what? Last year? We can't compare anything to last year because nothing is the same, all the territories are different and there was the drought. Safety incidents? That was Halliburton's fault. Bullies [and psychopaths] thrive in these environments where change is not managed, especially in organisations where many layers of management have been cut.

2) Managing change NOT is the easier option of offering total resistance to any change. Fundamentally people do not like change even though they know that nothing stays the same forever [except childhood]. It is always easier to do what you have always done. The path is already there to be followed. Trying new things, even new food can bring in unwanted new ideas, new tastes, new ways of thinking. YUKKKK. I never change who I am, at heart, I am Peter Pan, the boy who refuses to grow up BUT at times I am forced to adapt to a changing environment.

I am always a strong advocate for other people to change. I do this through a constant barrage of criticism, especially directed towards those that might compete with me for attention or promotion. This is important, if you are always criticizing others and lamenting their inability to change then you can get the reputation of being an innovator, whilst staying the same. The best training for being hyper critical is to have had parents that constantly criticised you when you were little. You can make other people wrong without even having to think.

Certain mood swings and peevish tirades that worked admirably as a teenager can still serve you well as a manchild, often with little or no modification. However, some tantrums, like holding your breath till you pass out, stop being cute when your body is bigger than a kiddies. Trust me, passing out mid tantrum is not a good look later in life. I've tried it, it didn't work and I "lost" an eyebrow and my pants. However, the same stubbornness and refusal to listen to anyone else that used to be dramatically conveyed by turning blue and falling over can be delivered effectively by simply shouting. Shouting is actually better because it can also intimidate. So change is not always bad but it has to be managed. It is vital that you provide at least the illusion of change, of growing up, whilst keeping your eye on the guiding light of immaturity that should underlay all your behaviour and can pay handsome dividends too.

It is essential in managing change that you put off having children of your own for as long as possible or forever whichever is the longest. You may think to yourself, "Oh, having kids won't change me" and for some of you that is true, because you'll have shot through well before the child is born. Some of you may also have developed your core selfishness to such a profound level that you may be immune to the "oooh I'm the so helpless and unconditionally loving child." In all honesty, few have attained that level of personal mastery. Children bring lots of change that you cannot control very easily, so avoid it, them. I am told that children also turn out to be a very expensive hobby.

Marriage is also to be avoided if possible. Why do it? Also be careful of de-facto relationship laws which might kick you in the ass-ets. If you are getting married understand this; your spouse is marrying you in the vain hope that he / she can change you. Your immature essence or personality will not change but financially losing half your wealth in a divorce will impose some unwanted, unwelcome changes on your lifestyle. Think about it and the reason that there are so many jokes about married couples not having sex after they are married? Well, ask a few. With divorce rates running at around 50% you do the cost benefit analysis.

Never getting married will also happily reduce the chances of becoming a parent. True story.

If it's too late for you and you are already married and have children and you feel so trapped that you cannot just run away as so many DNA donors do today, then there is still some hope for you but you have to fight the impulse to become the adult in the family with all of your being. Your choice of parenting style can help compensate for your earlier mistakes. Remember that the three parenting styles that will help you to avoid growing up the most are: 1) disengaged parenting 2) permissive parenting and 3). authoritarian parenting

Leaving Neverland

"The key to change... is to let go of fear."
--Rosanne Cash

28

Leaving
Neverland

(by Daniel Prokop)

We have had too many unaccountable, irresponsible Peter Pans wielding power inappropriately for too long. Unlike J.M. Barrie's creation, the Peter Pan's of today;

> "...got that way because nobody helped them grow up and because most of them were actually rewarded for childlike behaviour... The devastating fact is that most men are fixated at an immature level of development." (Moore and Gillette, 1990).

How many boys wearing men's bodies do you know? And how many girls do you know who have shunned the journey into healthy womanhood. Some argue that in Neverland 2.0 our girls are actually struggling more than the boys because of early sexualisation. Girls are also more vulnerable to advertising and body image expectations. Girls that are struggling are just much less "in your face" than the boys and given the strength of the "glass ceiling" few women run big corporations, yet.

Neverlanditis is pretty much a global pandemic (sort of spread by rats) and thankfully the conversation around growing up is finally getting some traction so whilst this book doesn't look at first glance much like a tractor, it is all about traction. All the stuff that Peter Pan talks about would be much funnier if there was not so much truth in what he says and I hope it made you laugh because:

"Even if there is nothing to laugh about, you can always laugh on credit." --Unknown

Lots of violent wars and oil spills have happened since man started writing his version of "his-story" down and my observation is that a lot of it (except the natural disasters) is pretty much the same thing with different manchild actors on the stages. Lots of positive things have happened too. It seems a lot of people today are busy surviving, trying to get those ends that seem to have opposing magnetic forces on them, to meet. Financial stress, personal isolation and long intense work hours do not help our communities and we have the opportunity now to build new strong diverse communities. There are more than enough resources on this planet for us all to live well and we will need to redistribute those resources better and spend less time and money on trying to kill each other for that to happen.

I didn't study until the night before an exam. As human beings it is the night before our biggest test. It is time to dig deep and find the strength and time to support one another, to listen with respect to other people's point of view, even when we disagree, to question the news and find sources that do not put profit before the truth, to educate ourselves, to make our own minds up about issues and to be guided by an open heart. We can and must hold corporations and politicians accountable and for many countries it is time to create a fairer democracy and for others, time to trust the people.

Reclaiming Rites of Passage is an important step in building healthy communities. Healthy adults make better parents than overgrown children for starters. Confident parents that spend time with their children are happier healthier adults. Healthy adults make better wives and husbands, business owners, politicians and even generals. Elders have access to a treasure chest of wisdom that can be shared but not necessarily googled. We have more knowledge being created in a year now than once existed in the famous library at Alexandria but without wisdom and respect it is only chaotic vibrating electrons. We have bowed our heads and given our power to experts when in many situations common sense would have served us as well if not better.

As the supposed adults in our society we have a lot of work to do to re-brand adulthood into something aspirational rather than something to be avoided at all costs (including your life). The first steps are actually not that hard. We can start by laughing more, having more fun, owning our emotions, taking responsibility for our actions and spending more time with our children. We could have full global employment tomorrow if we tried to fill all the vacancies that are available for healthy adult role models.

Michael Jackson has left Neverland forever. It's time for us to leave Neverland 2.0 too, our survival as a species may actually depend on it. It is time to go home....

The pathway to healthy manhood has been lost for a long, long time and will never be found in Neverland though it is highly convenient to look there.

> Under a streetlight, late one night, a man is looking for the keys that he has dropped. A group of passersby gather to help him look for his keys. Eventually one person asks the man, "Are you sure you dropped your keys out here?" The man replies. "Oh no, I dropped them in the yard over there but its dark over in the yard."

We will not find the path out of Neverland by looking where the light is currently focused. We can move the light to help us illuminate new possibilities.

In Western culture we have experimented with doing nothing, not marking any life stages besides marriage and the subsequent divorce, for a very, very long time and it hasn't worked very well. Neverland is not Nirvana...

Once upon a time, a long time ago, before writing, even before TV, in a Galaxy right under our noses, people lived together. They lived their own lives intertwined with those of their tribe and there were many ways they could live together: from councils of elders, to chiefs, to matriarchs. Vicarious living was not an option, there were no couches even for the potatoes and most importantly there was no word for "work" or "performance anxiety." The word for work and the ensuing definition of an imposed 60 hour week would have to wait for more "civilized" times. Oh, and once upon a time, everyone helped raise the children.

All so called "primitive" people marked important changes in the seasons with ceremonies and festivals that could last days and involved everyone often including people from neighboring tribes. Even the teenagers participated (it helped a lot that there was no word for "bored" or "whatever"). There were also a series of important rituals and events that marked a person's passage from one life stage to another.

Arnold van Gennep created the term "rites de passage" to identify the category of ceremonies that marked the passage from one role or social position to another, from birth, puberty, marriage, elder and death. Arnold published this term in Paris in 1909 in his book "Les rites de passage." Though the book was not translated into English until 1960 the term 'Rites of Passage' was quickly adopted by anthropologists.

Arnold was also the first anthropologist to observe and identify three stages that he found were common to all the Rites of Passage from the various groups that he studied. Whilst the ceremonies were often quite different, the following three stages were remarkably consistent across quite diverse cultural boundaries:

1. Departure or Separation from the known, the preliminary phase
2. Transition, the in between or the liminal phase
3. Incorporation or reintegration, the post liminal phase

The term Rites of Passage is not all that well known though everyone in contact with any form of modern media would be familiar with the mythology of Rites of Passage in a slightly different form. Van Gennep's work was a strong influence on Joseph Campbell who wrote the book, The Hero with a Thousand Faces. Most people today will be familiar with Campbell's work on the "Hero's Journey" though they may not have recognized it at the time.

Campbell divided the Hero's Journey into three parts: "Departure," "Initiation" and "Return." Many of the most popular books and movies ever created follow the hero's journey, for example, Star Wars (IV- VI and then I-III), Lord of The Rings (I-III and The Hobbit), The Matrix (I-III) and more recently Harry Potter (I-VII). It is not compulsory to use a trilogy to tell a Hero's Journey, however, there are commercial benefits in doing so especially if you can retain the worldwide merchandising rights. A Hero's Journey could be a short story, even a poem and given the success of Star Wars there is obviously no need for the Hero's Journey to be told as a sequential story either.

> {"Peter Pan" is a great example of a Hero's Journey, which of course makes me a Hero!}

> Well, actually Peter, "No" and "Yes". Peter Pan is not a Hero's journey, not for you, because you never complete the last two stages of the journey. You achieve departure or separation from the rest of society accidentally, by falling out of a pram …

{That's unfair! That pram was not baby worthy...}

Whatever. Peter, you fulfill the Departure stage, but whilst you are at times brave, verging on foolhardy, fighting the pirates and the Indians and anyone else you can, you are also capricious, mean spirited and childish. You never complete your liminal or initiation phase. You overcome some challenges but there are no men in Neverland to guide you. You never hear the stories of men. You are not acknowledged or honoured for your many gifts by men. You constantly self initiate but it is never enough because being cheered by lost boys is different to be acknowledged by men and then a community. Peter, you never take responsibility for your actions and you do not Return or Reintegrate. You decide to stay in Neverland, a child forever, churlishly defiant. There are many words for this type of behaviour, but Hero is not one of them. "Peter Pan" is a children's bedtime story, sure, written at a time in history when for a lot of people childhood was incredibly fleeting if visited at all. Yes you are a kind of idol but only to the Neverland 2.0 recruits who are desperately looking for someone to champion perpetual childhood for them.

{I am so a hero.} <sulk><bigger sulk>

In a healthy society you are a kind of anti-Hero. There is no transformation. You start as a child and you finish as a child. A child, who never grows up, eventually becomes an overgrown child, at best. At worst, they can be irresponsible, physically and mentally abusive bullies. Peter you are brave but bravery is not a quality exclusive to heroes. Bravery, when you know you are mortal and have a family and you are afraid and yet you do what needs to be done anyway is a deeper bravery than the semi-conscious bravery / bravado of someone who believes themselves immortal and therefore has nothing to lose.

{So um, I have a friend, well, an acquaintance really, what if he wanted to become a true Hero?}

Does this friend really want to be a Hero?

{What would he have to do?}

204

He would have to grow up. If your friend is from Neverland. Please let him know that unfortunately, Neverland was light on for good male role models (As is the oil industry and international banking). The pain and anger of being abandoned by your family can be difficult to let go of.

<silence>

You still there?....Hello?

{I'm thinking}

Ok, I'll continue then…

One way to identify an intentional Rite of Passage is that they are carried out in the realm of a sacred (safe) space, powered by intention and they are carefully crafted and guided by individuals that have already passed through that particular life stage and lived into it i.e. in Neverland, growing up is not possible because children can only initiate children further into childhood not adulthood. Children should never initiate children. It doesn't work and is actually unconscious ineffective self initiation with a cheer squad. It is not just the intent and the ritual that determines the effectiveness of the Rite, it is the support afterwards that keeps the transformation alive.

Rites of Passage are transformational which is why profound social, behavioural and psychological differences can result from relatively short periods of time. It is quite amazing that whilst the methodology of the actual rituals varied there was such strong consistency in the three part structure across such diverse distances and cultures.

Van Gennep regarded Rites of Passage as essential for maintaining a healthy society. Rites of Passage are normal, they are for everyone and they are not about "fixing" the young people. They are all about supporting the young people and the community. The Rite of Passage from child to young adult, for example was not just for "troubled" or "out of control" youth, it was for all children, when they were ready. It was not left up to the child to determine when they were ready. The intention of a Rite of Passage is that it is the catalyst that facilitates the necessary transformational energy to leave one stage of life behind and create the opening, the space for a new way of being to emerge ... with a new way of being, certain behaviour will fall away and certain behaviour will emerge. A Rite of Passage is required to overcome the psychic inertia, the years spent building a life stage, only to leave it behind.

It is possible for a person to experience an amazing life changing breakthrough and then gradually revert back to the old way of being. Whilst the behavioural base line may be higher than before the event, the actual way of being can look pretty similar. The little voice in the head, if left to its own sickly sweet way, can over time, diminish the significance of a Rite of Passage in a participant's mind. Traditional societies didn't need doctorates in psychiatry to understand this which is why the departure and return stages were so important as well as ongoing connection and cultural expectations.

In Western culture and in some other cultures intentional Rites of Passage have been lost and certain ones that have somehow persisted appear to have lost their potency as true Rites of Passage, becoming more about money and or prestige than about transformation. However, there is a growing world wide interest in Rites of Passage which is highly positive. For some life stages there has been a void for many generations. For the transition from child to young adult we have abandoned our young people to self initiate, unless there is a war going on. By so doing we have also forfeited the opportunity to reinforce our own experience of growing up through teaching them.

Consider this. When families were larger, communities more open and schooling less stratified, the older children actually helped look after and bring up the younger children. They had to think of someone else besides themselves. When their own children subsequently rolled down the birth canal they had their own relatively recent childhood and extensive hands on baby training to draw upon. As new parents they had some idea of what to expect when looking after their new born but their parenting style would of course faithfully replicate that of their parents.

Inside-the-family training to raise children rarely happens any more and with parents coming from smaller families, having even fewer children at older ages it means that a big gap has opened up in the parenting continuum. This is a challenge and it also presents us with the fabulous opportunity for warm, consistent, highly engaged and balanced parenting to emerge and for bullying, domination, command and control based parenting to fade away.

The continuum gap creates opportunities and along with it some challenges. The gap creates the space for parenting to break from the old authoritarian parenting style. The gap also means that the current generation of parents is the least experienced generation of parents to ever face a full disposable nappy. There is a huge opportunity to help men to become good fathers and learn how to look after a pregnant wife and a new infant and there is also the opportunity to help women to make the transition from woman to mother which is more than giving birth. If we do this well, then fewer men will abandon their responsibilities and their families and run away and we can do a lot to alleviate or eradicate post natal depression for women.

In our Western Culture and in the many cultures that it has overwhelmed there is a hunger, a niggling yearning for something that remains just beyond reach which is not a suppressed shopping urge or a desire for the neighbour's wife. There is a feeling that life was not meant to be so lonely, so disconnected and this feeling is manifesting in the high rates of global depression. The WHO estimate that within 20 years, more people will be affected by depression than any other health problem, but hey, those uncomfortable feelings can be numbed through business, TV, shopping, alcohol, drugs etc.

The boom of social networking Web 2.0 demonstrates, beyond contestation, the desire for human beings to connect with one another. Facebook now has over 500 million active users and was only launched in 2004. One of the challenges we face is how we can increase the amount of time humans have connecting with other human beings in person, exchanging hand shakes and hugs rather than just swapping electrons. We risk the atrophy of actual human to human social skills if we retreat too far into cyber space. More than at any other time in history we are aware that what happens in countries far away can affect us all. We are all connected, we all make a difference and our strength lies in our diversity, the diversity in our natural environment, in our countries, in our agriculture, seed stocks, in our communities and yes, diversity in business.

We live in a time when life expectancy at birth (in most countries) is at the highest levels ever seen for humans. Average, life expectancy at birth has gone from approximately 39 years for the USA in 1800 to 49 years at 1900 to 78 years in 2006[1]. These are profound changes and as with all statistics, the numbers need to be treated with some caution too, as much of the driver for the dramatic increases in life expectancy at birth are due to sharp decreases in infant mortality. Having given that caveat, it is true that people on average, are living much longer. The other dramatic social shifts have been a sharp decrease in the number of babies women are having, from an average of 7.01 children in 1801 to 3.85 children in 1900 to 2.1 children in 2001[2].

The shift in recent population dynamics have huge social implications and create an ever more urgent need to rediscover and provide contemporary, community based Rites of Passage, for our sake, for our children's sake, ffs. These changes help explain why Peter Pan has been so successful in expanding the borders of Neverland. Once the industrial revolution got steaming along, families were still large, houses small, death, particularly of infants and workers was common and children helped the family or slaved away in factories from as young as four years old.

Despite the protests of factory owners that any changes to labour laws would send them broke, "do-gooders" in the UK pushed through the UK Factory Act of 1833 which banned children under 9 years old from working in the textile industries and 10 -13 years olds were limited to just a paltry 48 hour week. Somehow industry recovered from these 'libertarian' changes that threatened to undermine the very fabric of society.

Children went from child to child worker, then eventually, from child to part time primary school student, to child worker, to parent. At the start of the 1900s High School was a relatively rare event with only 6 percent of teenagers graduating high school in the US. High School participation rates globally did not climb significantly until 1929, the Great Depression, when something, anything urgently had to be done with the large number of teenagers who were competing for work with men who were desperately trying to find work to support their big families.

What to do? What to do? "What about another world war?" "Nawwww, we're still full from the last one." "Hmmmm, there must be some way we can put all our teenagers into a kind of suspended animation just for five or six years, till we get through this crisis?" "Weeeellll, there's really no room for them but we could make all teenagers go to high school?" "Poifect!" and so they did. Teenagers were put into an environment where they could stay children until, well, until whenever...

So high school numbers jumped astronomically but given the tough economic times, funding for high schools did not. Some would say high school education is still playing catch up from this time of massive, unplanned, under funded, and under resourced growth. The 1930s role of high schools was to take youth out of the workforce until they could be absorbed by industry and industry needed workers trained to do what they were told. In return, the worker would be given work for life. A job for life no longer exists and whilst industry has to respond to changes like vinyl records to CDs or go bust, our education system does not have that imperative for change. There is a huge opportunity for our education system to reinvent itself.

Suddenly from the 1930s on, adolescence became a clearly defined marketing segment and a more significant and longer life stage. Adolescence is defined as being the period from puberty to adulthood. Adolescence has been growing ever longer and starts earlier in girls than in boys and for some it is a badge of pride to take adolescence from puberty all the way to death, skipping adulthood altogether, eh Peter?

{True, true, extended adolescence facilitated the expansion of Neverland 2.0}

By 1996 the percentage of teenagers graduating high school in the US was 85 percent and most states have now enacted legislation extending compulsory education laws to the age of 16 and there is talk of lifting it even higher.

Prolonged adolescence in evolutionary terms is not even out of its packaging. It is a brand new phenomenon and adolescents coming from small families where both parents are working and largely absent, or largely absent because they are parenting on their own and trying to work ... well, the paint is still drying on this as a social experiment. The other experiment, one that tragically Australia has embraced through successive governments but under the Howard "open trough" system reached it's market driven crescendo, subsequent collapse and tax payer bailout is the experiment of a generation of children placed in for profit commercial childcare centres.

Parents have been encouraged to put infants into child care because we need workers, dammit! Personally it makes my skin crawl to think of babies, sometimes only a few weeks old, being placed in childcare. That is my truth. I feel sad when I think about it and I can get that in some extreme situations it may be the best thing for a baby but only as the exception rather then the market driven rule. Abandoning a new born so that the woman can go back to work as soon as possible rather than care for her baby is something that I believe we will look back on in years to come and see it as an indication of just how disconnected a society we had become. Those parents may not ever bond with their child or discover what they missed and the baby, well, our communities will reap what they have sown at great cost whilst the economists crow about temporarily increased national productivity.

It seems in all the arguments about childcare that what is forgotten is that parenting children is at least a two way street (side streets may include grandparents, uncles, aunties). I have learned so much about the simple pleasures of life from my children. Mix a little sand and water and an entire afternoon can go by and as a bonus I get to laugh and exercise my imagination and creativity.

Governments and some parents talk about how valuable our children are (and some people refer to them as a resource or commodity, like any of those people have ever made a sandcastle). Children, especially small children, are so very precious because they love unconditionally. Their job is to help us open our hearts. But if someone else is parenting for us, if we put all our children into "efficient", centrally located child feedlots aka childcare centres then our society is the poorer for it. So are our families.

Whew. So moving right along, in summary, not so long ago, the period of childhood and adolescence was fleeting for many and for some, like those exploited as child labour today, they were sweating too much to notice that they had missed it. But they knew how to make great brand-name sneakers. When childhood was short, the thought of never growing up must have sounded pretty cool and may well have contributed to the enormous charm and popularity of Peter Pan when it was first published in 1906.

The Industrial revolution, bless it's greedy, steam driven heart, effectively removed the father from the home environment for over 60 hours a week, though in 1874 a law was passed whereby no worker was allowed to work for more than 56.5 hours per week, damn those soft hearted liberals. Fortunately that rule seems to no longer apply. The father hasn't made it back into the home much before six PM yet and when so little time is spent in the home, men feel like strangers rather than family members.

> *"When a father, absent during the day, returns home at six, his children receive only his temperament, not his teaching." Robert Bly*

Taking men out of the home has created a phenomenon never before experienced on this planet (Aren't we special, creating all these new things?) It is called;

> *"Father hunger.... That is unrecognized, unnamed, not seen as that. It is seen in the people who rage toward society, and in the need for authority – for someone to tell them what to do. Underneath all of that there is a father wound out of which comes a tremendous father hunger in our society that is showing its face in so, so many ways." Father Richard Rohr, from an interview "Naming the 'Father Hunger'", 1990.*

Steve Biddulph in his inspiring book *"Manhood"* wrote of father hunger in this way:

"The hidden grief... the deep biological need for strong, humorous, hairy, wild, tender, sweaty, caring, intelligent masculine input." Steve Biddulph

Steve estimates that only 10% of men have a good relationship with their fathers, 30% of men have no relationship, 30% have a prickly or hostile relationship and 30% only have contact out of a sense of duty. That is a sad indictment of past parenting practices.

Women have a hard time understanding this wound in men though they often have to deal with the impact of the anger and frustration associated with it. It is not just men that suffer from 'father hunger.' Absent and or emotionally unavailable fathers wound women in a different way, leaving a longing for male approval that can manifest in unhealthy relationships. Both men and women experience an illogical feeling that it is somehow their fault that their fathers didn't love them and or weren't available emotionally.

Long, harsh working conditions and a feeling of being trapped by a job and duty to the family did tend to teach men some sense of responsibility and then early marriage and parenting large families left them in no doubt that they were not the centre of the universe. Certainly parts of growing up happened through trauma and harsh working conditions but the cost was that men largely became estranged from their emotions and women also, to a lesser extent (women were not allowed to ever get angry). A sensitive man or a man showing vulnerability was a weak man, a nancy boy...

{Who exactly was Nancy and how many kids did she have? Oh and Darpan are you ever going to actually make a point?}

Getting there.

A hard drinking, hard man was a good, solid man and frequent violent outbursts were just part of the package. If a man had to choose between being feared or respected by his family he would choose feared 'cause that were his experience of his Dad, by gum. Thus the previous generation of men, in absentia, passed a damaged, confused, wounded manhood onto the next generation. Fury for this travesty has been replaced with anger then sadness and only now are men starting to shed the tears that can wash the wounded man and with the support of other men, make him whole.

".... this is the heart of the problem – men have lost the ability to pass on the wisdom and experience of their life and who they are. All they know how to do is to pass on roles, money and opinions, but not who they are." From "Naming the 'Father Hunger'" An interview with Father Richard Rohr by Anthony Schulte, 1990.

In the past there were certainly some privileged individuals, gentlemen and otherwise, who were able to avoid any responsibility, hard physical work and growing up. Some of these individuals, considered the "champions" of industry, had no qualms about forcing workers to endure dangerous conditions and abandon their families for negligible pay. It was what made profits fat for these cunning businessmen. "It's not personal old chap, survival of the fittest, don't you know?" The champions of industry fought unions with tooth, nail, gun, nail gun and in some cases whole private armies. There was a sharp line between management and workers; "it's us agin' them." Each would cut off the nose to spite the face if given half of half a chance (a quarter of a chance).

I've taken a pretty broad brush here, more of a roller really and while painting the walls I noticed that the ceiling needed painting too but it was worth writing a little more about the Neverland we live in. Time to move onto some specific Rites of Passage...

[1] Source : Gapminder.org
[2] Source : Gapminder.org

Child to Young Adult Rite of Passage

Globally we have had some recent experience with little boys tearing down (mismanaging for their own selfish advantage and taking no responsibility for their actions) the structures of culture (the international banking system, the ecosystem of the Gulf of Mexico) just to feel the warmth of the cash. We also have many politicians behaving badly - is it any wonder that some young people are struggling and some are out of control?

Of all the Rites of Passage and all the various festivals and events that made up the rich fabric of village life the ritual that traditional societies put more time and energy into than any other aspect of community life was the rite of passage from child to young adult. The rite of passage for boys to manhood could take years. Helping the young people make the transition to adulthood was even more important than the vital we still gotta eat to stay alive, planting and harvest festivals.

It is important to note that traditional societies allocated their limited resources this way when there was a whole village to help raise the children, when there were healthy role models available, when the village would actually have two or three adults assigned to each boy to watch over them, spend time with them, teach them. These societies knew that their very survival depended on having healthy men and women as community members, their very survival, get it? Do I need to say survival again? I don't want to labour this point too far but they knew that they could all die (not survive) if some idiot man-child usurped power or did something monumentally stupid like invading another country or drilling for oil in deep water with an emergency response plan written on the back of a soiled napkin.

There has been no widespread, non-military Rite of Passage for western young people for thousands of years (with a few exceptions e.g. Bar Mitzvah's).

Oh and in case you haven't noticed, there is no village anymore to help raise the children but we do have cable and shopping centres and a big block of flats where that messy green space used to be and role models? Ummm, sports stars? Movie stars? oh? You mean GOOD role models and you want men or women that also have time to spend with actual flesh and blood teenagers rather than cyber teens? Sorry, we're too busy and we're done fresh out of old people who do have some time 'cause we put them out to wither and die out of sight and sound - but aren't gangs a terrible thing? Young people these days, when I was young.... Sorry, I'm starting to sound like Peter. My point is that we have done less than nothing for a long while. What we have done is put up many obstacles to growing up.

> *"What is becoming clear is that where no socially sanctioned markers are provided, young men – and I believe young women – will create their own markers. Too often these will be clearly aimed at creating a separate cultural identity by shock tactics such as: binge drinking, drug use, 'unsafe' sexual activity that will impress and engage their competitive peers. Their message appears to be something like "I am no longer a child. I am powerful. I am independent and I will do as I wish rather than what I am told to do." Whilst these are clearly statements of independence they are made the more satisfying if they carry an additional layer of rejection, shock and challenge for authorities such as their parents and elders." Don Bowak, Marking Life's Stage, 2008.*

Self initiation is the name for what happens when we do nothing. Self initiation also includes hazing. Hazing or ragging refers to activities that humiliate, shame or risks emotional and/or physical harm as a way of initiating a person into a group e.g. in gangs, military units, clubs (think fraternities) and some workplaces. Hazing is often prohibited by law because it has resulted in a number of deaths and injuries but it still happens.

In addition to the examples cited above other forms of self initiation includes self mutilation or cutting, driving powerful cars too fast, piercing, more piercing and fighting pirates.

{Fighting pirates?}

That was just for you, Peter.

{I'd like to see these whimps take on the Cap'n.}

You're still living in the early 1900s, aren't you?

{You're going to tell me to grow up aren't you?}

Sorry, got distracted. Acts of self initiation are not designed to add the amazing fire of youth to the hearth of community. The intent of self initiation is to piss on the community fire and to take away as much wood as possible and start a different and better fire somewhere else. Self initiation in young people is a biologically induced, hormone fueled attempt to seek acknowledgement of the recently added "adult" body mass whilst simultaneously rejecting anyone with the wisdom and ability to bestow the gift of acknowledgement that is so desperately yearned for.

Self initiation cannot install the new "adult" operating system that is optimized to run the larger, more powerful and vibrant young adult body. The adult.exe file will not auto install in a timely fashion on its own. A bug and relatively neurosis free installation requires a carefully planned and lovingly executed ritual. The other alternative is application of personal trauma sufficient enough to dislocate the aspects of the child that no longer serve and replace them with healthy adult thinking. Of course it is mandatory to survive the trauma so that the install can eventually complete.

Self initiation is not really about transformation it is often about taking childish behaviour to new levels of infancy and or danger or both. In Australia and in many parts of the world there is a phenomenon called "schoolies" which occurs just after high school students finish the final exams that mark the completion of high school.

I remember the sense of complete and total under whelm that I felt when I finished my last High School exam. Ok, so I had just finished 13 years of schooling (including the year of the crayon – kindergarten) and ummm, so what now? Schoolies came about as a way for young people to come together to celebrate the end of high school, to fill the "What now?" void. It marks the end of schooling which is a change of doing rather than being.

Schoolies is sometimes referred to as a Rite of Passage. It is not a Rite of Passage and unless something changes it will never be a Rite of Passage because children cannot initiate children into adulthood they can only initiate children further into childhood. Children should never initiate children. It doesn't work and without elders and healthy adults to help guide and craft the process serves only to reinforce self obsessed, irresponsible, instant gratification seeking behaviour. Children initiating children is a wrong of passage and it is the reason that growing up is not possible in Neverland.

Acts of self initiation often wound rather than grow a person and they can send the innate fire wild and no matter how risky the act, it will never satisfy the hidden hunger for acknowledgement, for honouring as a man by men or as a woman by women thus leaving a psychological hole which peers cannot see and so they cannot fill it, though they can and do try. There are a lot of men today in their forties or older who when asked "when did you

215

become a man?" don't know. They don't know if they are a man or not because they have never been acknowledged as a man by other men and there are a lot of women who continue to behave like little girls even after giving birth to children of their own.

It does not take a lot to create ceremonies to welcome men to manhood. The Pathways Foundation offers a four day Leadership Training program which achieves this. Tracks Trust in NZ has a two day program called "Good Men Making Tracks." I haven't done the two days but I have spent time with the Tracks team and they are inspiring. Tracks is guided by wise and inspiring Elders (on ya Jim Horton and Duncan) and they are balanced by their sister organisation Tides. (Girls Rites of Passage.)

Getting back to young people, there is another group of young people out there, young people who do not even attempt to self initiate. These young people are terrified of getting anything wrong, of breaking any rules, of upsetting anyone. Their fire, if not wholly quenched, smoulders in deeply hidden places. These young people suck up anxiety, anger and frustration and either take it to their grave (or cremation jar) or wait until sometime, some place when the damped fire comes roaring to life. Then all the suppressed feelings come vomiting forth often in an inappropriate though spectacular manner. In mid-life these people can have trouble suppressing their emotions and they hit crises and begin a process of self discovery or self repression which can be painful and for some lethal.

Most of my experience is obviously with the rite of boys to manhood both as a leader and also as a father. I have been as inclusive as possible, talking about child to adult where applicable because Rites of Passage are important for both boys and girls and indeed I have been told that there are some programs in Europe that are run for whole families though I am not familiar with them. The journey into adulthood for girls and boys is very different but the same three stages of a Rites de Passage are followed for both. I will share my observations and what I have learned from working in this area for the past five years and I do speak with an Adam's apple … but first …

Initiation through War or the Military

> *"As a general rule, the more a tribe practices warfare, the harsher its rites of initiation are for boys. In such cultures, the main purpose of the initiation rites for males is to turn civilian boys into military men." Fire in the Belly, On Being a Man by Sam Keen, Bantam Books 1991.*

The most common form of rite of passage for boys over the past millennia or so is one where the intent is not to help a boy become a healthy independent man and a loving, responsible and emotionally available husband and father. Rather the intention has been to make a boy become a fierce, compliant soldier, a useful puppet with strings pulled by men who will never know him. If in the moulding of the soldier, the numbing and domination required for compliance make him a less than ideal husband and father afterwards then whatever, he has served his purpose and that other stuff is somebody else's problem / cost centre.

The archetype of the noble, masculine warrior has been around for a long time. Unfortunately, when war became more profitable and more organized with much bigger, highly expendable teams, the "warrior" accidentally dropped the soap in the shower and he has been getting boned senseless by the "soldier/lobbyist archetype" ever since.

Certain positive attributes of "The Warrior" resonate deep in our collective psyche. These have been manipulated in a way that dishonours the archetype by a well funded, highly lathered and lethal war machine to spread fear, create and vilify enemies and do anything humanly possible to justify ever spiraling spending on "defense" whilst simultaneously declassifying the "human being" status of children and women and reclassifying them as acceptable "collateral damage."

Oh and anyone who questions ever bigger and better toys and the consequently astronomical military spending is attacked as a traitor who wants to leave their country defenseless against just the kind of cross border drone attacks that the US regularly launches on its allies like Pakistan all the time. Drone attacks are based on hard "military intelligence," where the military is appointed judge, jury and executioner despite its appalling record on the really big things, like Iraq. And so the trust has been broken and the warrior shafted. After so many examples of military cover-ups in many different countries who can believe the military anymore? Military power without consequence and no accountability that can't be covered up is unwise, very unwise.

The scales of justice do not seem to have a receptacle that holds murderers in uniforms or the besuited individuals that green light the killing of innocent people. On April 5th, 2010, Wikileaks released to Youtube decoded footage of a US Apache helicopter engagement in New Baghdad that left 2 Reuters employees dead (www.collateralmurder.com). There had been an investigation. The military investigation did not correlate with what the footage reveals. The footage is not graphic but it is highly disturbing and how many times has this happened where no Reporters have been involved? And where the coded footage has not been leaked?

The International Criminal Court (ICC) as of March, 2010 has 111 countries signed up with a further 37 countries who have signed but not yet ratified the treaty. China has always opposed the court and given China's record in Tibet and elsewhere, no surprises there. Significantly the US, Israel, and Sudan have "unsigned" the treaty. The US and Israel cry "terrorist" often and loudly but they fight terror with terror and when footage such as that released by Wikileaks is viewed it is easy to understand, but difficult to forgive them for not signing. They will not allow an Independent court to investigate US and Israeli war crimes. Sudan has "unsigned" because the ICC has issued an indictment against the Sudanese President, Omar al-Bashir for war crimes and crimes against humanity in the Darfur region. What can the world do to bring all these countries under the ICC?

What about an immediate cookie blockade? No cookies might bring them to the table where a nice warm glass of milk will be ready. Dunking but not water boarding would be permissible. China with only the fortune cookie to munch on (it is a turd of a cookie, totally undunkable) might just be open to a cookie intervention. That was a bit random but the book is nearly finished.

Bushido is the traditional code of the Japanese samurai warrior. Traditional warrior codes were codes of behaviour that stressed honour, respect, self-discipline, bravery, being in service and protecting the weak. If the military systems of this world codified independent strong warriors living by an appropriate code they could have made themselves redundant. One very good reason why this has not happened. The military industrial complex seems intent on perpetuating warfare rather than creating enduring peace. Honourable warriors could never have served the oily industrial and colonial masters that have pulled the strings for so long. In some warrior cultures, a warrior could choose to follow a leader or not. Bad leaders would have few followers and good leaders would have many.

A soldier is told who to follow and follow they must, even if they despise the person that commands them and killing can now be done from the comfort of an air conditioned office via a video screen in the USA and the people that give the kill command that results in innocent people dying, can go home and have dinner with their families. "How was your day dear?" "Not too bad, Darling, a little collateral damage, fortunately all foreigners, got the wrong house, again. Can you please pass the peas?"

Before we can give the "warrior archetype" a chance for his busted ring to heal, enough for him to finally sit down again and have a rest, we need to defuse the power of the well paid, conscience free lobbyists and or maybe let them do a tour of duty near sites where depleted uranium has been used? Make them sit down and listen to families that have lost loved ones on both sides of the conflict, let them explain why they pressed the button that killed their sons and daughters and let them hear how hollow that sounds and maybe all witnesses could just leave the room for a bathroom break if the conversation gets a little non-verbal?

"War" or We Are Right, is a part of the word "War-rior." After 5,000 years or more of conflict and domination maybe the war-rior can sit out for a bit, give the Peace-rior a chance. If we replace "hawks" with Elders we can have leadership rather then self serving Alpha-bet males. Bullies in a uniform are still bullies.

Veterans of the highly avoidable First World War believed that it was the war to end all wars. They knew what a horrific experience it was. They saw and felt the death of friends, the wounding of spirit and flesh. They smelt the smoke, saw the devastation of cities and children and women and they believed that no one that had experienced the unimaginable horror would ever allow war to happen again and they were right and wrong. Right, in that it should never have happened again and wrong, because the people who make the wars never have to take responsibility for or face the consequences of their actions. Leadership today is from as far away as possible, instead of leadership from the fray. Fear and terror are used by "leaders" to control populations. Maybe they have finally cried "wolf" once too often?

The soldier half of the soldier lobbyist archetype are trained to do exactly what they are told without question, even if it is the wrong thing to do. Soldiers usually destroy things rather than create them. This is not a criticism of the men and women who are in the armed services at this time. I pray that you come home safe. It is a criticism of the system and some of the "top brass." I believe that the powers that be have been less than honest and have marketed warrior attributes to attract enlistments whilst delivering soldier duties. Whilst it is called a defence force, after Iraq, that marketing description is no longer valid.

Surely we must be reaching the point where we can restrict and control the sale of the weapons and move towards a strong, responsive, more centralized military system based on a more democratic and more effective and open UN Security Council system? Surely?

There are men who have experienced camaraderie with other men through the military, through shared experiences, even battle experiences. The experience of connection and trust has touched them deeply and as a result of this bond they open up their emotions and are able to talk about what is going on in their lives. Their comrades become their brothers. Because the military has been a positive experience for them, some believe that every child must have the same experience and they assume that it will be the same for those children. They also believe that it is the only way that men can experience such camaraderie.

Compulsory conscription has been put forward at different times as a good thing to toughen up our young people, to teach them a little discipline, teach them 'how to be a man'. As I mentioned earlier there is a lot of baggage that comes along with that way of thinking.

Let's bring back Rites of Passage instead of bringing back conscription.

Camaraderie amongst men (or women or men and women) can be achieved simply by creating a safe respectful space, a circle where everyone is at the same level and an intention to share from the heart. Small opportunities for this can be very healing. It helps to have a facilitator, someone to hold the space, perhaps a candle or something in the centre of the circle to focus on. It works if everyone agrees and is clear that the space is not about "shoulding" on people. "You should do this..." "You should do that..." or making sweeping philosophical statements such as "we all...". The space is for "I" statements ... "I feel ..." "when I did.."

To the hawks that think that we need ever more militarization to be "safe" I have three words to say, "Enough is Enough" you psycho military pretzel person (I have no idea why I wrote "pretzel", but I liked it and it is much more polite than the alternatives.)

"Fighting for peace is like fucking for virginity"
Unknown

OK, I've vented a little, and that was a lot, and I mean a lot tamer than the first five drafts. I'm OK now. "Don'cha think 5,000 years of war is enough?" "Huh?" "How much military spending will ever be enough?" "Ooh please can I just have one more billion dollar stealth toy, please, please, please?"

The role of the military is not to create independent, self actualized free thinkers. That would be potentially dangerous and you can't have soldiers refusing to destroy a "terrorist safe house" located in a foreign country, with a smart bomb from Virginia because they question the "intelligence" (did I mention that the word "intelligence" has divorced the word "military"?) and / or the proximity of a hospital. That would not do at all. You can't have people leaking all the little secrets either...or can we? There are men that claim that war has done so much for world peace. These same men "make a killing" by dealing munitions to the highest bidder, be they warlord or dictator or cartel.

You get the idea. Self initiate, do nothing or let the good ol' folks that help spend US$1.50 trillion dollars[1] globally on the business of killing human beings look after our young people's emotional well being? Oh and a special mention has to go to the United States of Idiots whose people have been numbed, lied and bullied into allowing the US's military spending to reach 48% of the world's total military spending[2]. A lot of starving kids in the US and outside the US want to say "Thank You" because ...because ... I ...<sigh> I can't find anything more preposterous to write, sorry. I'm speechless but fortunately I can still type ☺.

The US Department of Defense (DOD) budget for 2010, including "overseas contingency operations," is $663.8 billion which equates to approximately 28% of the estimated tax revenue for the whole of the United States. When defense related expenditures that are outside of the DOD budget are included, defense expenditures make up between 38 to 44% of total estimated tax revenues[3].

You don't have to be an emeritus professor of economics to know that that is not sustainable or wise and that the fan is just about to fall into the sewerage treatment plant. Imagine telling your wife:

> "Honey, no food for another month but I got that new tank because I'm pretty sure that Mr. and Mrs. Smith next door are about to buy a pistol. Ohh, yeah about that, the guy I bought it from was real nice. I twisted his arm and I got us a no interest for the first 50 years, 450 year loan. Honey, just don't worry your

pretty head about paying it back, that's why we had lots of children. Yeah, I'm not stupid, of course I know the house is about to fall down around our ears. Weren't you listening woman? I just done got us a tank. Yeah, so what? We can all sleep in the tank. Night time? No problem 'cause this tank glows in the dark, the paint has a special metallic finish called "depleted uranium grey." Darling we can sleep peacefully knowing that I can defend the rubble that was once our house with more firepower than the rest of the city combined. We might be starving but God dammit woman, we are SAFE!"

Respect to the men and women serving in uniforms around the world. My beef is not with you. It seems MAD that so many resources, that are so desperately needed elsewhere, are tied up in armies and on expensive, deadly ordinance for "Departments of Defence But if We Deem it Necessary Offense." I think even Peter Pan would rather starving children were fed rather than buying another missile.

{Well... um... technically... we don't really have starving kids in Neverland.}

Really? How is that?

{Ahem... ummm... well, they die too easy and, death is not welcome and kids with arms like pretzels, well, they aren't very good at adventures and when it's time for make believe all they can make believe is that they can have some food and clean water to drink and well, we can't be responsible for them can we?}

And what would have happened Peter if you had been left to starve after you fell out of your warm pram instead of being sent to Neverland? What if the rules were; "Boys so stupid as to fall out of their prams should be left to starve to death thereby cleansing the gene pool of these fools?"

{Sorry, had to pee, what did you say?}

Initiation has been used to create soldiers and military training follows the stages of separation, transition and incorporation. The young men (and now young women too) go to boot camp (separation) where transition happens, where they are initiated by the drill sergeant and the old way of being is replaced with unquestioning obedience to authority and finally the return and the celebration of graduation.

In contemporizing Rites of Passage it is important to keep this in mind; some Rites of Passage in the past were designed to create warriors and to separate a boy from the feminine rather than transform his relationship with the feminine. The feminine is not the enemy of men nor is the masculine the enemy of women. In any Rite of Passage, if the balancing energy is defiled or derided then balance is not going to be an outcome of that Rite. A man who has been intentionally and lovingly initiated into manhood has;

> "....no need to be macho. An insecure, uninitiated man has to be: he takes on the symbolic, exaggerated masculine [role] because he has never been given the real thing." Father Richard Rohr, "Naming the 'Father Hunger'" Interview, 1990.

Sam Keen explains the cost of culturally selling the warrior archetype as the exclusive domain of a man;

> "So men, the designated warriors, gradually form "character armor," a pattern of muscular tension and rigidity that freezes them into the posture that is appropriate only for fighting - shoulders back, chest out, stomach pulled in, anal sphincter tight, balls drawn up into the body as far as possible, eyes narrowed, breathing foreshortened and anxious, heart rate accelerated, testosterone in full flow. The warrior's body is perpetually uptight and ready to fight." Sam Keen "Fire in the Belly."

How many men do you see walking around in character armor? Taking enough steroids will also produce the same effect. That posture in a man will elicit the same posture in other men and when you add alcohol, stupidity or a lit match like a woman - the fight will easily be on. A true warrior would never be so insecure as to precipitate a confrontation from hubris.

---

[1] Stockholm International Peace Research Institute (SIPRI) research. Launch of the SIPRI Yearbook 2010
http://www.sipri.org/media/pressreleases/100602yearbooklaunch
[2] The Centre for Arms Control and Non-Proliferation (The FY 2009 Pentagon spending request – global military spending.)
http://www.armscontrolcenter.org/policy/securityspending/articles/fy09_do d_request_global/
[3] http://en.wikipedia.org/wiki/Military_budget_of_the_United_States Wikipedia

The Good News

Many traditional Rites of Passage prevented the development of individuality. These were handed down without change and without question for long periods of time. Often permanent scarring was a feature so that the initiate wore a reminder of the rite for the rest of their life. The benefit of this rigidity was that men and women knew who they were and where they were going and that they belonged to the tribe. Conformity was ensured because there was no adolescence, no gap between childhood and adulthood. The downside of this was that;

> *"The son was cast in the same mold as the father. The sacred ways of the ancestors were repeated without alteration. Tribal peoples kept their eyes focused on the past, determined that they should keep the faith of their fathers, repeat their virtues, and remain loyal to their visions of the world."* Sam Keen, Fire in the Belly, On Being a Man.

The world is changing very rapidly and some Rites of Passage viewed from a year 2010 western perspective can be seen as cruel, even brutal, for both boys and girls. For some practices to continue today, just because that's what we have always done, may not be good enough for meeting the needs of today where adolescence is longer and the rate of change quickening.

Male circumcision of infants is on the wane. I considered it for my son only because I had been circumcised myself, no other reason, no medical reason, no religious reason. Beth was firmly against it and I wasn't keen on it but the power of the past can be strong especially when questioning the past is not encouraged or even possible. Whilst I was still thinking about this, our mid wife told us that Samuel, only a week old, had a small tongue tie. The frenulum, the small fold of tissue under his tongue was restricting his tongue a little, making it more difficult for him to suckle.

Our mid wife suggested we get a tiny snip done to release the tongue, a very simple, safe and quick snip. Sam went from being on the breast feeding to a tiny quick nick by a doctor, a momentary squawk of pain and then Sam was straight back on the breast feeding. He was fine, I was not so fine. I hated it. It was very quick and professional and I felt the squawk of my son's pain in my gut. It left me shaking. Beth was worried that I was going to punch the doctor for hurting my cub. Sam's suckling improved. After that experience, there was no way I would allow Sam to be circumcised just because I had been circumcised.

It brought up for me the "Why would you put an infant through the unnecessary pain and agony of cutting his penis for no good reason?" Why would you deliberately traumatize an infant in that way? Especially if they have only just arrived into a world of air and bright lights and loud sounds. They haven't even had time to even play with it yet.

I understand that the WHO (not the band) are now saying that there is compelling evidence that in Africa male circumcision can help reduce the risk of heterosexually acquired HIV infection by approximately 60%. Babies are not sexually active, so give them a break.

Female Genital Mutilation (FGM) is a different matter and there is a lot of evidence that it only results in physical harm to girls and women in many ways. In my opinion, just because it has been done in the past is not a good enough reason to continue this practice. What is the intent behind it? And does anyone even know? Foot binding of women in China continued for 1,000 years and the "small feet are beautiful" bullshit argument hid the intention that it was started to dominate women and control them by crippling them. It went on for so long because after a while no one questioned it and then, despite the agony, it became accepted and even propagated by the women.

It seems that with FGM, the original intention was to deny women sexual pleasure as a way to exert control over them. It was justified then or later as being a way to prepare a girl for womanhood. I am blessed to have a daughter. When I read about FGM I have a physical response to it which is an involuntary shiver of disgust and sadness that such a thing still happens on such a large scale. Approximately 3 million girls in Africa are at risk of this and the WHO and many other agencies are working and have been working for many years to stop this practice.

It is not necessary to remove or damage healthy female genital tissue in a way which then interferes with the natural functions of a woman's body to welcome her into womanhood. There are many, many examples of contemporary and traditional Rites of Passages for girls that do not involve mutilation of her genitals. Even as I write this the irony is that western women are now opting for vaginal cosmetic surgery but that is a totally different subject and maybe if they saw what happens to girls in Africa and elsewhere they would not be so keen to pay good money for a vag job. Hey, maybe have another look and choose to be happy with what you have and donate the cost of the cancelled cosmetic surgery to the UN programs that are working to stop girls and women having their fannies butchered. Or grow your pubes back? Just a thought.

Whewwww, that was a lot of heavy stuff <deep breath.>

{I had to leave the book for a while there.}

I'm sure you did.

{I can't imagine something like that happening to Wendy.}

No it is pretty sad, must be tough living with the thought that this happens in Neverland

{I never think about it 'cause that doesn't happen in Neverland}

Oh, I thought you had nearly taken over the world? Which would include the 100 to 140 million women that have been subjected to FGM.

{No way, Dirk, you can't pin that one on Neverland.}

Hell, yes, foot binding to me is the same as FMG, all initiated by Alpha-bet males to dominate and control women, Neverland behaviour through and through.

{I can't accept that, no way}

Of course you can't, because then you would have to start to question all the other stuff in Neverland that you ignore or you justify as boys being boys, or harmless fun or high spirits. I could bind your feet for you, Peter, starting by breaking your toes so I can bend them back under your...

{STOP, stop!}

People are getting hurt, Peter, a lot of people are getting hurt, we don't just have lost boys anymore we have sad, depressed boys and girls and men and women. A lot of children are being sexually abused, 1 in 4 girls and 1 in 6 boys, the Earth's ecology has been fucked with badly by humans, we have no idea what is going to happen to our environment and until we leave Neverland Peter, we've got fuck all chance of doing much about it ... but by all means continue to pretend it all away.

226

{Neverland is just supposed to be fun, a place to stay young forever, nothing to worry about, no responsibility or cares....}

Adults can have fun too, Peter. We're not very good at it yet but our children help us and in strong communities children can play free and safe and the adults will be happier too but we need to grow up.

{I need a bit of time to think about this....}

Sure, I've got a bit more to write, feel free to chime in.

We live in a non-traditional world, a rapidly changing world and there is so much we can learn from traditional societies, especially around community, living with nature rather than dominating and destroying our natural world, and parenting healthy children to name a few.

The period called adolescence is new and it's not going away. This is the period when contemporary Rites of Passage will take place and it means that our rituals will be different to when adolescence did not exist. We have created adolescence where;

> "the not-yet-adult is allowed to rebel, to play and
> to experiment" (Sam Keen, Fire in the Belly).

The questioning, experimenting and play can renew our rituals keeping them alive and relevant. Especially if the questions are answered and any changes tempered by the wisdom and experience of elders. Elders that hold traditions gently, reverently and are open to being questioned and can answer honestly. Sometimes the answer will be "I don't know. We've just always done it that way."

We can give our young people an alternative to self initiation or military initiation and it is high time we did so, for our sake, for ... well you know the rest and while we are doing this we might just do a bit of growing up ourselves. Just as spending time with a small child is a wonderful reminder of simple pleasures and joy and laughter for no good reason, so too being involved in Rites of Passage is a reminder of what it is to grow up, to behave like an adult, a role model for the young (and there will always be a few who have an immunity to growing up.) Rites of Passage are not just for the individual; they also benefit the whole community.

BUT before we go any further we're going to visit (again) the realm of the bleeding obvious. Even the dullest tool in the shed knows that men and women are different. For example, women can easily be paid up to 15% less for doing the same (if not better) job than a man, big difference. If men and women are different then it stands to reason that boys and girls are different too. Pretty safe ground so far. After a few years boys and girls look different which is very convenient, they communicate differently, they play different games...

> {And they pick their noses differently. Boys are fearless, they mine deep, deep up, sometimes poking their brains as the second knuckle disappears entirely. Whereas girls are much more dainty pickers, preferring to capture their prey on the nail alone.}

Despite these obvious differences, in our education system there is great rigor on insisting that boys and girls are treated exactly the same. Perhaps it is time to review this practice.

The Rites of Passage for boys to manhood and girls into womanhood follow the same basic three stage structure, and were always carried out in gender circle (males with males, females with females). The actual methodology for boys and girls is quite different.

> *"Boys became a man in chronos, social time; girls in kairos, body time, natural time, moon time. This crucial difference became the basis of men's and women's different sense of time, their views of death, their experience of their bodies and their personality structure." Sam Keen, Fire in the Belly.*

A girl's first bleed or menarche is a definite marker of her body becoming the body of a woman, she has become fertile. For boys, the body of a man is generally not marked by his first ejaculation, as exciting and sometimes surprising as that is.

The other huge difference between boys and girls is the way their bodies respond to physical stress / danger. Boys get a boost of adrenalin, which accelerates their heart rate, dilates their pupils, results in vasoconstriction, their senses sharpen and they feel excited. They go into 'fight or flight' response and in the right circumstances they immediately want to do it again, and again (the child character of "Dash" in the movie *The Incredibles* does this magnificently.) Girls on the other hand get a shot of acetylcholine (a hormone that lacks a good publicist.) When this happens girls can become dizzy, slow thinking, physically they can freeze, they find it stressful, unpleasant even nauseating[1] and can have unaccustomed trouble expressing themselves.

Boys' journey into manhood is more of an external journey. Physical challenge is a very important element. Girls have a physical challenge built in with their menstrual cycle. The girls' journey is more of an internal journey and the honouring of their body rhythms is a critical element of their journey.

In traditional societies, when the separation occurred, parents would not go with their children to the transition phase but they would know and trust all the men or women who would be responsible for their child during their Rite of Passage. They would have assisted on Rites of Passage for other youth from the community. They had to let go of the child to welcome back the young adult. The mothers would be supported by the women to grieve the loss / ceremonial death of the child to create the space and the changes necessary to support a new relationship with a young adult. Similar support would be available to the men. For simplicity the following is about boys to manhood. With the caveats above much of it is translatable for girls into womanhood.

Whilst in the transition phase the boy would hear stories of their people, of their tribe or community, their land. The boys would hear stories from men about their journey to manhood, about grief, challenges they have faced, relationships and sex. They would be able to ask questions and share their own stories. The men would support them through various challenges and these varied depending on the tribe and the physical land they lived on. For some it was a vision quest, to be alone in the wilderness for a period of time, for some it was jumping off a high bamboo platform with vines tied to their legs, swimming a river, climbing a cliff, enduring physical pain or hunting a wild animal. The challenges were designed so that the boy with effort would succeed. If he was a natural athlete then the challenge could be more mental and if he was a natural mental (just checking to see if you are paying attention) if he was clever then his challenge could be more physical. In some instances if he did not succeed at first he could try again and again until he did succeed.

With the contemporary, community based Rites of Passage I have experienced; the father accompanies the boy through the transition phase. In a time of single mothers and fractured families the dad may not be able to or be interested in participating and so quite a few boys are accompanied by uncles, grandparents or a mentor. The reason for this has already been touched on, we live in a time of great father hunger and generations of men that have not had their own Rite of Passage. For the Dad to truly understand what is going on for his son, he has to have some experience of it. This shared experience, the time together, the space to share stories, make it a richer experience for all involved.

I am constantly amazed and inspired by men, by the willingness of men to dig deep and share beautifully, to be so generous with their spirit and emotions. The unleashing of creativity and beauty that happens when people work co-operatively together to create rituals and ceremonies is fantastic to witness. The miracles of synchronicity that manifest so regularly when the intention is to work with nature and the rain, hail or shine (and sometimes all three together) is exactly what is needed at that particular time. No screenwriter could ever imagine nor a director ever co-ordinate the rainbows, the shooting stars, the clouds or the rays of sunshine that appear at the most sublimely perfect moment.

I have already mentioned the return, the reintegration to community where the young men are welcomed back. The community now expects behaviour consistent with being a young man and the young man now expects to be treated as a young man not a boy. Sometimes this would be also marked by being allowed to wear different clothes, different hair style, a new name or a symbol of his new social rank. In some communities he would be allowed to marry and assume full adult responsibilities and to continue his journey through other marker journeys of manhood, then to eldership and finally to dust.

Whilst the men and boys are away the mothers have time to process and let go of their boys. One of the key transformations that a Rite of Passage achieves is a transformation in the relationship between a mother and her boy. Traditionally the mothers would spend time together grieving for the loss of her boy because for a young man to be born the boy must die. Not being a mother I can only be in awe of a mother's love for her child and without an event to mark the end of childhood a mother can continue to mother a child beyond the time when that serves them both.

Peter jokes about men wanting two mothers, their biological mother and a wife. The apron strings that tie a boy to the mother have to be cut for him to step out on his own and for the mother to let go of the child. This does not mean that the boy stops loving his mother. The goal is that the love changes from one of dependence to one of independence. This frees the young man to seek an independent rather than co-dependent relationship with the feminine. What do we want? For the young man to meet the feminine as a strong, equal and respectful partner or to meet the feminine in a dependent way where he equates love to having his partner to do everything for him? Or worse still where he is insecure in his masculinity and when he meets the feminine he thinks that he has to dominate the feminine to be a man.

When this transformation is done well, the gratitude and respect increases in both the young man and the mother. The fear of "losing" something chokes the possibility of the mother/son relationship evolving. It can be done gracefully and support for mothers by women makes it a lot easier and prevents the relationship from reverting back to mother child. There are a lot of women who have infants to look after. When they also have a demanding child that is supposed to be her husband, things do not always go well.

One of the other key outcomes of contemporary, community based Rites of Passage is that it is not just the boy's relationship with the mother that shifts. On one program, I remember one mother saying "I sent two boys out on camp and I got a man and a young man back." When Rites are done well respect for the feminine is increased for all the men. Men's business can and does honour the feminine for the many gifts that the feminine brings.

I believe that it is possible to use the existing infrastructure of the education system to make contemporary Rites of Passage available rapidly through out the western world. There is a thirst for this work, for ritual outside a religious context and a compelling need for it. This work can be used to help transform our education system for our young people, for us all.

> *"I do beseech you to direct your efforts more to preparing youth for the path and less to preparing the path for youth." Judge Ben Lindsay*

With the vast knowledge resources of the whole internet now at the tip of a students hand via their web enabled phone, surely it is time to start teaching life skills to our young people and trust that as we put our hearts and communities to this task, reading, writing and 'rithmatic will require less effort and be learnt better as well. How can a depressed child concentrate? How can a child terrified of being bullied even make it to school at all? How many talented teachers would like to start to really teach? The great possibility is that with school based Rites of Passage programs they can be run over a whole year with regular follow up possible and mentoring built in as part of the program structure.

The Rite Journey is a Rites of Passage program that is running in ten schools here in Australia and one in NZ and it is an exciting initiative. The founders Andrew and Graham are both very experienced teachers and passionate men. There are other programs that I have read about but have no experience of. ROPE has three stages and has been running in the USA since the

1980's. There are schools that are working in this direction with their outdoor education programs. Scouts, Guides, Rovers, and many other organisations are waking up to the potential of incorporating elements of Rites of Passage into work they are already doing. My heartfelt best wishes for all working in this area and a request to remember to include parents at some point in any school based programs.

I have experienced the beauty of community programs in Australia with the Pathways Foundation and this work is also held magnificently by the Tracks Trust tribe in New Zealand. Rites of Passage are happening in many other places in the world

Follow up for young people and for the families that have participated in Rites of Passage work is really important. A Rite of Passage helps a young person to locate and clear the start of a path that leads to healthy adulthood. The pathway is long and windy and as I know, it is easy to get lost along the way. Regular follow up of programs is very helpful. Many pieces of life's puzzle are revealed during a Rite of Passage. Follow up and mentoring helps to integrate some of the pieces:

> *Each lifetime is the pieces of a jigsaw puzzle.*
> *For some there are more pieces.*
>
> *For others the puzzle is more difficult to assemble.*
> *But know this: you do not have within yourself all of*
> *the pieces of your puzzle.*
>
> *Everyone carries within them at least one and*
> *possibly many pieces to someone else's puzzle...*
>
> *When you present your piece, which is worthless to*
> *you, to another, whether you know it or not, you are*
> *a messenger from the most High.'*
> *Rabbi Lawrence Kushner*

My work with Rites of Passage has helped me with my puzzle. For more information on the methodology of creating an effective Rite of Passage I highly recommend "Marking Life's Stages" by Don Bowak. I have included a list of the books that I have found useful in the appendix.

Why Gender Matters: What parents and Teachers need to know about the Emerging Science of Sex Differences by Leonard Sax (New York: Doubleday, 2005)

The Shadow of Rites of Passage

In Jungian psychology the shadow is that aspect of the human psyche that comprises repressed 'negative' qualities. When illuminated and understood however, this archetype has much to teach us. I have already written about the shadow side of Rites of Passage, that they can be abused in a way that dominates rather than produces healthy men. As Rites of Passage become revitalized it is important to understand that there can be a shadow. We need to ensure that authentic Rites of Passage programs are not diminished by programs that use the term as an advertising slogan rather than something to be treated with great respect.

Rites of Passage are powerful work and they are so heartfelt and make such a difference to the lives of families that it resonates and inspires people in an amazing way which is fantastic. The shadow of the light of attraction is that Rites of Passage can attract well meaning people who may not be suited to supporting the work and it can attract interests that may try to corporatise the uncorporatisable.

Some of the shadow stuff is your bog standard shadow stuff, of ego and pain bodies. Strong processes and governance, transparency and a culture of supporting healthy adult behaviour is important. Contemporary Rites of Passage is the work of a new paradigm which is served by a co-operative management style. Support from Elders that are experienced in the work is really important.

With Rites of Passage, a certain amount of mystery surrounding the detail of some processes adds vitality to the work. The trick is to ensure that the cloak of confidentiality is not used to protect unhealthy practices. The presence of Elders and men and women operating from healthy adult thinking protects the work. An intentional Rite of Passage is a path very different to self initiation but a poorly intentioned, badly executed Rite of Passage can be as wounding as self initiation.

> *"In any such endeavour, if there is power in the action, then that power may be used for good or ill. It is my hope that by encouraging public discussion, the collective eyes of men [and women] in our society will focus upon this process. It is in secrecy that evil flourishes...."* Don Bowak, Marking Life's Stages 2008.

Other Life Stages

There are two other life stages that stand out as priorities for attention. Eldership is one and Eldership is vital in supporting the other Rites of Passage. The good news about Eldership is that as it is a way of being, an ongoing way of being and so it can be taught by elders to olders. Certainly life experience that comes with passing a number of years does help with the transition. It is transformational work and just as with the rite of passage from child to young adult our challenge and opportunity is to create a contemporary passage into eldership and then to support our Elders when things get a bit sticky and the temptation is to retreat into numbness.

In our older folk we have a treasure of experience to be unveiled. Some of our treasure is lonely, angry, frightened or bewildered but together we can lift the shoulders, raise the chin, smile and look confidently back at our communities. There are many examples of amazing Elders in our communities who have never been honoured or acknowledged for this role. Ray Ellis you are an Elder to me and an inspiration.

The other life stage that I am going to mention briefly is the life stage of becoming a parent: from man to father or from woman to mother. I tried to go from child to father and I almost didn't make it. Babies are so precious and in many of the OECD countries there are fewer of them around than not so long ago.

We can do so much to help men become good fathers. Simple and inexpensive things like giving them a safe space to share the excitement as well as the feelings of panic and lack of knowledge for being a father with other expectant dads. For some men they have to face the fear of becoming like their own father and how do you fold a nappy? Men don't like asking directions and some men won't ask how to fold a nappy because of the fear of looking like a dill (as in pickle).

We need men to help men so they know how to look after a pregnant wife and how to support their wife when she becomes a mother in those first few weeks and months whilst they are breast feeding. Men need to explain to men that sex is not physically comfortable for a woman after giving birth to a child. Lack of "action" is not to be taken personally. "Dude, you're going to be wanking more often for a while, get over it." And fathers can share with expecting dads and new dads stories of the feelings of outrageous joy and love that holding a baby can invoke and how important it is to make time for their child *mano e mano* or *mano e girlo* and as a family. Parenting is a wonderful journey and to hear how incredible it can be helps with the times when it can also be frustrating and difficult. "Are we there yet? Are we there yet? Are we there yet?"

The Fatherhood project runs Expectant Fathers programs which I believe should be linked to or paid out of any government baby bonus money that is available. We can achieve so much with very little. I know that there are also Expectant Fathers programs being run in the UK.

There is a lot of focus on the birth and supporting mothers with birth is great. There is a lot women can do to support women after the birth in particular with breastfeeding and how to look after themselves. Mid wives can help with some of this and hearing from other women can be powerful. As a new parent there is just so much we don't know and a graceful start to parenting helps the emotional bonding which helps. Parenting is the most important job on this planet and we can start to value it more.

There are many other life stages that can be marked but going from zero to three might be enough for one book. This first book or one or perhaps many.

The Epilogue

Even the war and the navy,
couldn't bring him to maturity
He keeps referring back to school days
 and clinging to his child
Fidgeting and bullied,
his crazy wisdom holding onto something wild
He asked me to be patient, well, I failed
 "Grow up!" I cried
And, as the smoke was clearing, he said,
 "Give me one good reason why!"
Lyrics from "Strange Boy" by Joni Mitchell

There are many reasons why growing up is important. I could spend a whole book on them ☺. Times they are a changing. Transparency, accountability and responsibility (TAR) are tools that can be used to encourage the little boys to put the cookie jars down. They need to leave the corner offices and go play where they can do no harm or they can grow up or both.

Strength lies in diversity and big corporations run by perpetual boys create monoculture (monopolies) rather than multiculture. Sit in a café near a busy street and just watch people walk past. Tall people, short people, "small people," big people, blue eyes, brown eyes, black hair, grey hair. Watch for a little while. We are all so different and yet we are all the same. We are all brothers and sisters, we are all connected. Who knows which person is going to be that 100th Monkey but instead of washing root vegetables (which is a top idea) we will start to celebrate our life stages with Rites of Passage that include our communities as we all move around the wheel of life.

Now is the perfect time to revitalize Rites of Passage, to contemporize them. It is time to show respect to one another and to this amazing blue planet that we share. For me it starts with me.

The better I model healthy adult behaviour, the easier it will be for my son and daughter to grow up. Having people around me to hold me to my word makes it easier and more fun (and a bit annoying at times). The more I can lighten up on myself and others and enjoy life, the more attractive adulthood will be to my children and when it is time for them to have children I intend to be there to welcome my grandchildren, to remember the unconditional love that children offer freely.

Life is a grand adventure. I have seen miracles in my life time. The Berlin Wall coming down, the dismantling of Apartheid, peace in Northern Ireland and Tibet enjoying true autonomy, oh, wait a second that last one hasn't happened yet, but I think China is strong and confident enough to do it

I was brought up in the 60's in the USA and was led to believe that Russia was not only an enemy of the United States but of the Catholic Church as well. I was taught that the only good Russian was a dead Russian and I expected that there would be a third world war and that I would have to fight, on the side of right. Why plan for the future when that was what it was going to be? I was taught to have an enemy and it was all very black and white. We were good and they were bad. A series of lies told often and well on each side of the world held up the illusion of separation of us vs. them. The illusion was a house of cards and eventually it came falling down.

There is a song that still reverberates for me, the song "Russians" by Sting. Sting asked a question that helped pull a card from the bottom of the house of cards. The simple question was: "Do the Russians love their Children too?" It is very important to ask questions? Why do we need so much secrecy? How much is enough? I would ask you to consider now: "Do the Iraqi's love their children too? Do the Iranians? Did Peter Pan's parents?

{Did they? Really?}

I'm sure they did, you were lost not abandoned.

{Really?}

Really.

{Wow, I just... I never thought that they loved me.}

It is time to Leave Neverland, for our sake, for our children's sake, for Peter's sake.

{Despite how crowded it is in here, I get a bit lonely. I'm gonna think about what you've written...<pause> Daniel.}

Thanks Peter.

Notes Page

Rites of Passage Programs: Boys and Men

Pathways Foundation: National except S.A. Registered charity since 2002. Tel: 1300 850 766 . Mailing Address: PO Box 416, Narooma, NSW 2546. All donations tax deductible Email: info@pathwaysfoundation.org.au Website: www.pathwaysfoundation.org.au.

Pathways to Manhood: A contemporary, community based Rite of Passage for boys, 13-15 yo and their fathers or a mentor, 5 or 6 day bush camp. Mothers are supported by experienced women facilitators.

YoungStars: A fun, adventure filled, camping weekend that celebrates the boys' (6-10 yo) relationship with their fathers or a mentor.

Men's Leadership Training: A unique, program that provides opportunities to deepen leadership qualities in a range of environments including ongoing involvement as a Leader on Pathways programs

The Rite Journey: Successful national and international program. Website: www.theritejourney.com.au Running in schools in Australia and NZ. Based in SA. Contact Andrew 0432 603 655. School based Rite of Passage program for boys and girls which is designed for year 9 students. The program runs for the whole of the school year and includes a mentoring component. Reinvents the traditional process of a Rite of Passage to assist in transforming the adolescent from dependency to responsibility.

Tracks Trust: Has Offered Rites of Passage programs in NZ since 2002. Based in Takaka, Golden Bay. Website: **www.tracks.net.nz** email: **info@tracks.net.nz** Ph: 64-3-525 8778. Phase one: is a 5 day program. Second phase return as Young Leader to complete Rite of Passage. Mothers supported by experienced women. Good Men Making Tracks: 2 day men's program and the way to become involved in becoming a Tracks leader. Registered charity.

The Uncle Project: Helping Boys Become Men. Website: www.uncle.org.au. Phone Marc Gasson 02-66808582. Runs regular social events. Supports boys through providing healthy male mentoring. Based in Byron Bay. Incorporated community association. Started in 1997. All donations are tax deductible.

Finding Your Wisdom: Eldership Program. Contact: Allan Rudner 0411 191 354, Email allanrudner@gmail.com A carefully crafted program that considers a man's journey from birth, to the present and into the future. Enjoy an opportunity to acknowledge and embrace the special, sacred role of the Elder within this unique and intense 3½ day exploration.

The Fatherhood Project: Contact: 02 6621 4839, Mail :PO Box 594, Lismore NSW 2480. Website: **www.fatherhood.net.au** Email: **info@fatherhood.com.au**. Celebrates fatherhood with an annual festival also provides Rite of Passage for man to father via Expectant Fathers programs which can be made available nationally.

Fathering Adventures: Darren Lewis Founder. Based in Townsville, QLDEmail:info@fatheringadventures.com.auWeb:www.fatheringadventures.com.au Programs:2 Night Father Son Adventures (7-13 year olds with their Dad or a mentor), 5 night Father Son Adventures (13 -70 year olds) with their Dad or a significant male other.

Bush Ventures: John Guy Founder Ph:0755 443232 Email:info@bushventures.com.au Web: www.bushventures.com.au

Rites of Passage programs: Girl's and Women

Pathways Foundation: National, all states except S.A. Registered harm prevention charity. All donations tax deductible Tel: 1300 850 766 . Email: info@pathwaysfoundation.org.au Mail:POBox 416, Narooma, NSW 2546. Website: www.pathwaysfoundation.org.au.
Pathways into Womanhood: A contemporary, community based Rite of Passage for girls 12-15 yo and their mothers or a mentor, 5 day program. Fathers supported by experienced male facilitators.
Women's Leadership Training: A unique, program that provides opportunities to deepen leadership qualities in a range of environments including ongoing involvement as a Leader on Pathways programs

The Rite Journey: Successful national and international program. Website: www.theritejourney.com.au Running in schools in Australia and NZ. Based in SA. Contact Andrew 0432 603 655. School based Rite of Passage program for boys and girls which is designed for year 9 students. The program runs for the whole of the school year and includes a mentoring component. Reinvents the traditional process of a Rite of Passage to assist in transforming the adolescent from dependency to responsibility.

Tides Trust – Offers Rites of Passage programs for girls. Based in Takaka, Golden Bay, NZ. Website: **www.tides.net.nz** email: **contact@tides.net.nz** Ph: 64-3-525 7610. For girls 13 to 16 yo and their mother or a caregiver. 5 day program. Available twice a year in first week of April and in September school holidays. Registered charity.

Source Books and Suggested Reading

Andrews, Peter: Back from the Brink ABC Books 2009

Biddulph, Steve: Manhood Finch Publishing 2002

Bly, Robert: The Sibling Society Heinemann Australia 1996

Bowak, Don: Marking Life's Stages Don Bowak 2008

Brooks, Karen: Consuming Innocence: Popular Culture and Our Children University of Queensland Press 2008

Campbell, Joseph: The Power of Myth Doubleday, NY 1988

Pathways to Bliss: Mythology and Personal Transformation New World Library 2004

Hero with a Thousand Faces New World Library c2008

Forward, Susan: Toxic Parents: Overcoming Their Hurtful Legacy and Reclaiming Your Life Bantam Books 1990

Grille, Robin: Parenting for a Peaceful World Longueville Media 2008

Hamilton, Maggie: What's happening to our girls?: how our kids are overstimulated, oversold and oversexed Viking 2008

Keen, Sam: Fire in the Belly Bantam New York 1991

Lashlie, Celia: He'll Be OK Harper Collins 2007

Leimbach, C.& McShane, T. & Virago, Z: The Intimacy of Death and Dying Allen & Unwin 2009

Liedloff, Jean: The Continuum Concept Arkana 1986

Marshall, Joseph, M III: Walking With Grandfather Sounds True 2005

Mellors, Ken & Elizabeth: Teen stages: how to guide their journey to adulthood Sydney, NSW: Finch Publishing, 2004

Moore, R & Gillette, D: King Warrior Magician Lover: Rediscovering the Archetypes of the Mature Masculine Harper San Francisco 1990

Norberg-Hodge, Helena: Ancient Futures: Learning from Ladakh Rider 2000

Pfeiffer, T & Mack, J.E: Mind Before Matter: Visions of a New Science of Consciousness O Books 2007

Plotkin, Bill: Nature and the human soul : cultivating wholeness and community in a fragmented world New World Library c2008

Resources for Developing Personal Responsibility & Emotional Intelligence

Byron Katie   Loving What Is: Four Questions That Can Change Your Life Rider 2002

Debbie Ford   Why Good People Do Bad Things: How to Stop Being Your Own Worst Enemy HarperOne 2008

The 21-day Consciousness Cleanse: A Breakthrough Program for Connecting with Your Soul's Deepest Purpose HarperOne 2009

Deepak Chopra, Debbie Ford & Marianne Williamson The Shadow Effect: Illuminating the Hidden Power of Your True Self HarperOne 2010

Eckhart Tolle   A New Earth: Awakening to Your Life's Purpose Michael Joseph 2005

Hale Dwoskin The Sedona Method: How to Get Rid of Your Emotional Baggage and Live the Life You Want Element 2005

Joe Vitale and Ihaleakala Hew Len Zero Limits: The Secret Hawaiian System for Wealth, Health, Peace & More Wiley, 2008

Landmark Education: Personal transformation, international, high integrity, training company. Best known for The Landmark Forum.

Mabel Katz   The Easiest Way: Solve Your Problems and Take the Road to Love, Happiness, Wealth and the Life of you Dreams. Based on Ho'oponopono. Your Business Press, 2004

Marshall Rosenberg Nonviolent Communication: A Language of Life Puddle Dancer Press 2003

Sura Heart & Victoria Kindle Hodson Respectful Parents, Respectful Kids: 7 Keys to Turn Family Conflict Into Co-operation Puddle Dancer Press 2006

All these sources can be found on the web, with many offering free online courses and support.

Lightning Source UK Ltd.
Milton Keynes UK
UKOW05f2138180913

217478UK00019B/1698/P